# LONDON UNDER LONDON

## A subterranean guide

### NEW EDITION

One of the most popular books on London (reprinted many times since it was first published) *London under London* has now been updated to take into account the latest subterranean developments. A new section covers: the pioneering deep level water main 50 miles in length, twice as long as the Channel Tunnel; new power tunnels and the enormous substation beneath Leicester Square; new underground railways; glass fibre communications; and much more. Clearly, metropolitan man is burrowing as actively as ever.

The London we know and see is only the tip of the iceberg. Beneath the familiar surface lies an unknown city, a Hades of buried and forgotten rivers, sunken sewers, underground railways, pipes and passages, tubes and tunnels, crypts and cellars. These lifelines of the metropolis twist and turn hidden beneath the pavements of the city – fifteen hundred miles of Neo-Gothic sewers, a hundred miles of Neolithic rivers, countless miles of tube tunnels, twelve miles of government tunnels and hundreds of thousands of miles of cables and pipes. Layer upon layer, they run their urgent errands, carrying people, delivering water, removing sewage, passing currents, sending messages, conveying parcels.

Drawing extensively from the literature and visual archives of the underworld, *London under London* traces the history of the tunnellers and borers who have pierced the ground beneath the city for close on two thousand years. The authors trace the routes taken by man and nature, and enable us to follow them from the comfort of our armchairs. They also tell us, gazetteer-style, exactly where we can get below and see the strange world which they depict, whom to ask for permission, and which of the public service authorities organizes trips underground.

**'*London under London* is knowledgeable, lively, opinionated and utterly fascinating'** *Evening Standard*

**Richard Trench** has worked for the *Observer*, the *Guardian* and the *Financial Times* on a freelance basis, and from 1982 to 1987 he wrote the *Time Out* Guide to Paris. He is also the author of *Forbidden Sands*, an account of his crossing of the Sahara to the salt mines of Taoudenni, *Arabian Travellers*, *George Philips's London* and *Travellers in Britain*.

**Ellis Hillman**, a passionate enthusiast about subterranean London, is Chairman of the London Subterranean Survey Association, founder and president of the Lewis Carroll Society, principal lecturer in environmental studies at the University of East London and a councillor for the London Borough of Barnet.

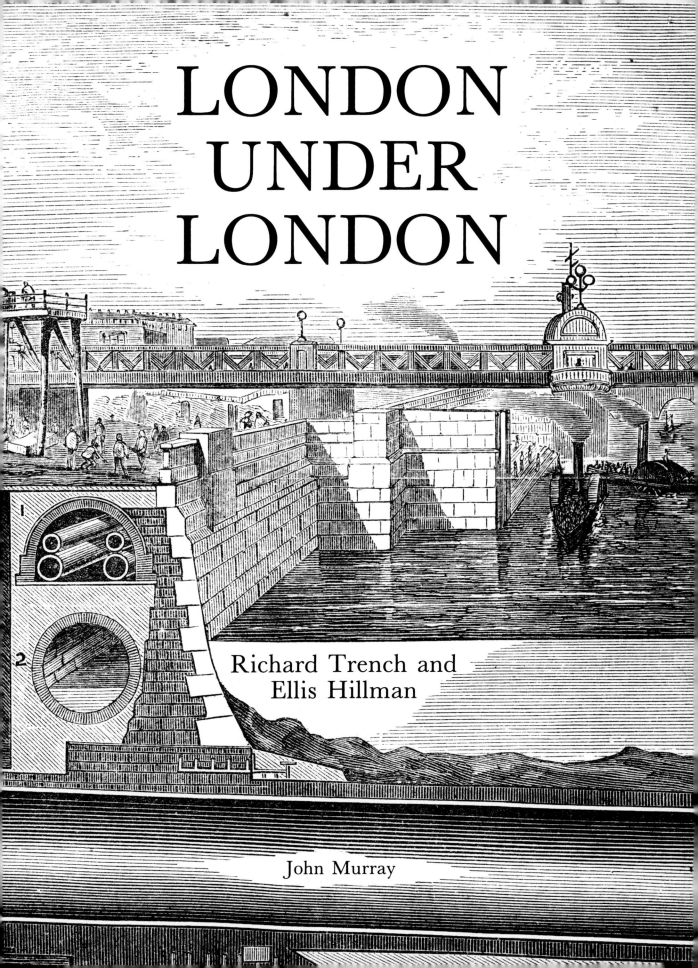

# LONDON UNDER LONDON

Richard Trench and
Ellis Hillman

John Murray

To Louise and Eli,
Eleni and Jack

*Title-page: London under London in 1867 – a section of the
Thames Embankment showing the subway (1), the low-
level sewer (2), the Metropolitan District Railway (3),
and the pneumatic railway (4)*

© Richard Trench and Ellis Hillman 1984, new material 1993

New edition 1993
Reprinted 1994, 1996, 1998, 1999, 2000, 2001, 2002

First published 1984
by John Murray (Publishers) Ltd
50 Albemarle Street, London W1X 4BD
Reprinted 1985, 1986, 1988, 1989, 1990, 1992

Printed in Great Britain by
Butler & Tanner Ltd, Frome and London

Produced by Rock Lambert
123 The Promenade, Cheltenham

British Library Cataloguing in Publication Data
Trench, Richard
London under London.
1. London (England)—Underground areas
I. Title   II. Hillman, Ellis
914.21        DA689.U5

ISBN 0-7195-4617-6

# Contents

Acknowledgements   6

Preface: The Organisms Below   7

1   The Underworld War   11

2   Smothered Streams and Strangled Rivers   23
*The Walbrook, the Fleet, the Tyburn,*
*the Westbourne, Counter's Creek,*
*Stamford Brook, the Neckinger and*
*Earl's Sluice, the Effra, Falcon Brook,*
*Hackney Brook, Lost Rivers*

3   The Bowels of the Earth   55

4   Patterns of Pipes   81
*Water, Hydraulic Power, Gas*

5   Tunnels under the Thames   105

6   Trains Underground   129

7   The Nerves of the City   165
*Electricity, Telecommunications,*
*Cable Television*

8   The Defence of the City   193

9   Orphanage for Oddities   205

10   Subterranean Futures   218
*The 80s, 90s and Beyond*

Bibliography   233

Gazetteer   234

Index   236

Since this book was first published the Greater London Council has been
abolished and many of the utilities have been privatised, reorganised,
sometimes re-named. We have not altered the names however. This is a
snapshot of underground London at moments in its life and does not aim
at describing a continuous development.

# Acknowledgements

A word of thanks to all who have helped this book. To Roger Morgan of the London Subterranean Survey Association; Ralph Hyde of the Guildhall Library; Terry Cannon of NUPE; Graham Cox, Dorothy Sealy, John Bridges and Laurie Moles of the Thames Water Authority; Paul Nitze of the National Joint Utilities Group; Romilly Leeper and Ursula Sharpley of William Halcrow and Partners; Dr H Fitzhugh of London Transport; Chris Bulford of the Post Office Engineering Union; Frank Kelsall of the GLC's Historic Buildings Division; and Messrs Crawley and Tiboo of the London Electricity Board.

To them we are grateful for particular help. But there are others to whom a debt is owed: Desmond Hennessy, Cedric Price, John Smith, Peter Davis, Sandy Foy and the late Howard G Kennedy, of the London Subterranean Survey Association, and George Brosan for their enthusiasm; Robert Collingwood and Anna Mitzi for their encouragement; Kathy Lambert and Tim Rock for their wearisome task of editing and picture researching; and authors Nicholas Barton and Michael Harrington who helped lead the way.

## Sources of Illustrations

While every effort has been made to trace sources, it has not always been possible.
Bryan Alexander, 41; Allen Lane/Paul White, 72B; Architectural Press Ltd, 170, 215; B T Batsford Ltd, 83T, 83B; BBC Hulton Picture Library, 130R, 131; British Gas, 94, 95T, 97B, 98, 103; British Telecom, 186; Syndics of Cambridge University Library, 42B; Central Electricity Generating Board, 171, 172; Daily Telegraph Colour Library/D Kasterine, 56; Elton Collection, Ironbridge Gorge Museum Trust, front cover, 112, 128; Mary Evans Picture Library, frontispiece, 30T, 36, 65B, 80, 88T, 117T, 127B, 137T, 179R, 213B; Ferranti Archives, 168R; The Greater London Council Photograph Library, 54, 57T, 59B, 77B, 124B, 198B, 200-201, 204, 207; Guildhall Library, City of London, 22, 23, 26B, 28, 30B, 31B, 32, 33, 34-5, 38, 48, 51, 61B, 62, 67, 68, 69, 70, 73B, 74, 75, 76B, 83C, 84T, 85L, 86T, 87T, 87BL, 97C, 102, 104, 106, 107, 108BR, 109, 110B, 111, 113, 114, 115, 117C, 134B, 136, 213T, 138, 140, 144L, 209, 213T; Sir William Halcrow & Partners, 163; Illustrated London News Picture Library, 27, 73T, 77T, 79, 96T, 122-3, 124-5, 126, 127T, 133, 134T, 137B, 141, 143T, 145, 151, 155, 179L, 180, 183L, 193, 194T, 210; Trustees of the Imperial War Museum, 11, 12T, 13L, 14TL, 14TR, 14BR, 15, 16T, 17, 18, 19, 20T, 82L, 198T; Institute of Electrical Engineers, 168L; Peter Jackson, 63, 84B, 167T, 169L, 202; Keystone Press Agency Ltd, back cover, 59T, 59C; London Electricity Board, 164; London Transport, 12B, 119C, 132BL, 132BR, 143, 145, 149, 152, 153, 156, 157, 158, 160, 161, 162, 196; Mansell Collection, 116; Eric de Maré, 72T, 142, 212; Markham & Co Ltd, 119T; Joseph McKeown, 93, 95, 97T, 169TR, 205; Clive Milner, 118; Henry Moore Foundation, 10; Museum of London, 26T, 31T, 37B, 64, 148L; Peter Noble, 108BL, 109T; Hugh Phillips, 42T; Plessey Co PLC, 197; Post Office, 183BR; Robert L Priestley Ltd, 120; Corinna Rock, 110T; Trustees of Sir John Soane's Museum, 82R; Tarmac Construction Group, 119B; David & Rosemary Temperley, 108T; Trustees of Tate Gallery, 13R, 14BL, 16B, 20C; Thames Water, 58, 71, 76T, 87BR, 89T; Richard Trench, 203, 217; Xenophon (Roger Morgan/Subterranean Survey Association), 20B, 47, 86B, 117BR, 135, 148R, 150, 154, 177, 183TR, 194B, 195.
The authors wish to thank the following for the illustrations in chapter 10. Thames Water, 218, 219, 220; London Electricity (W.W. Richards) 222; London Underground Ltd 223, 224, 225; London Underground Ltd (Norman Foster) 226; London Underground Ltd (Michael Hopkins & Partners) 227; Docklands Light Railway 228, 232; CrossRail 230, 231 (*bottom*); CrossRail (Duncan Lamb) 231 (*top*).

# Preface: The Organisms Below

Every time we turn on the tap, pull the chain, pick up the telephone, there is an underground movement: a gurgle of water, an impulse along a wire. Sometimes we are conscious of this movement; more often we are not. As we bask in the electric sunshine of our city surface, we are quite unaware of the subterranean labyrinth honeycombing the ground beneath our feet. Very occasionally, in time of war, strike or flood warning, we become aware of this troglodyte city, London under London. But *only* in exceptional and extraordinary times. In our everyday lives our ignorance of the world below extends to profound depths.

How many miles of muck and sludge does a sewage worker wade through on a working shift? What is the connection between a Greathead Shield and the Tower of London? What is the Brigade of Guards doing under Bloomsbury Way near the British Museum? How does London Transport use the atmospheric pressure principle to get rid of asbestos in London's Underground? What are 'fluffers' doing under London in the small hours?

Despite our ignorance, London under London is there, palpable but hidden; without it, life on the surface would become uncomfortable, unhealthy, even deadly. Like the human body, London hides its organisms within it. There are arteries bearing the body's fluids, lungs enabling it to breathe, bones giving it support, muscles endowing it with strength, nerves carrying signals, and bowels disposing wastes.

Before descending to these internal organs, we should put London in its ecological and geological setting. First, there is no simple pattern: sink a bore-hole at Golders Green and it will pass through 259 feet of London clay, 49 feet of sand and pebbles, 15 feet of Thanet sand and 329 feet of chalk, along with several layers of flint and two layers of fossils. Sink a bore-hole at The Angel, Islington (only seven stops on the Underground along the Northern Line), and it will pass through 18 feet of gravel, a mere 43 feet of London clay, 51 feet of sand and gravel, 34 feet of Thanet sand and 293 feet of chalk.

London, on its uneven bed of gravel, clay, sand and chalk, lies astride the Thames, sunk into a depression formed by the hills of Neasden, Hampstead and Hornsey to the north, and Streatham, Dulwich and Forest Hill to the south. Shaped in the Eocene period, it is a million years old. Half a million years later, London's terrain was reshaped by the Ice Age.

> Once a tongue of ice came as far as Finchley, bringing with it boulders of rock far from the north, as well as clay and finely crushed rock from the lands over which it had travelled. When the ice melted the boulders embedded in the clay were left behind in the deposit we know as boulder clay. So it is that we find lumps of chalk from Lincolnshire in the tongue

7

of boulder clay that today stretches from Whetstone to East Finchley
Station.                                      (RSR Fitter: *London's Natural History*)

The glaciers that carved and scored the London basin formed
valleys, rivers and tributaries, breaking out through the clay from the
water-soaked chalk depths. There are some dozen rivers still flowing
under London to the Thames. And it was at the confluence of one of
these rivers – the Walbrook – with the Thames that Britain's
Roman conquerors built their capital and called it Londinium.

Since Roman times, at first slowly and then at an increasing rate, a
separate city has been created beneath ground – a service industry for
the life above. Going below ground in London today is like going
through the green baize door of a country house in its heyday. But
unlike the strict order of life below stairs, the life beneath London has
grown haphazardly, with little coordination.

Thus, if you try to find a map or A-Z of subterranean London, you
will be unlucky. A journey through it begins without a map.

It is not that maps of underground London do not exist. The North
Thames Gas Board has maps at 60 inches to the mile; the London
Electricity Board has maps from 60 to 25 inches to the mile; the
London Telecommunications Region has scales from 100 inches to the
mile (becoming smaller the further you go out from central London);
the Public Health Department of the Greater London Council has
scales of 88 inches to the mile, plotting London's main sewers; the
local boroughs have maps of the same scale to plot local sewers; and the
Geological Museum has maps at 6 inches to the mile. But none, except
the boroughs' and the Geological Museum's, is available to the public.

What makes such underground surveys possible today is the
development of digital mapping techniques. The way they work is
very simple. The Ordnance Survey map is placed on a drawing board
with tens of thousands of tiny crosswires, like a grid, on it. The
crosswires define the points horizontally. Each point is then defined
vertically by its depth. This is translated into computer language and
stored in forty 'layers' or 'views', which can then be reproduced three-
dimensionally. Cross-sections and longitudinal sections are available
at the touch of a button, and perspectives can be programmed at the
turn of a dial. You can weave a route, or a pattern of routes, across a
digital map just by instructing a computer.

As no comprehensive map exists, we have been forced to make our
own, exploring the archives of the Guildhall, the British Museum and
the Public Records Office, delving into the basements of office
buildings, libraries and estate offices. Slowly, as we searched through
records of geology, history, archaeology, sociology and geography,
our map emerged, like the forty layers of a digital map. We could not
plot such a map on a two-dimensional piece of paper, so instead we
have had to store it, using our memories as a computer, with its cross-
sections, longitudinal sections, and bird's eye perspectives.

But our map contains more than that, for it peers through time as well as space. In the London Electricity Board tunnels under the Thames at Barking and Battersea, we knew we were in the twentieth century. In the low-level interceptory sewer, we felt we were mid-way through the nineteenth century. But tramping the alignment of the River Walbrook, the main artery of Londinium Augusta, and the site of a hundred mediaeval tanneries, we sometimes imagined that we had marched back in time to another age and another consciousness.

Yet, despite the rich history that lies buried and largely forgotten, London, alone among the major cities of the world, has no obvious underground myth. Every other major city – Paris, New York, Warsaw, Vienna – has its underworld and its myth: a living underworld serving present needs and a buried one encapsulating past needs. In each of these cities, the darkness and mystery of the underworld have caught the imagination of the world above.

'Imagination', wrote John Hollingshead – author of the Victorian *Underground London* and one-time proprietor of the Alhambra and Gaiety theatres – who was even more obsessed with London's underground than most of his Victorian contemporaries, 'generally loves to run wild about underground London, or the subways of any great city. Take away the catacombs of Paris . . . and a keystone of a mass of French fiction falls to the ground.'

Out of the imagination, myths have grown up from the nether-world: the Phantom of the Opera fleeing through the catacombs of Paris, crocodiles slithering through its sewers; obese alligators living under New York; Resistance fighters hiding in Warsaw's sewers; the fingers of Harry Lime clawing at the Vienna pavement grille.

Alas, though it is true that New York's alligators were once flushed down its lavatories, no alligators prowl the sewers of the city today. But the fertile imagination that gave them birth is still alive and well. The latest underground myth from New York concerns marijuana seeds. Flushed down the lavatory too, they have been nurtured by the rich nutrients of the city's sewers. Accordingly, a new, super-strong variety has grown up beneath the streets, called 'Subway Silver'. Unfortunately no one can get at it, because – you've guessed it – it's guarded by alligators.

In London, the damp and tattered posters warning that 'Careless Talk Costs Lives', still visible on the platforms of the disused King William Street station, provide the key to London's underground myth. For, in the summer of 1940, subterranean London was rediscovered.

> Under the surface of flux and fear there is an underground movement,
> Under the crush of bureaucracy, quiet behind the posters,
> Unconscious but palpably there – the Kingdom of individuals.
> (Louis MacNiece: *The Kingdom*)

Underground London had found its myth.

# 1 The Underworld War

They arrived in droves with their children and blankets, paid 1½ d for tickets to the tube platforms. Those who found the first station they selected was too crowded, moved over to the next. Some arrived with bulging shopping baskets, old coats, parcels of food, bottles of milk and ginger pop, and suitcases on which they squatted. One old woman proudly announced that she had brought enough cheese and tea cakes for a fortnight, and indeed it was noted that she did not leave the East End railway platform which she had chosen for fourteen days, except to get a 10-minute breath of fresh air when there was no raid in progress.

(Charles Graves: *London Transport Carries On*)

*'They arrived in droves with their children and blankets . . . with bulging shopping baskets, old coats, parcels of food, bottles of milk and ginger pop, and suitcases on which they squatted.' The interior of Stoke Newington shelter on 8 November 1940.*

The war gave subterranean London its finest hour: seventy-nine Underground stations, together with the Aldwych extension (which was reserved for children) and the disused King William Street tunnel, which could hold 100,000 people, were taken over by shelterers.

At first, London Transport discouraged the practice:

UNDERGROUND STATIONS MUST NOT BE USED AS AIR-RAID SHELTERS. The public are informed that in order to operate the railways for essential movement underground stations cannot be used as air-raid shelters. In any event a number of stations would have to be cleared for safety in certain contingencies.

Later notices were more concise.

During air-raids, passengers only admitted.

The public's response was characteristic. They purchased the cheapest underground ticket available and went down below.

Henry Moore has given a vivid description of his own rediscovery of the London Underground:

One evening after dinner in a restaurant with some friends we returned home by Underground taking the Northern Line to Belsize Park. As a rule I went into town by car and I hadn't been by Tube for ages. For the first time that evening I saw people lying on the platforms at all the stations we stopped at . . . I had never seen so many reclining figures and even the train tunnels seemed to be like the holes in my sculpture. And amid the grim tension, I noticed groups of strangers formed together in intimate groups and children asleep within feet of the passing trains. After this evening I travelled all over London by Underground . . . I never made any sketches in the Underground. It would have been like drawing in the hold of a slave ship. I would wander about sometimes passing a particular group that interested me half a dozen times. Sometimes, in a corner where I could not be seen, I would make notes on the back of an envelope so that I would be reminded when I sketched next day . . . Naturally, of the Underground Stations, I had my favourites. I used to go quite often to Cricklewood and I was fascinated by a huge shelter at Tilbury which was in fact the basement of a warehouse. But Liverpool

*Opposite:*
*Henry Moore's* Air Raid Shelter Drawings: Gash in Road, *1940. Bombed buildings above are based on reality; figures underground on his imagination.*

*Sloane Square Underground station after a bombing raid on 12 November 1940.*

**Billy Brown of London Town**

Down below the station's bright,
But here outside it's black as night.
Billy Brown will wait a bit
And let his eyes grow used to it.
Then he'll scan the road and see,
Before he crosses, if its free;
Remembering when lights are dim
That cars he sees may not see him.

*Printed for*
*London ⊖ Transport*

*The sanctimonious 'Billy Brown of London Town' dogged Underground travellers and shelterers relentlessly during the war years.*

Street Underground Extension was the place that interested me most. The new tunnel had been completed except for the rails and at night its entire length was occupied by a double row of sleeping figures.

In people's minds the Underground provided not just safety but an escape from 'moral loneliness'. For some, however, it was to prove a death trap. Twenty people were killed by a bomb at Marble Arch on 17 September 1940. A month later a bomb blew up in a tunnel between King's Cross and Farringdon. The next day a bomb exploded in Sloane Square station. Eighty-two people were injured, but the cast-iron pipe carrying the water of one of London's dozen underground rivers, the Westbourne, remained intact. Later on, a bomb at Balham fractured a water main and 600 people were drowned. The following year a bomb broke through the pavement at the foot of the Duke of Wellington's statue outside the Royal Exchange, dropped into the crypt of St Mary Woolnoth, bounced down the escalator of Bank station and exploded on the platform, killing 117 people.

Regrettably, however, the enemy failed to kill that dreadful and despicable creation of the London Passenger Transport Board's publicity department, 'Billy Brown of London Town', a smug little man with a Neville Chamberlain pair of trousers and a John Selwyn

 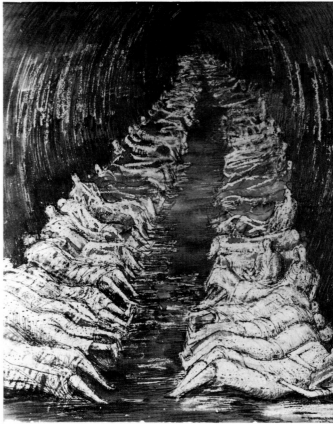

Gummer face, who used to exhort passengers with insufferable verses:

> He never jostles in a queue,
> But waits his turn. Do you?

To which one shelterer added in pencil:

> You annoy so much, you really do.
> I wish you dead. Do you?

People felt happier sheltering below ground. Despite the bomb at Marble Arch only days earlier, 117,000 people are recorded as having slept in the Underground on the night of 27 September 1940. A whole subterranean society developed. Stations had their own lending libraries, canteens and first-aid posts. The Unity Outside Show put on underground theatre, the London County Council ran evening classes, and shelterers elected 'station committees'. Station loyalty developed, 'lice to lice', people said, and invasion by outsiders was resented. Swiss Cottage even had its own newsletter, *The Swiss Cottager*, two issues of which are now in the British Museum.

> Greetings to our nightly companions, our temporary cave dwellers, our sleeping companions, somnambulists, snorers, chatterers and all who inhabit the Swiss Cottage Station of the Bakerloo nightly from dusk to dawn. This is the first in a series of announcements issued in the name of

*Above left:*
*Tube becomes shelter – tracks on the Central Line east of Liverpool Street Station filled in with tarmac to accommodate more people.*

*Above right:*
*Henry Moore's* Tube Shelter Perspective. *'I saw hundreds of . . . Reclining Figures stretched out along the platforms . . . even the train tunnels seemed to be like the holes in my sculpture.'*

13

co-operation so that we may find what comfort and amenities there may be in this our nightly place of refuge.

Swiss Cottage, with its disproportionate number of middle-class professionals, intellectuals and drama students, was not typical of London, but its sweaty smells, comradeship and lack of amenities were universal. To go to the lavatory meant either taking a train to Finchley Road or using a public bucket.

The discomfort was deliberate in the early days of the Blitz. There was much disapproval for the Underground shelterers, who were (if they were men of a certain military age) called 'Tube Cuthberts'. The *Daily Express* reported gleefully on these 'Cuthberts'; one of them told its reporter that he was a pacifist and promptly threatened to punch him on the nose. Fortunately, the *Railway Gazette* was able to reassure its readers. 'We are happy to record that a vast majority of offenders are members of alien races, or at least alien extraction' – a view shared by Harold Nicolson's housekeeper:

Mrs Groves had tried to spend the night in the tube, but when she got there she found the whole place full up with 'foreigners'. 'Greeks, they were, sir, by the look of them, and they made themselves comfortable with mattresses and suchlike. I never did hold with foreigners. My father was an Indian Mutiny veteran and always warned me against them since I was a child.

London Transport's tunnels were not the only places in London's underworld taken over by sanctuary seekers. The two great subterranean warehouses in the East End – 'Tilbury' under Commercial Road and Cable Street, and 'Mickey's Shelter' under Stepney – were broken into and occupied by East Enders.

Mickey's Shelter was run by Mickey Davies, a three-foot-three-inch-high hunchback, who created order out of chaos under Stepney by sheer personality. He was elected chairman of the shelter committee, and when an 'official' shelter marshal was appointed by the Minister of Home Security, the shelterers demanded Mickey's reinstatement. He soon became a celebrity. Marks and Spencer donated a complete canteen to the shelter committee, and Wendell Wilkie, American presidential candidate, visited Mickey's Shelter on his tour of Britain.

The best description of Tilbury comes from Mass Observation, a nationwide voluntary organisation set up in 1937 by the poet Charles Madge, the film director Humphrey Jennings and the anthropologist Tom Harrisson, using thousands of amateur sociologists, crypto-chroniclers and genuine busybodies, to record human behaviour in everyday life. They turn out to have done the history of London an invaluable service. The Mass Observation archives, housed at the University of Sussex, are raw and immediate. Here is a Mass Observer's description of Tilbury on 14 September 1940.

First impression was of a dim cavernous immensity. The roof is made of

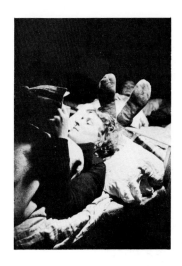

*Cheek by foot in a south London shelter.*

*Opposite, above right:*
*'As from your graves rise up, and walk like sprites,/To countenance this horror!'* (Macbeth) – *a night's rest snatched during the Blitz in an East End crypt.*

*Above right:*
*Edward Ardizzone's* Shelterers in the Tube.

*Below left:*
Woman Seated in the Underground *by Henry Moore.*

*Below right:*
*An Indian family in an East End crypt, photographed by Bill Brandt.*

15

*Latrines overflowing into the corridor of a shelter. The worst aspect of the underground shelters was the smell; many people preferred to face bombs above than stench below.*

*The cavernous Tilbury warehouse, drawn, like his tube shelters, from Moore's notes and memory. 'I never made my sketches in the Underground. It would have been like drawing in the hold of a slave ship.'*

metal girders, held up by rows of arches, old and solid . . . The entrance to this vast, dim, cathedral-like structure is narrow and insignificant – just a break in the street wall that could easily be missed by a passer-by. But once through this gap, one finds oneself in a large stone courtyard, sloping away in two directions down into the earth . . . By 7.30 pm every bit of floor-space is taken up . . . people lying everywhere, on the railway tracks, among the margarine crates, everywhere. The floor was awash with urine . . . Some horses were still stabled there, and their mess mingles with that of humans.

Gradually links were forged amongst the frightened strangers, shelter marshals elected, cleaning squads set to work, and hygiene rules enforced.

There were, however, lighter moments. 'A girl in a scarlet cloak danced wildly to the cheers of an enthusiastic audience; a party of negro sailors sang spirituals while someone played an accordion,' the journalist Harold Scott recorded. A Mass Observer noticed another group, at about the same time: 'In the middle arch, on Friday, a girl played an accordion, while men danced burlesque dances round her. She was a tall, pale girl with long straggly hair, and played effortlessly with a vacant face.'

A vivid physical picture of Tilbury emerges from the notes that Henry Moore made for his drawings.

Figures showing faces lit up – rest of body in silhouette. Figures lying against platform with great bales of paper above also making beds. Perambulators with bundles.
Dramatic, dismal lit, masses of reclining figures fading foreground. Chains hanging from old cranes. Sick woman in bathchair. Bearded jews blanketted sleeping in deck chairs. Lascars Tunnel (bundles of old clothes that are people.)
Bunks with women feeding children.
Dark wet setting (entrance to Tilbury).
Men with shawls to keep off draughts, women wearing handkerchiefs on heads.
Muck and rubbish and chaotic untidiness everywhere.

Yet the dominant features of Tilbury, evident both in Moore's drawings and in the Mass Observation reports, remained resignation and apathy.

4 pm. A poor working-class woman makes her way slowly down the aisle, carrying a heavy bundle of bedding tied with string, and a fish net basket filled to overflowing. Though only middle aged, her hair is grey and her face wrinkled . . . She dumps her parcel down . . . and starts to unfold it to its full width; finds her baggage in the way, picks it up again and moves further away. She takes well over a minute unfolding the rug, breathing hard all the time. Having done this she sits down on it heavily, leans against the partition, and stares in front of her for several minutes without doing anything . . .

5 pm. Still sitting there surrounded by the things she has brought. Stares

expressionlessly at first one lot of people then another. After some minutes a man, about 45, picks his way towards her across the crowded platform. She looks at him as he approaches, and as he lowers himself onto the rug beside her. Neither of them say anything. He sits for a minute doing nothing, then slowly begins to loosen the laces of his boots. He takes a very long time doing this; then pauses in the middle of it:
'What you got there, Mum?'

*An old woman uses a beer keg as a pillow. Crypts, cellars, tubes and warehouses were all pressed into service as shelters.*

The appalling conditions in both the Underground and the subterranean warehouses during the Blitz were a breeding ground for radicalism. *The Swiss Cottager* in its November issue complained of 'indifference amounting almost to callousness, neglect, soulless contempt for elementary human decencies . . . red tape, authoritarianism and officialdom'. That week in the station a child had died of meningitis. Communist militants gained control of Tilbury, started a campaign for the provision of deep-level shelters, and even organised an 'Inter Station Conference of Tube Shelterers'. The moderate and middle-class Swiss Cottage Committee participated in the conference but later withdrew, complaining that it had been taken over by extremists.

Official disapproval for the Underground shelterers did not,

*'Red Ellen' Wilkinson, Churchill's junior minister responsible for shelterers, inspecting her subterranean domain with Admiral Sir Edward Evans and the cartoonist David Low.*

however, extend to the top of the hierarchy. The arrival of Winston Churchill at Downing Street resulted in a new mobilisation of subterranean London. He first sent Lord Horder into the Underground to report on conditions there; then took a special interest in the Holborn extension, which was reserved for children; and soon appointed the radical MP 'Red Ellen' Wilkinson as a junior minister with special responsibility for shelterers.

Churchill was attracted to the idea of a people down below waging war against the forces of darkness above. He himself was an underground buff of the first order, and his description of his subterranean fortresses in *Second World War* reveals far more than the guardians of our official secrets would have allowed from the less illustrious.

From his War Rooms under the Treasury, Churchill extended the Whitehall tunnel, which had been excavated in the 1930s to carry cables between government departments under Broad Sanctuary and Great Smith Street, to his new subterranean citadel in the old gasworks at the Rotunda off Horseferry Road (now the foundations of the Department of the Environment); equipped the entire Whitehall complex with Lamson pneumatic tubes; and extended and improved the 'Hole in the Ground' (a subterranean office block built in 1933 under the Treasury at Storey's Gate) with six new lifts. Beyond Whitehall he built more citadels below ground: in the basement of the MI5 building in Curzon Street, in the Post Office's Faraday House Exchange, and, appropriately enough, under the Geological Museum, which became the London Civil Defence headquarters. Then he dragged his Cabinet off to their emergency headquarters at Dollis Hill:

> We held a Cabinet meeting at 'Paddock' [the Cabinet Office's citadel built in the 1930s under the Post Office Research Station] far from the light of day, and each Minister was requested to inspect and satisfy himself about his sleeping and working apartments. We celebrated this occasion with a vivacious luncheon.

The day-to-day problems of building below ground were left to Lord Beaverbrook:

> Lord Beaverbrook was . . . entrusted with the task of making a large number of bomb-proof strongholds capable of housing the essential staffs of many departments of state, and a dozen of them, several connected by tunnels, survive in London today.

Not content with digging under London, Churchill even invented his own tunnelling machine. He had first suggested in November 1916 a device for getting soldiers safely across 'no man's land' on the Western Front. It proved impossible to build. In 1936 he approached Sir Stanley Goodall, Director of Naval Construction, with a revised idea; again he was turned down. By 1940 he was Prime Minister and impossible to turn down. It fell to the Admiralty's Naval Land

Equipment Section to translate Churchill's proposal into reality. The project was mischievously code-named 'White Rabbit No 6', but was renamed at Churchill's suggestion 'Cultivator No 6', and later 'Nellie 1'. The Prime Minister had not enjoyed the joke; not for him Lewis Carroll's fantasy world.

The machines were constructed by Ruston-Bucyrus of Lincoln. They resembled large, turretless tanks with a six-foot steel plough in front and a long conveyor-belt behind. They could advance at three miles an hour, dig a six-foot trench and pile the spoil on either side. The infantry were then supposed to follow in the trench behind the machines. Fortunately for the infantry, the war was over before Nellie could be tested under real conditions.

We shall never know whether Churchill intended to turn his mind to a machine for tunnelling under London. What is certain is that he was concerned for the safety of civilians.

Before the war Sir John Anderson, then Lord Privy Seal, had set up a conference to investigate shelters. Its report, in April 1939, reflected Anderson's own views: shelters, it said, would create stampedes, would be too expensive, and, once in them, people might not want to come up again.

Throughout the Blitz there had been calls for deep-level shelters for Londoners, as well as for the government, and the Prime Minister, overruling most of his War Cabinet (who supported Anderson), insisted on excavations 100 feet deep. The change of policy was announced by Herbert Morrison in November 1940. 'The deep shelter provided in London by the tubes will be extended by tunnelling.' But he added a warning. 'Anything like a universal policy of deep shelters . . . is beyond the bounds of practical possibility.'

Originally the government planned to build ten deep-level shelters – two under the Central Line, at Chancery Lane and St Paul's, and eight under the Northern Line, at Clapham South, Clapham Common, Clapham North, Stockwell, Oval, Goodge Street, Camden Town and Belsize Park. Work at the Oval was defeated by the River Effra, while work at St Paul's was stopped because of fears that it would undermine the cathedral (the half-completed workings were handed over to the Central Electricity Generating Board and annexed to their underground headquarters). Of the remaining eight, Chancery Lane and Clapham Common were used as emergency citadels in anticipation of the V1 and V2 rockets; Stockwell was turned into a hostel for American troops; and Goodge Street became General Eisenhower's underground headquarters. The public was allowed to use the other four.

The tunnel shelters, completed in 1942, are all similar. Each lies directly underneath its Underground station, and was to be linked after the war into a high-speed tube line (this never happened). Each shelter consisted of two parallel, 1200-foot tunnels, divided into an

*Churchill and his tunnelling machine, 'Nellie 1', alias 'Cultivator No 6' and 'White Rabbit No 6'. Fortunately the war was over before Nellie was tested in battle conditions.*

*Latrines (Bill Brandt) and bunks (Henry Moore:* Shelter Scene: Bunks and Sleepers*) – two unwholesome but essential features of life underground. The bunks were dismantled in 1941, on Clementine Churchill's insistence, because of lice.*

*Down Street station was used in January 1940 for a meeting of the railway executive committee.*

upper and a lower floor, and furnished with iron bunks. There were extensions at right angles for first-aid posts, wardens' rooms, ventilation equipment and lavatories – which posed a particular problem, since the shelters were below the level of the sewer system.

> At each shelter, eight lavatory tunnels were driven 12 feet in diameter. Closets are of the Elsan type. At the far end of each lavatory a hopper has been installed into which closets are emptied. To keep out bottles, boots, clothing etc. all of which have been found to give trouble in other shelters, it was necessary to install a wire screen. The hoppers are connected by piping to a closed ejector placed in the bottom of the staircase shafts, and the contents of the ejector periodically forced out by means of compressed air through a rising main, 6 in. diameter, up to sewer level in the street above. (*The Engineer*, 18 September 1942)

You can still spot most of the shelters today – at Belsize Park, Goodge Street and along Clapham Road – with their distinctive shaft-head buildings, which look like a cross between an electricity sub-station and a house designed by Le Corbusier.

A string of disused Underground stations was also commandeered for the duration of the war. Down Street was used during the Blitz as an underground citadel by the Railways Executive Committee and by Winston Churchill, who described it as 'a considerable underground office in Piccadilly . . . 70 ft below the surface and covered with high strong buildings'. You can still recognise it – as you can many other lost Underground stations – from its distinctive maroon-tiled facade. It is now a solicitor's office.

Dover Street, one stop to the east of Down Street, became London Transport's emergency headquarters; its abandoned lift shafts were later used to shift spoil during the excavation of the Victoria Line. Brompton Road (close by the Oratory), three stops west along the Piccadilly Line from Down Street, which had operated as an Underground station from 1909 to 1932, became an anti-aircraft control centre, and was taken over by the Territorial Army after the war. They still use it. South Kensington, one stop on from Brompton Road, provided two deep-level tunnels – intended for a high-speed, deep level District Line, which was never built – for London Transport's emergency engineering equipment, with links, via the public tunnel under Exhibition Road, to the underground Civil Defence headquarters beneath the Natural History and Geological Museums.

To many, the benevolent interest taken both by Churchill and the Communists in subterranean London destroyed the spontaneity of the earlier days. The bunks (later taken out because they were found to be a breeding-ground for vermin), the canteen trains and the awful Billy Brown of London Town, destroyed the soul for which the Young Communist League and the Women's Voluntary Service had been competing.

While the poor took shelter in the Underground and under the East End, the rich took to the 'bomb-proof' nightclubs, the Savoy shelter and the subterranean Turkish baths at the Dorchester Hotel. Cecil Beaton wrote of the Dorchester in his diary:

> There the noise outside is drowned by wine, music and company, and what a mixed brew we are! Cabinet ministers and their self-consciously respectable wives; hatchet-jawed iron grey brigadiers; calf-like airmen off duty; tarts on duty; actresses (also); déclassé society people, cheap musicians and motor-car agents. It could not be more ugly and vile.

Such contrasts of squalor and luxury bred resentment. On 15 September 1940, the Communist MP Phil Piratin led a hundred East Enders into the Savoy shelter. The Savoy could not lawfully keep them out. They left after the raid, remembering to tip the staff on the way out.

American journalist Ralph Ingersoll also found the self-conscious luxury distasteful: 'It was like an overdone movie, beautifully costumed but badly directed by a man who had made B-movies all his life. There is too much reality in London for make-believe.'

On 8 March 1941, the subterranean Café de Paris, which had been modelled on the ballroom of the *Titanic*, was hit by two fifty-kilo bombs. Thirty-four of Beaton's 'ugly and vile' nightlifers were killed.

Much of what was 'ugly and vile' in wartime subterranean London has been forgotten. In 1975 Tom Harrisson contacted as many of the original Mass Observers as he could find, and asked them to rewrite from memory what had happened. He then compared the two descriptions. His conclusion:

> There is little or no logical relation between the two sets of accounts, 34 years apart. Memory has glossified and sanctified these 'finest hours'.

The myth has taken over. But the reality, although almost forgotten, is still there. The stations, with their harsh lights and black tunnels, deep shafts and endless arguing corridors and passages, still lie under London. They are part of the city's history. But they are only a part. To understand the full complexity of what lies under London, we must begin with her subterranean rivers. Only they, always flowing and always there, provide continuity: explaining not only what London was, but what it is, and perhaps what it will be. As E M Forster wrote: 'Only connect'.

**CLERKS-WELL.**

A View of the Pump near Clerks Well : Ray Street in the Parish of Clerkenwell : with its descriptive Iron Tablet : as it appeared in 1827. — Also a plan of the Site and Vicinity.

It was near this Well that the Parish Clerks of London in the year 1390 the 14th of King Hen. 4th are said to have acted in a Scene representing a Play which Play touches from the Creation of the World : in the presence of most of the Nobility and Gentry of England.

London : Published 1st Nov. 1829 by Robert Wilkinson Burchard Street &c.

On the South side

**The CONDUIT, near BAYSWATER,**

in the parish of Paddington, stands in a meadow, opposite the north side of Kensington Garden, between Paddington church & the road to Uxbridge. It was erected, and is kept up, by the corporation of London, to preserve a large spring of pure water, which rises at the place, and was formerly conveyed by leaden pipes into Cheapside and Cornhill. This water appears to have been granted to the citizens by Gilbert Standford, 21 Hen. 3. anno 1236.

Stowe, Howell, Dunant's Lond. > alit. and Lyson's Midd. page 331.

Over the door

REPAIRD

conjecture 1657, or 1658

Pub. Aug. 10. 1796 by N. Smith, Rembrandt's Head, 3a Mays Buildings, St Martins Lane; & J. T. Smith, 18 Frith Street, Soho.

THE ORIGINAL GARDEN-ENTRANCE TO BAGNIGGE WELLS, ESTABLISHED IN 1680.

# 2 Smothered Streams and Strangled Rivers

There are over a hundred miles of rivers in London, fed by over a hundred springs and wells, which once flowed and gurgled through meadows and valleys. Villages sprang up on their banks. As London grew the villages turned into suburbs and the streams into sewers. Hidden from view, recalled only in street names, they trickle through a succession of platforms, ravines, caverns and culverts under the city: still there in spite of their long and tortuous transition from spring to stream to sewer, and from ditch to dyke to drain.

Central London lies in an alluvial flood plain, formed by the meandering Thames, the northern banks of which rarely rise above thirty feet, and the southern banks of which are reclaimed marshland. Hemming in this plain are the *petits massifs* of Hampstead, Highgate and Hornsey to the north, and Dulwich, Streatham and Sydenham to the south. Beneath the flood plain is a layer of non-porous clay, beneath the clay a layer of porous chalk. Where the clay is thin, the water breaks through, forming streams that flow down to the Thames, and springs impregnated with chalybeate, which traditionally gave them medical and miraculous powers.

Some of the streams, like the Wandle, Ravensbourne and Beverley Brook in south London, are still above ground. Others, like the Shoreditch, Cranbourne and Langbourne, are completely lost, their courses a mystery, if, indeed, they ever existed at all. Most of them – Walbrook, Fleet, Tyburn, Westbourne, Counter's Creek, Stamford Brook, Neckinger, Effra and Falcon – are still there, just, flowing beneath us.

*While London's rivers were being buried underground, her springs became fashionable spas, where people could 'drink waters that do you neither Good nor Harm, provided you do not take too much of them'.*

As for the springs, many, like St Chad's, St Agnes', St Bride's and St Pancras Wells, and Holywell itself, became holy wells, their healing qualities attributed to the benevolent influence of saints and virgins. Others, like Sadlers' Wells and Hampstead Wells, were turned into fashionable spas, where, according to a French visitor to London in 1719, 'you drink waters that do you neither Good nor Harm, provided you do not take too much of them'.

These springs are referred to in the first detailed description that we have of London, by William Fitzstephens. Fitzstephens, who was secretary or 'dictator' (he who is dictated to) to Thomas à Becket, prefaced his *Life of St Thomas* with an account of the city in which they had both grown up:

> On the north side are fields and pastures, and a delightful plain of meadow land, interspersing with flowing streams, on which stand mills, whose clank is very pleasing to the ear . . . There are also round London, on the

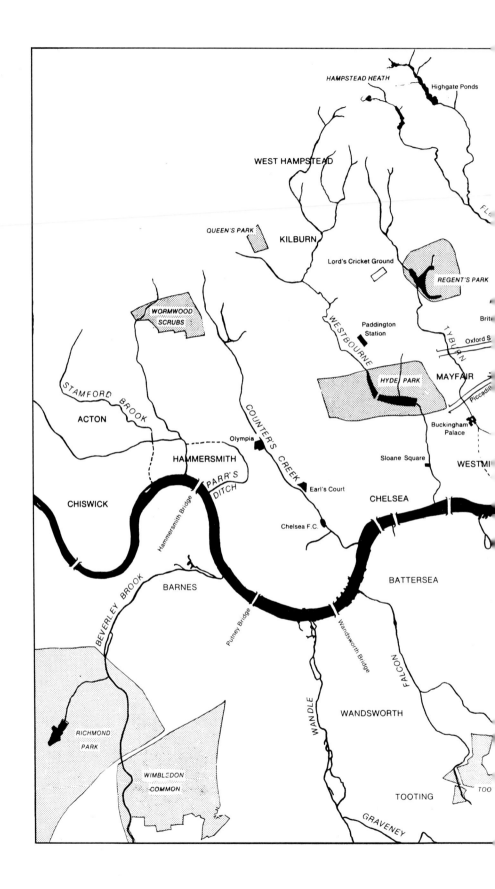

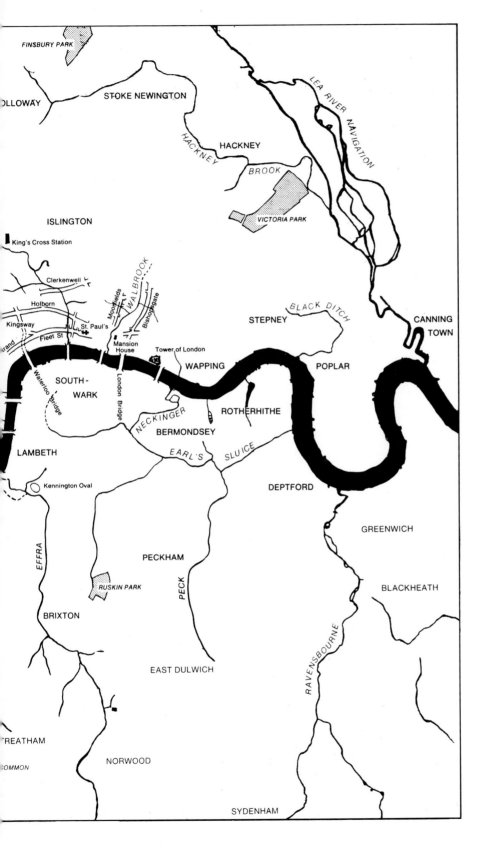

*A map showing where London's rivers run; most of them flow in tunnels and pipes beneath city streets.*

FINSBURY PARK

OLLOWAY

STOKE NEWINGTON

HACKNEY

HACKNEY

HACKNEY BROOK

ISLINGTON

VICTORIA PARK

King's Cross Station

LEA RIVER NAVIGATION

Clerkenwell

Moorfields

WALBROOK

Bishopsgate

STEPNEY

BLACK DITCH

CANNING TOWN

Holborn

Kingsway

St. Paul's

Strand

Fleet St

Mansion House

Tower of London

WAPPING

POPLAR

SOUTH-WARK

London Bridge

Waterloo Bridge

NECKINGER

ROTHERHITHE

BERMONDSEY

EARL'S SLUICE

LAMBETH

Kennington Oval

DEPTFORD

GREENWICH

EFFRA

PECKHAM

RUSKIN PARK

PECK

BLACKHEATH

BRIXTON

RAVENSBOURNE

EAST DULWICH

TREATHAM

COMMON

NORWOOD

SYDENHAM

25

northern side, in the suburbs, excellent springs, the water of which is sweet, clear and salubrious, 'mid glistening pebbles gliding playfully, amongst which Holywell, Clerkenwell and St Clement's Well are of the most note, and most frequently visited as well by the scholars of the schools, as by the youth of the city when they go out to take the air in the summer evenings.

They are referred to again by the second of London's great chroniclers, John Stow, a contemporary of Shakespeare, who devoted a lifetime's study to London ('My feet . . . have borne me many a mile'), giving us in his *Survay of London* the most comprehensive picture we have of London before the Great Fire.

> Anciently until the Conqueror's time, and for two hundred years after that, the Citie of London was watered (besides the famous river of the Thames on the south part) with the rivers of Wels, as it was then called, on the west: with the water called Walbrooke, running through the midst and with a fourth water or Bourne, which ran within the Citie through Langbourne Ward, watering that part in the east. In the west was also another great water, called Oldbourne . . . And after this manner was this citie served with sweet and fresh waters, which being since decayed, other means have been sought to supply the want.

These springs and streams continued to provide London with 'sweet and fresh water' until the thirteenth century, by which time their lower reaches had become so polluted that they were abandoned as sources of drinking water for other streams, wells and conduits bringing clear water from the outlying villages of Bayswater, Hampstead and Islington. The waters were used instead by tanners for dyeing, merchants for transporting and millers for grinding. Yet their upper reaches, flowing through the fields and meadows surrounding the city, remained 'sweet, clear and salubrious, 'mid glistening pebbles gliding playfully' until the middle of the nineteenth century.

The burying of London's rivers was a gradual process, beginning with the lower parts in the sixteenth century, when London burst out of its walls, spreading out towards the surrounding villages. The rivers formed natural valleys; valleys were natural roads; houses sprang up along roads; roads required drains; drains flowed into rivers; rivers became sewers; sewers became culverts.

You can still follow the courses of these residual streams, from the hills that look down over London, through the gentle valleys and backyard ravines, to the Thames. Each of London's underground rivers can be walked in an afternoon, though for some of them you should make it a long afternoon. You don't need a compass and a file of Ordnance Survey maps. An A-Z is sufficient. You can check your course by the slight pressure of the gradient on your ankle. And should you tire, your feet aching, remember John Stow.

## THE WALBROOK

The City, the heart of London, has its own river. The Walbrook rises from a series of rivulets in Islington and Hoxton, which then merge into two streams just south of the old Roman wall and run through the City into the Thames near Cannon Street Station.

The western source starts in Islington, runs down City Road (where, until the early nineteenth century, it remained open at the City Road Turnpike, powering a lead mill) and under the western side of Finsbury Pavement. At the Roman wall, now London Wall, it passes into the City through a culvert, described by Stow as 'an iron grate in the channel which runneth under the watercourse of Walbrook before ye come to the posterne called Moorgate'.

The eastern source begins about a mile away, at Waterson Street in Hoxton. From there it continues south-west down Hackney Road, then south down Curtain Road, with the London College of Fashion on its left bank and the National Safe Deposit Company (where the Walbrook was uncovered during excavations in 1873) on its right, and runs on, parallel to the Broad Street railway line, beneath the burial grounds of Bethlem Hospital (the original 'Bedlam'), now an NCP car park, under Liverpool Street – skirting the eastern side of Finsbury Pavement – to a culvert in London Wall. The eastern culvert was uncovered during building work in 1842 and matches Stow's description of the western culvert:

> Opposite Finsbury Chambers, at a depth of 19 feet, what appeared to have been a subterranean aqueduct was laid open. It was found to run towards Finsbury, under the houses of the Circus for about 29 feet, and at the termination were iron bars fastened into the masonry to prevent the sedge and weeds from choking the passage. The arched entrance, 3 feet 6 inches in height, by 3 feet 3 inches in width, had evidently been above ground as quantities of moss still adhered to the masonry.

*The Walbrook's 'Dowgate torrents falling into the Thames' – a reconstruction by Alan Sorrell of the mouth of the river.*

Evidently these two culverts were insufficient to contain the waters of the Walbrook, which not only regularly flooded the City Ditch, but also spread into Moorfields, where – according to Fitzstephens – the youth of London skated in winter, 'when that vast fen which waters the walls of the City towards the north is hard frozen'.

The Walbrook, beyond London Wall, divided the Roman city into

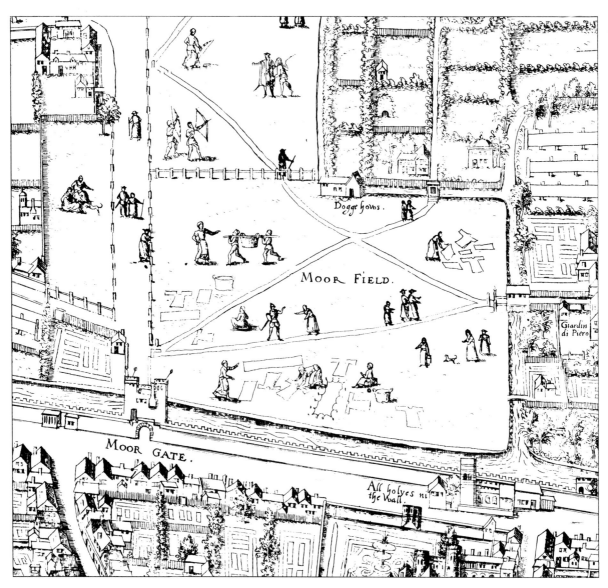

*A detail of Moorfields from one of the earliest maps of London (1558), showing the upper reaches of the Walbrook flowing into the City Ditch. Below the City walls the river was already underground.*

two, 'which division is till this day constantly and without change maintained', wrote John Stow, describing the tradition by which juries were selected. The City Ordinances of the Middle Ages lay down that 'the proceedure, according to the ancient usage of the City of London, is wont to be that eighteen men must be chosen from the east side of the Walebroke, and eighteen men from the west side'.

28

Stow described the Walbrook in the two centuries after the Norman Conquest as a 'fair brook of sweet water'. By the thirteenth century it was neither 'fair' nor 'sweet', providing mediaeval London with its most convenient open sewer, 'worse cloyed and choken than ever before'. In 1288, during the reign of Edward I, it was ordained that 'the watercourse of Walbrook should be made free from dung and other nuisances', and in 1300 its lower reaches were covered in.

In 1374, during the reign of Edward II, the Walbrook at Moorfields was leased to Thomas atte Ram, a brewer:

> upon the understanding that the same Thomas shall keep the said Moor well and properly . . . cleared of dung and other filth thrown or deposited therein . . . he taking for every latrine built upon the said watercourse 12 pence yearly . . . And if so cleansing it, as aforesaid, he shall find aught therein, he shall have for his own all that he shall so find in the dung and filth thereof.

After London Wall the two streams join under Drapers' Hall, and run under Angel Court, the site of several mediaeval tanneries. The united Walbrook continues under St Margaret's Lothbury – which was built over it on vaults – to Sir John Soane's Bank of England, where, as late as November 1803, it was visible 'still trickling among the foundations of the new buildings of the Bank'. From there it curves west under Poultry, then south under Bucklersbury. This was the highest point at which the river was navigable in Roman times, and it was here that they built their port and a temple dedicated to Mithras.

The covering-in of the Walbrook's middle and lower reaches took place in 1463, when a Royal Act ordered that 'such as have ground on either side of the Walbrook, should vault and pave it over as far as his grounds extended'. All this took a century, and by Stow's time its entire course, except for the City Road Turnpike at its source and Dowgate at its estuary, was underground.

Continuing towards the Thames, past Wren's church of St Stephen Walbrook, the Walbrook flows just to the west of the street which bears its name, under Cannon Street (where its unseen presence is marked by a dip in the street's surface), and down Dowgate Hill. Here the river was open in Stow's day, and had such a swift course that in 1574, 'a lad of eighteen years old, minding to have leapt over the channel, was borne down that narrow stream towards the Thames with such violent swiftness as no man could rescue or stay him, till he came against a cart wheel that stood in the watergate, before which he was drowned and stark dead'.

From Dowgate the Walbrook crosses Upper Thames Street and flows into the Thames near Dowgate Pumping Station. If you sit on the terrace outside The Bouncing Bowler in Cousin Lane, by Cannon Street Station, you can still see its remains after a heavy rainstorm coming out of the Walbrook Sewer, a mere ghost of an outlet compared to Ben Jonson's 'Dowgate torrents falling into the Thames'.

## THE FLEET

Parallel to the Walbrook is the Fleet, best-documented of London's rivers. Sometimes called the Holbourne, the River of Wells or Turnmill Brook, it rises in Hampstead and flows through Camden Town, King's Cross and Clerkenwell, joining the Thames near Blackfriars Bridge. The inspiration for Ben Jonson's *Famous Voyage*, the sweaty backdrop for Pope's *Dunciad*, and the research ground for Samuel Pickwick's *Speculations on the Source of Hampstead Ponds with some Observations on the Theory of Tittlebats*, it is the most literary of London's underground rivers

Whatever the source of Hampstead Ponds, together with Highgate Ponds they are the source of the Fleet, which flows from Hampstead Ponds down Haverstock Hill, and from Highgate Ponds down Highgate Road, uniting under Hawley Road, just north of Camden Town Underground station, and from there flows down Pancras Way, once called Pancras Wash, to King's Cross.

For the Fleet, as for London's other rivers, it was the expansion and development of London – turning lanes into roads, roads into highways, and highways into high streets – that buried the river. Its upper reaches, from King's Cross to Hampstead, remained open until the beginning of the nineteenth century, when the excavation of the Regent's Canal in 1812 and the development of Camden Town submerged the stretch of river from King's Cross to Camden Town.

*Sources of the Fleet: Hampstead Ponds (below), and Highgate Ponds (bottom), in Kenwood.*

The continuing development of Hampstead in the nineteenth century made the final cover-up from Camden Town to Hampstead and Highgate Ponds, and its diversion into the high-level interceptory sewer in 1872, inevitable.

The Fleet continues between Gray's Inn Road and King's Cross Road (formerly Bagnigge Wells Road) in the valley now used by the Metropolitan Line. Meandering between Mount Pleasant, Black Hill and Saffron Hill, it became a pivot of revolutionary London's defences against the Royalists in 1643, when a vast number of earthworks were built on either side of the Fleet to protect the City's northern approaches from Prince Rupert. One newspaper reported:

*Top:*
*The Fleet running alongside Bagnigge Wells Road, now King's Cross Road, in the valley presently used by the Metropolitan Line.*

*Above:*
*'Mr Deputy Dumpling and Family enjoy a Summer Afternoon' at Bagnigge Wells.*

> Many thousands of men and women (good housekeepers), their children and servants, went out of the several parishes of London with spades, shovels, pickaxes, and baskets, and drums and colours before them; some of the chief men of every parish marching before them, and so went into the fields, and worked hard all day digging and making trenches from fort to fort . . . and late at night the company came back in like manner they went out, and the next day many more went, and so they continued daily, with such cheerfulnesse that the whole will be finished ere many days.

The Fleet continues along the railway line by Farringdon Road, with Turnmill Street (which gave the river the name of Turnmill Brook) on its left. Frequently referred to as Turnbull Street, it was a well-known place for whoring and villainy. The Rose Tavern was said

*The Red Lion – Jonathan Wilde's house and Dick Turpin's hideout – from the front (top), and from the Fleet at the rear (above).*

to be the scene of many of Falstaff's and Justice Shallow's youthful exploits, while the Red Lion (Jonathan Wilde's house) was reputed to have been the hideout of Dick Turpin. 'Vice of every kind was rampant in this locality,' wrote William Pinks, a nineteenth-century John Stow and historian of Clerkenwell, 'no measures being effectual for its suppression; the appointed officers of the law were both defied and terrified.' Turnmill Street was also the site of a series of watermills, with 'a good stream and current that will turn a mill to grind hair-powder or liquerish or other things', according to an advertisement in the *Daily Courant* of 1741.

The line of mills continued down Farringdon Road as far as Carthouse Street, where a tributary, Faggeswell Brook, joined it from Smithfield. Here the slaughterhouses and tanneries turned the Fleet red. Tanning was one of London's leading mediaeval industries, and the source of many complaints from others who used the Fleet. In 1307, Henry Lacey, Earl of Lincoln, told Parliament that 'whereas in times past the River Fleet has been of such depth and breadth, that ten or twelve ships with merchandise were wont to come to Fleet Bridge, and some of them to Old Bourne Bridge, now the same course, by the filth of the tanneries and such others, and by the raising of wharfs, is stopped up.'

With Snow Hill on its left as it flows through a valley so steep that it is almost a ravine, the Fleet continued to be of strategic value to London. It was the western boundary of Londinium Augusta, and as the City grew it took on a new function – that of separating Westminster from the City. The possession of its bridges was vital for any revolutionary uprising:

> About the latter end of October, Monmouth said to Sir Thomas Armstrong and Lord Grey that it was necessary for them to view the passage into the City, which accordingly they did from the lower end of Fleet Ditch next the river to the other end of it at Snow Hill . . . At Fleet Bridge we designed to use our cannon upon the land carriages, and to make a breast works for our musqueteers on each side of the bridge next us, and to fill the houses on that side the ditch with men, who should fire from the windows, but the bridge to be clear.
>
> (Lord Grey: *Secret History of the Rye House Plot and Monmouth Rebellion*)

The Fleet continues down Farringdon Street under Holborn Viaduct (where there had been a bridge since Stow's time). Here in mediaeval days, according to Stow, another tributary joined the Fleet, the Old Bourne, which:

> broke out about the place where the bars [Temple Bar] do stand, and it ran down the whole street till Oldbourne Bridge, and into the river of the Wells or Turnmill Brook. This bourne was likewise long since stopped up at the head, and in other places where the same has broken out, but yet till this day the said Street is called High Oldbourne Hill, and both sides thereof, together with all the grounds adjoining, that lie betwixt it and the river Thams remain full of springs, so that water is there found at hand and hard to be stopped in every house.

It was at Holborn Bridge that those two attractive lunatics, Sir Ralph Shelton and Sir Christopher Heyden, made their epic journey in Ben Jonson's *Famous Voyage*, in which the Fleet eclipses in foulness all four rivers of Hades:

> At Bread-streets Mermaid, having din'd and merry,
> Propos'd to goe to Hol'borne in a wherry . . .
> And many a sinke pour'd out her rage anenst'hem . . .
> But still their valour, and their vertue fenc't'hem . . .
> And so they did, from *Stix* to *Acheron*:
> The every-boyling floud. Whose banks upon
> Your Fleet-lane Furies; and hot cookes doe dwell,
> That, with still-scalding steemes, make the place hell . . .
> Upon your eares, of discords so un-sweet?
> And out-cryes of the damned in the Fleet?

Flowing on south, the Fleet crosses Newcastle, Fleet and Seacoal Lanes, sites of large coal wharfs in the seventeenth century. At Fleet Lane the river was spanned by another bridge, which, wrote John Stow, was

> a bridge of stone, fair coped on either side with iron pikes; on which, towards the south, be also certain lanthorns of stone, for lights to be placed on winter evenings, for commodity of travellers.

*Holborn Bridge was built by Wren as the ornamental end of the 'New Canal' in 1674. The architect Sir William Tite wrote in 1840, four years before this engraving was made: 'The Sewer of Holborn Hill was opened, & as I was passing, I saw the southern face of the Bridge which crossed the Fleet at this place uncovered to some extent. It was built of red brick, & the arch was about twenty feet span.'*

Samuel Scott's 'Mouth of the River Fleet', showing the New Canal and Fleet Bridge, built by Wren at a cost of £74,000. Ten years after his death, the entire river was arched over and hidden from view.

Beyond the bridge the Fleet supplied the moat around Fleet Prison on the eastern side of Farringdon Street.

Most of the great wharfs that flanked the river at this point were destroyed in the Great Fire of 1666. In his design for rebuilding London after the Fire, Wren envisaged six bridges spanning the Fleet, but his plans were rejected. The river was, however, deepened from Holborn Bridge to the Thames, its banks built up with brick and stone, and a new bridge erected by him at Holborn. The 'New Canal', as this stretch of the Fleet was renamed, was cut to a standard width and a depth of five feet; it was spanned by four bridges with storage vaults under their ramps and pillars. The labour was beset with difficulties: workmen were press-ganged into the Navy, construction was delayed by silting and the cost of the enterprise trebled. It was an unprofitable speculation. The toll was high and the rate of traffic low, while its banks became focal points for the lower forms of London life.

The New Canal hardly possessed the romantic appearance of Samuel Scott's painting of the Mouth of the River Fleet, while Ned Ward, in his *London Spy*, questioned the expense lavished on it:

> From hence on we took a turn by the Ditch side, I desiring my friend to inform me what great advantage this costly brook contributed to the town, to countervail the expense of £74,000, which I had read in a very credible

author was the charge of its making: He told me he was wholly unacquainted with any, unless it was now and then to bring up a few chalfron of coals to two or three peddling coal-merchants, who sell them never the cheaper to the poor for such a conveniency, and as for the cellars you see on each side design'd for warehouses, they are wholly useless except . . . to harbour frogs, toads, and other vermin. The greatest good that I ever heard it did was to the undertaker, who is bound to acknowledge he has found better fishing in that muddy stream than ever he did in clear water.

Swift's *City Shower* confirms Ned Ward's view:

> Now from all parts the swelling kennels flow,
> And bear their trophies with them as they go:
> Filth of all hues and odours seem to tell
> What streets they sailed from by their sight or smell.
> They, as each torrent drives its rapid course,
> And in huge confluence joined at Snowhill ridge,
> Fall from the conduit prone to Holbourne Bridge;
> Seepings from butcher's stalls, dung, guts and blood,
> Drown'd puppies, stinking sprats, all drenched in mud,
> Dead cats and turnip-tops, come tumbling down the flood.

By the early eighteenth century, the Fleet's days in the open were numbered; but before the river finally disappears from view, one last

*Overleaf: Bridewell Bridge, from Pope's* Dunciad, *with the Bridewell itself on the right. Originally a palace, the home of kings, it became a prison, the home of whores. Hogarth made it the setting for the fourth episode of 'The Harlot's Progress'. Its most notorious inhabitant was Mistress Cresswell, a contemporary of Nell Gwyn. On her death she left a legacy of £10, upon conditions. 'By the will of the deceased, it is expected that I mention her, & say nothing but what is* well *of her. All that I shall say of her, however is this: she was born* well, *she lived* well, *& she died* well; *for she was born with the name of Cress*well, *she lived in Clerken*well, *& she died in Bride*well.'

35

*Here strip my Children! here at once leap in*
*Here prove who best can dash thro' thick & thin.*

Dunciad Book II.

literary bouquet thrown into it should be recalled: Pope's *Dunciad*, his Dantesque journey through the inferno of London, in which he meets all the critics, hypocrites, scoundrels and hacks whom he has encountered in his human life.

> This labour past, by Bridewell all descend,
> (As morning pray'r and flagellation end)
> To where Fleet-Ditch with disemboguing streams
> Rolls the large tribute of dead dogs to Thames,
> The King of dykes! than whom no sluice of mud
> With deeper sable blots the silver flood.
> 'Here strip, my children! here at once leap in,
> 'Here prove who best can dash thro' thick and thin.'

In 1732, just ten years after Wren's death, Parliament gave permission for the Fleet to be arched over from Holborn Bridge to the Punch Tavern at Fleet Street. In 1765, its lower reaches, from Fleet Street to the Thames, were also arched over. The Fleet had become a sewer – its role enshrined in the mid-nineteenth century by William Pinks, when he called it 'the *Cloaca Maxima*' of the metropolis.

The arching-over of the River Fleet provided eighteenth-century London with an underground myth comparable with the alligators under twentieth-century New York – an obese pig lost in the sewer. Soon whole species of subterranean pigs were reported to be living under London. The story first appeared in the *Gentleman's Magazine* on 24 August 1736:

> A fatter boar was hardly ever seen than one taken up this day, coming out of the Fleet ditch into the Thames. It proved to be a butcher's near Smithfield Bars, who had missed him five months, all which time he had been in the common sewer, and was improved in price from ten shillings to two guineas.

The last description we have of the arched-over New Canal comes from the Victorian artist Anthony Crosby:

> There are no less than four bridges over the Fleet River at that part called Holborn-bridge. They are joined together at their sides, two of these evidently having been added at different periods to widen the passage of the original bridge; and the additional bridge, which was erected by Wren,

*Top:*
*The Fleet Canal during its brief period of rehabilitation after the Great Fire. The 'New Canal' was cut to a standard width and depth of five feet, and spanned by four bridges.*

*Above:*
*Bridewell, 'To where Fleet-Ditch with disemboguing streams/Rolls the large tribute of dead dogs to Thames'.*

37

South View of Fleet Bridge.

Deposition
of
Mr Thomas Calladine, one of the
Brothers of the Charter House, London.
Made at his own Room in the Charterhouse
No 18.

Saith he is now aged Ninety Six
years of age, that is to say he was Ninety
five on the 24 of April last. He well remembers
Fleet Bridge, having often gone over it
when a Young Man. It was a Stone Bridge
of One Arch. It had, to the best of deponents
recollection no stone parapet, but a Wooden Rail
and posts on the South side - and was joined
on the North to Fleet Market, as seen in the
above view. drawn on this same half sheet of
paper. Deponent at the time he used to go
over the Fleet Bridge (which went from Fleet
Street to Ludgate Street, and which bridge was
flat and had no ascent) was serving his
Apprenticeship to Mr Edward, Tailor, of Wine Office
Court. Deponent signs this his relation this
thirteenth day of December One thousand Eight
hundred and thirty Nine, at p 6. P. M.

Tho Calladine

Witness to the above deposition
and signature by deponent.

Thomas Hall of the Charty
Anthony Crosley Esqr      Brothers Charterhouse

38

was introduced not only to secure that object, but to supply a beautiful terminus to the grand canal that was formed after the great fire of 1666 by the cutting and embanking of the River Fleet from Holborn to the Thames. The whole of these bridges are now hidden . . . and of the thousands who still daily pass over them perhaps there is scarcely one who has ever heard of their existence.

Crosby's description was to prove the Fleet's epitaph; seven years later, in 1846, the river – quite literally – blew up, its rancid and foetid gases bursting out into the street above. At King's Cross the road was impassable; in Clerkenwell three poorhouses were swept away in a tidal wave of sewage; and a Thames steamboat was smashed against Blackfriars Bridge.

The rebuilt Fleet continues its ducted course under Ludgate Circus (touching Fleet Street) and on down New Bridge Street, with the Bridewell on its right and the Carmelite monastery of Whitefriars on its left. (In 1290 the monks of Whitefriars had complained that the smell of the Fleet overcame the incense burnt at Mass.) It continues past Baynard Castle to the Embankment at Blackfriars. There, on rainy days, you can still see the Fleet tumbling down to its final destination as the river 'rolls the large tribute of dead dogs' to the Thames.

West of the Fleet flows the Tyburn, sometimes called the Aye, or King's Scholar's Pond, and often confused with Tyburn Brook, which runs past the place of execution. Originally called 'Teo Burns' (Two Brooks), it was first referred to in an amateur forgery by Anglo-Saxon monks, the Charter of King Edgar (anno 951), which granted the lands of Westminster to Archbishop Dunstan. Unfortunately for the forgers, Edgar was not crowned until six years after the supposed Charter, while Dunstan did not become Archbishop of Canterbury until ten years after that.

The eastern source of the Tyburn is a spring just behind Hampstead Town Hall on Haverstock Hill. It flows along Belsize Avenue ('Belasis' – beautifully situated), across Adelaide and Avenue Roads to the crossroads of Norfolk and Woronzow Roads.

The western source, which also emerges on Haverstock Hill, springs up from behind the imitation French château, once called Shepherd's Well, on Lyndhurst Road, and runs through the eastern side of Fitzjohn's Avenue, under the Central School of Speech and Drama, behind the Hampstead Theatre and under Adelaide Road, to join the eastern source at Woronzow Road. From there the united streams, flowing in the valley between Primrose Hill and Ordnance Hill, cross Prince Albert Road and run over the Grand Union Canal in a cast-iron pipe built within the brick footbridge.

These upper reaches were meadows until the mid-nineteenth-century housing boom swallowed Hampstead, but the river's lower

## THE TYBURN

reaches had been recognised as a sewer as early as 1672. By 1860, when John Hollingshead made a journey down it, it had been entirely bricked over.

His voyage through the bowels of Victorian London has all the excitement, adventure and melodrama of the search for the source of the Nile:

> The entrance to King's Scholar's Pond Main Sewer, that I decided to go down by, is close to the cab-stand at St John's Wood Chapel . . . The side entrance is a square brick-built shaft, having a few iron rings driven into two of its sides. These rings form the steps by which you ascend and descend, putting your feet on one as you seize hold of the other . . . When the daylight was shut out, a closed lantern was put in my hand; I was led stooping along a short yellow-bricked passage, and down a few steps, as if going into a wine cellar, until I found myself standing knee-deep in the flowing sewer . . . Turning ourselves towards the Thames we waded for some time, in a stooping posture, through the sewer, three of my guides going on first with lanterns, and two following me. We passed through an iron tube, about three foot high and two feet broad, which conveys the sewage over the Regent's Canal, through the crown of the bridge. It was not until we got onto some lower levels, towards Baker Street, that the sewer became sufficiently large to allow us to stand upright.

Beyond the Grand Union Canal, the Tyburn runs south under the American Ambassador's residence through Regent's Park to the artificial lake, where it is joined by a small tributary that rises under London Zoo; it then continues down Gloucester Place and swings east under Baker Street, Aybrook Street and Marylebone Lane. At Wigmore Street, it makes a small zigzag to the east – 'turned by order of the City' in 1738 – and crosses Oxford Street, almost under the present HMV record shop – where it was turned by the proprietors of the Central London Railway in 1899.

Under ground the intrepid Hollingshead continued his journey:

> At different parts of our course we passed through the blue rays of light, like moonlight, that came down from the ventilator gratings in the highway above. Under one of these we heard a boy whistling in the road, and I felt like Baron Trenck escaping from prison . . . Although underground, we passed over the Metropolitan Railway in the New Road, and then along the line of Baker Street, under Oxford Street, and through Berkeley Square . . . As we got lower down our great underground channel, the roof became higher and higher, and the sides broader and broader; but the flooring, I am sorry to say, became more jagged and uneven. The lower bricks had been washed out, leaving great holes, down which one or other of my legs kept slipping, at the hazard of my balance and my bones, We peeped up at an old red-bricked, long-disused branch sewer, under some part of Mayfair, that was almost blocked up to the roof with mountains of black, dry, earthy deposits.

In 1875, just fourteen years after Hollingshead made his momentous voyage, workmen excavating a sewer in Stratford Place,

40

just off Oxford Street, came upon a stone structure. It was London's first reservoir, built in 1216 to store water from the Tyburn for the Great Conduit, which ran eastwards from Oxford Street to Cheapside, supplying the City with water.

Not far away, at the corner of North Audley Street, workmen uncovered a Roman bath which had once been fed by the Tyburn. The main room was about four foot by twelve, supported by eight arches. In the middle of the room was a stone bath, still half-full of water.

On the other side of Oxford Street, the Tyburn runs parallel to Bond Street, across Brook Street and round Berkeley Square in the valley between Hay and Grosvenor Hills. It turns west into Curzon Street, under the concrete headquarters of the British Secret Service and the Third Church of Christ Scientist, behind Lord Palmerston's London house, across Piccadilly into the valley of Green Park, dividing into a delta that radiates out from under Buckingham Palace.

Our Victorian explorer's next stop was the Palace itself:

> In Piccadilly we went up the side entrance, just to get a mouthfull of fresh air, and a glimpse of Green Park, and then went down again to finish our journey . . . We had not proceeded much further in our downward course when . . . the guides stopped short, and asked me where I supposed I was now? I thought the question quite unnecessary, as my position in the sewer was pretty evident . . .
> 'I give up', I replied.
> 'Well, Buckingham Palace', was the answer.
> Of course my loyalty was at once excited, and, taking off my fan-tailed cap, I led the way with the National Anthem, insisting that my guides should join in the chorus.

From Buckingham Palace, the eastern branch of the Tyburn (once diverted to feed Rosamond's Pond in St James's Park) flows under

*A sewer worker descends into the bowels of Buckingham Palace. In 1860 he would have been doffing his cap and singing the national anthem alongside that intrepid and patriotic underground explorer, John Hollingshead.*

41

*Top:*
*Rosamond's Pond, like the Serpentine in Hyde Park, was an artificial stretch of water in St James's Park, fed by the River Tyburn.*

*Above:*
*Thornea Island, 'that awesome place called Westminster'. St Peter blessing the church on the island, from an apocryphal mediaeval manuscript.*

Wellington Barracks, along Petty France, to Tothill Street (once Tothill Fields, the site of King's Scholar's Pond), where it divides again. One branch goes east along Broad Sanctuary, across Parliament Square, under the Treasury, across Whitehall and into the Thames by the 'old' New Scotland Yard. The other goes south under Great Smith Street and into the Thames at Millbank. The island formed by the two branches, variously called Thornea, Thorneye or Thorney Island, is at 'that awesome place called Westminster' (Offa's Charter, 785).

The southern branch of the Tyburn leaves Buckingham Palace and runs down Palace Street, across Victoria Street under Willow Place, across Vauxhall Bridge Road and down Tachbrook Street, falling into the Thames under the Tachbrook Estate. For that final part of his journey John Hollingshead travelled by punt:

> The journey was wanting in that calmness, light and freshness which generally belongs to boat journeys, and while there was a good deal of Styx and Charon about it in imagination, there was a close unpleasant steam about it in reality . . .

> By this time our bark had floated out of the broad archway of the sewer – an arch as wide as any bridge-arch on the Regent's Canal, and we were anchored on that pea-soup-looking open creek that runs for some distance along the side of the Equitable Gas Works. The end of this creek, where it enters the Thames, is closed with tidal gates, which are watched by a kind of sewer lock-keeper, who lives in the cottage immediately over the sewer. He cultivates flowers and vegetables at the side of the channel, and his little

dwelling is a model of cleanliness and tasteful arrangement.

That last stretch of the Tyburn remained open until the 1970s. In spite of that the river is almost forgotten. Possibly because of the Tyburn's confusion with Tyburn Brook, which runs into the Westbourne, and its false association with the place of execution, it is the only one of London's underground rivers not to be remembered in place or street names. There is a Brook Street and an Aybrook Street, but there is only one 'Tyburn' in central London, and that marks the executioner's block, not the river's course.

## THE WESTBOURNE

The Westbourne, the most westerly of central London's rivers, emerges from Hampstead Heath just a few hundred yards from the western source of the Fleet. But for the narrow ridge near the Vale of Health (so named because it was a refuge for Londoners during the Plague) the Westbourne would have ended up as another source of the Fleet. Also called Bayswater Brook, after Baynard's Watering Place, and – more realistically – the Ranleigh Sewer, it runs from Hampstead Heath, through Kilburn and Paddington, across Hyde Park, where it formed the Serpentine, to the Thames at Chelsea. It is still remembered in the names of fourteen streets, avenues, places, gardens, groves, roads and terraces along its route.

The Westbourne rises at the Whitestone Ponds by the top of Heath Street, near Jack Straw's Castle. From there it runs under the vandalised drinking fountain and down the steep slope of Branch Hill to Redington Gardens, where it is joined by two tributaries, one from Oak Hill and the other from Telegraph Hill. The combined streams, running south-west, cross Finchley Road and West End Lane, joining Kilburn High Road near Hermit Place and Kilburn Priory.

Here the Westbourne is joined by another tributary, the Kilbourne (Cunebourne in Anglo-Saxon), which springs from the fish pond by Frognal Lane, crosses Finchley Road and joins the Westbourne at Kilburn Priory.

The Priory, which dates from the reign of Henry I, was the home of the hermit Godwyn, who built his cell by the side of the Kilbourne at Hermit Place, between the Punch Tavern and the Decca Records' offices. The Kilbourne supplied the Priory's moat until the dissolution of the monasteries in 1536, when it was described as the 'Nonnerie of Kilnborne'. The Priory's tessellated tile flooring, as well as a bell's clapper, a Gothic key and traces of human bones, was uncovered when workmen were widening the railway line from south Hampstead to Willesden Junction in 1850.

From Kilburn Priory, the Westbourne crosses Maida Vale and continues south-west along Kilburn Park Road to Shirland Road, where it is joined by another tributary from Willesden. It continues across Elgin Avenue, turns south to Dorchester Road under the Grand

Union Canal, the Westway flyover and the main line out of Paddington station. It turns west at Bishop's Bridge Road (a famous spot for fishing in the days of William Blake), then south under the gardens between Gloucester Terrace and Brook Mews, across Bayswater Road and into Hyde Park a little to the west of Lancaster Gate.

In Hyde Park the Westbourne formed eleven small pools. It was dammed in 1730 by Queen Caroline, wife of George II, at a cost of £20,000 (a mere £14,000 above the original estimate) and called the Serpentine. There the Westbourne receives another small tributary, Tyburn Brook, which rises under the flats of Portsea Hall and joins the Serpentine by the boat house to the west of the two small islands.

The river remained open in its reaches above the Serpentine until 1856. But as first Bayswater, then Hampstead, and finally Kilburn grew, so the river became more polluted and crowded in by buildings. By 1834 the housing expansion in Bayswater had so sullied the Westbourne that its waters were diverted by pipes from the Serpentine – which had become a cess-pit – and its lower reaches were completely covered over.

At Knightsbridge, where the Westbourne comes out of the Park at Albert Gate, the river was spanned by a bridge, the Knight's Bridge, a favourite spot for highwaymen. In 1593 a contemporary of Stow had described it as 'a dangerous place for a true man without good garde, unless he can make his party good, as did Sir H Knyvet, who valiently defended himselfe, there being assalted, and slew the master theefe with his own hands'.

On the other side of Knightsbridge, the Westbourne passes under the Park Tower Sheraton, down William Street and Lowndes Square, on under Cadogan Lane, crossing the staid east end of King's Road at Cliveden Place. This was the site of Bloody Bridge, another dangerous bottleneck for night-travellers, where Lord Harrington's cook, amongst others, was robbed and killed by highwaymen.

From King's Road, the Westbourne used to flow into the Five Fields, a desolate swamp which stretched from the suicides' cemetery in the gardens of Buckingham Palace to the Thames. By 1817, when Edgar Allan Poe was at school near Bloody Bridge, it had degenerated into a vast cess-pit:

A barren waste existed, fetid, damp,
Cheered by the ray of no enlivening lamp.
A marshy spot, where not one patch of green,
No stunted scrub, nor sickly flower was seen;
But all things base, the refuse of the town,
Lothsome and rank, in one foul mess was thrown.

The swamp was reclaimed in 1827 by master-builder Thomas Cubitt on behalf of George Basevi, Disraeli's uncle, the designer of Belgrave Square. Cubitt diverted and channelled the Westbourne, removing the surface clay from under the swamp, and turning the clay into bricks. The foetid swamp was transformed into one of the most fashionable districts of London,

> . . . Where Palaces do stand,
> Where dwell at ease the magnates of the land.

Cubitt moved on to Pimlico, a muddy lagoon on the Thames, where – using the clay as bricks again – and replacing it with soil excavated from the newly constructed St Katharine's Dock, he built a whole new district of London.

The Westbourne crosses the District and Circle Lines at Sloane Square and continues down Holbein Place and under Chelsea Barracks. There it divides into two. The western branch crosses Chelsea Bridge Road and Ranelagh Gardens, falling into the Thames between Embankment Gardens and Chelsea Bridge. The eastern branch crosses Ebury Bridge Road, where it once fed the old Chelsea Waterworks, and enters the Thames at the Grosvenor Canal, under the railway tracks leading to Victoria Station.

Two miles west of the Westbourne runs Counter's Creek, or Billingswell Ditch – so named after Billing's Well, the medicinal springs at Earl's Court. It rises on the edge of Harrow Road and Kensal Green Cemetery and flows south under the Grand Union Canal, through Little Wormwood Scrubs, to Kelfield Gardens (still open fields in living memory), where it receives two tributaries from Ladbroke Grove. The combined streams continue south-south-east under the arches of the Westway flyover, then beneath the flats of Freston Road and down St Ann's  Road to Royal Crescent. It runs diagonally under the Shepherd's Bush roundabout, along the railway line to Olympia, where it was once spanned by a bridge built in 1421 by the Countess of Oxford and referred to as 'contesses-brogge'. It was from this that the name of the river was derived.

From Olympia the river runs along the lines of the West London Railway as far as the Thames. Originally the two-mile cut was a canal. Built in 1828, a hundred feet wide and able to carry vessels of 100 tons, it was opened by Lord Kensington – after whom it was named – and christened by a procession of barges, headed by Lord Kensington's. Like the Fleet Canal, it was a financial disaster. Less than twenty years later it was sold to the West London Railway, who drained it, laid tracks, and even made it profitable.

With its course marked by the railway line, it continues alongside Harland Road, Warwick Road and Finborough Road, past Earl's Court Exhibition Centre and Brompton Cemetery. It crosses Fulham Road at Stamford Bridge (where there was first a ford and then a bridge) and is joined by another tributary from Eel Brook Common. In its final stages it crosses King's Road and runs parallel to Lots

**COUNTER'S CREEK**

Road, with Fulham Gas Works on its right bank, to the stagnant slime of Chelsea Creek, and from there – with effort – to the Thames.

**STAMFORD BROOK**  Stamford Brook, last of north London's rivers to be turned into a sewer, runs from Wormwood Scrubs through Ravenscourt Park to the Thames at Hammersmith. It was still open in its upper parts at the beginning of the present century, when it became a sewer. 'You can now, if you get permission, walk up the Stamford Brook as far as Acton,' wrote Sir William Bull in the *Parish Magazine of St Mary's Stamford Brook* of November 1929, 'It is in size a little smaller than a tube railway tunnel.'

From Wormwood Scrubs, Stamford Brook runs to Old Oak Common, touching the south-western corner of the Common, in the garden of the old Acton Wells Assembly Rooms, famous in the days of Queen Anne – when Wormwood Scrubs was infinitely more fashionable than it is today – for their purging waters.

The story of Acton Wells typifies what happened to so many of London's wells. They were fashionable until the days of the American Revolution. An advertisement on 3 July 1771 stated:

> By the recommendation of Physicians and the encouragement of the nobility and gentry Acton Wells are newly opened for the benefit of the public. Every Monday, Wednesday and Friday from Lady Day to Michaelmas are public days for drinking the waters and breakfasting.

But by 13 April 1776 the wells seemed to have lost their following: 'As Mr Owen finds the demand for the water very trifling, the sale is suspended to subscribers.' By 1815 the Assembly Rooms were taken over by a boarding school, and by 1889 anyone in search of the wells had to 'run the gauntlet (to one's nose) of the disgraceful open sewer which was once a purling crystal brooklet, that skirts the Way', Kemp wrote in his *West London Sketcher*.

From Acton Wells Stamford Brook runs south down Old Oak Common Road and Askew Road as far as Davisville Road (where the contours of the land suggest a sharp S-bend) and across Goldhawk Road into Ravenscourt Park, where it fed the artificial lake and once provided a moat around the park.

At Ravenscourt Park it is joined by two tributaries. One, the Warple, rises just north of Acton mainline station and runs south-east to Ravenscourt Park. The other, Bollo Brook, begins on the slopes of Hanger Lane, follows Bollo Lane for about a mile as far as Chiswick Park Underground station, for which, in the 1880s, according to Kemp, it was well-known for 'the agile but thoroughly voracious tittlebat', then runs west along the Piccadilly Line through Bedford Park to Ravenscourt Park.

Beyond the park, Stamford Brook hardly survives as a stream. Almost immediately it divides into three separate branches. One branch, a minor one, turns south-east under Ravenscourt Gardens and runs across Hammersmith to the Thames, a little downstream from Chiswick Park. The second, and more substantial, branch, comes out of the park at Paddenswick Road and flows south, down Middle Lane to the Thames just above Hammersmith Bridge. The most interesting branch flows east to the Metropolitan Line sidings near Hammersmith station, erected on the marsh where it once spread out. Beyond the Metropolitan Line, the brook was drained by Parr's Ditch, an artificial boundary stream, thought to be over 1000 years old, which divides the parishes of Hammersmith and Fulham. Carrying the waters of Stamford Brook, it runs along Brook Green, under Hammersmith Road and Talgarth Road and into the Thames beside the Riverside Studios.

South of the Thames things are different. They always are. Here were marshlands where south London's rivers, coming down from Forest, Denmark, Knight's, and Streatham Hills lost themselves in the flat and flooded reaches of Bermondsey, Southwark and Lambeth. Though south London can boast of three rivers which are still open – the Ravensbourne (which runs through Bromley and Greenwich), Beverley Brook (through Richmond Park) and the Wandle (which is itself fed by the semi-underground Graveney and runs through Wandsworth) – she still secretes four major rivers: the Neckinger, Earl's Sluice, the Effra and the Falcon. Of these the Neckinger and Earl's Sluice are the most easterly.

The Neckinger is probably the best known of south London's rivers. Small compared to the Westbourne or Fleet, its name comes from Neckinger Wharf, or 'Devil's Neckenger', where Thames pirates were executed with a rope known as the 'Devil's Neckcloth' until the mid-eighteenth century.

It rises under the naval guns which front the Imperial War Museum by Lambeth Road and makes a half-circle eastwards along Brook Drive, around the back of St Thomas' Hospital (named after Thomas à Becket and formerly the Almonry of Bermondsey Abbey), and under Elephant and Castle. On the other side of Elephant and Castle roundabout it runs alongside New Kent Road, then crosses over Spurgeon Street then over Dover Street and Tabard Street to Prioress Street, where it turns sharply north-east under the Green Walk to Tower Bridge Road and into Abbey Street. Abbey Street incorporates the site of Bermondsey Abbey, founded in 1082 by Cluniac monks. In the thirteenth century they built a stone bridge across the Neckinger and ran two large mills. One was on the Neckinger and the other, a tidal mill, on the Thames at Rotherhithe, where Albion and Canada Docks now stand. After the dissolution of the monasteries the Rotherhithe mill was converted into a water-raising machine to pipe

## THE NECKINGER AND EARL'S SLUICE

*The Wandle, one of the three south London rivers still flowing above ground.*

*The Ravensbourne, also open, but now entirely urban, runs from its source at Bromley (right), through Greenwich, and into the Thames at Deptford (below).*

MOUTH OF THE RAVENSBOURNE.

water to Southwark and Bermondsey. The other mill, by Millstream Road, became the first gunpowder factory in England to be powered by water. Later both were rebuilt as papermills and became the first mills in England to make paper from straw.

The river was also used by tanners, who often complained that the owner was 'shutting off the tide when it suited his purpose to do so, to the detriment of the leather manufacturers'. The conflict came to court and 'the ancient usages of the district were brought forward in evidence, and the result was that the right of the inhabitants to a supply of water from the river, at every high tide, was confirmed, to the discomfiture of the mill-owners', wrote Sir Charles Knight in 1842.

Tide-mills were dependent on a multitude of reservoir catchments called tide-streams, which filled with water every high tide. At low tide, water was let out through bottlenecks and powered the mill. This is why the Neckinger, and its neighbour, Earl's Sluice, often get lost in the artificial ditches and watercourses on the south bank of the Thames, their exact course a mystery.

Beyond Abbey Street the river crossed Jamaica Road and divided into two branches. Between the two lay Jacob's Island, one of the most squalid blots on the Victorian landscape. The *Morning Chronicle* of 24 September 1849 lampooned it, not only as the 'Venice of Drains', but as the 'Capital of Cholera'. It described the water surrounding it as 'the colour of strong green tea'. Charles Dickens called Jacob's Island 'the filthiest, the strangest, the most extraordinary of the many localities that are hidden in London', and immortalised it in *Oliver Twist*, as the backdrop to Bill Sikes' terrible end.

> In such neighbourhood, beyond Dockland in the Borough of Southwark, stands Jacob's Island, surrounded by a muddy ditch, six or eight feet deep and fifteen or twenty wide when the tide is in, once called Mill Pond, but known these days as Folly Ditch . . . Crazy wooden galleries, with holes from which to look upon the slime beneath; windows, broken and patched, with poles thrust out, on which to dry the linen that is never there; rooms so small, so filthy, so confined, that the air would seem too tainted even for the dirt and squalor which they shelter; wooden chambers thrusting themselves out above the mud and threatening to fall into it – as some have done; dirt-besmeared walls and decaying foundations, every repulsive lineament of poverty, every loathsome indication of filth, rot, and garbage: all these ornament the banks of Folly Ditch.

*'Every repulsive lineament of poverty, every loathsome indication of filth, rot and garbage' characterised the houses on Folly Ditch from which Bill Sikes made his last desperate bid for freedom. A contemporary illustration by George Cruikshank for* Oliver Twist.

South of the Neckinger, and possibly one of its tributaries, runs Earl's Sluice, which flows down Denmark Hill to the Old Kent Road and Rotherhithe, joined there by a tributary from Peckham, the Peck.

At the Old Kent Road there was a watersplash, later replaced by a bridge. It was known as Thomas-à-Watering, after Thomas à Becket. It was the first stop for pilgrims on their way to Canterbury, and Chaucer refers to it in *The Prologue*:

And forth we ridden, a littel more than paas,

Unto the wateryng of Sain Thomas,
And ther our hoost bigin his hors areste.

From Rotherhithe New Road, where it enters the swamps of south London, criss-crossed with mill-ditches and tidal-streams, its course becomes uncertain. One theory is that it joins the Neckinger in Bermondsey. Another is that it falls into the Thames near Rotherhithe station. A third says that it reaches the Thames at South Dock by St George's Steps. Like the corpse of Bill Sikes, the answer lies forever buried in the mud and slime beneath the streets of south London.

THE EFFRA    West of the Neckinger and Earl's Sluice is the Effra. Rising in Norwood and running through Dulwich and Brixton to the Thames at Vauxhall, it is the longest of south London's rivers, comparable in size to the Fleet and the Westbourne. Sir Walter Besant wrote in 1889:

> Forty years ago nightingales in great numbers made their homes in the sequestered portions of the Effra's banks, and flocks of larks might have been seen swooping over Rush Common. The river was then wider than at present, with the current racing along faster than a man could walk. Although its channels were very deep, a day or two of heavy rain invariably caused an overflow, which laid South Lambeth, Kennington and a portion of Brixton, under water.

From its springs in Norwood, between Beulah Hill and Central Hill, the Effra crosses under the A214 and runs down the valley between Salter's Hill and Knight's Hill to Norwood Cemetery. It runs north-east, crossing Thurlow Park Road (the South Circular) under West Dulwich Station, and into Belair Park (where, for a quarter of a mile, it is still open) inhabited by duck and overlooked by Robert Adam's Belair House. It continues along Croxted Road, skirting the eastern side of Brockwell Park, to Herne Hill, where Ruskin used to live. There the river is joined by two tributaries and continues under Railton Road and Coldharbour Lane. Though now known as 'The Front Line', it was until the mid-nineteenth century open country: Walter Besant's Rush Common.

From Brixton the river was just about navigable to the Thames. Over 1000 years ago, King Canute sailed down it: digging a canal from the Neckinger and Earl's Sluice to the Effra so that his troops could bypass London Bridge and attack London from downstream. Seven hundred years later, Queen Elizabeth I sailed up the Effra to Brixton on a visit to Sir Walter Raleigh at Raleigh House.

An old inhabitant of Stockwell traced the course of the Effra with a reporter from the *South London Press* in 1891:

> To speak of the Effra as a river, he confessed, was an extravagance, for in point of fact the 'river' partook more the character of a moderately capacious stream, consisting mainly of the surface water arising in the higher ground of Norwood and the then agricultural neighbourhood of

Brockwell and Herne Hill. The Effra was, at all events, a troublesome stream in the lower levels of Stockwell and Kennington, for a downfall of rain, even of a moderate character, would flood the basements of the houses thereabouts.

In Brixton Road the course of the Effra is clear – defined by the steep banks on either side of the road. Here the river was twelve feet wide and six feet deep, running through the front gardens on the eastern side of Brixton Road, with each front door linked to the pavement on the other side of the river by a little bridge. It continued up Brixton Road to St Mark's Kennington, where it was spanned by Hazard Bridge.

Although the Effra's upper reaches remained open until late in the nineteenth century, its lower reaches beyond Hazard Bridge were already a sewer by 1640, when a butcher, Robert Adison, was made responsible for scouring the river from Hazard's Bridge by the Surrey and Kent Commissioners of Sewers. The systematic building over of the lower reaches took place between 1837 and 1857 – St Mark's Kennington paying £322 towards the costs.

The river continues across Clapham Road to Merton Bridge, named after Merton Abbey, whose monks were responsible for its upkeep. On the other side of Clapham Road the Effra runs under the eastern side of the Oval cricket ground (its raised banks were built with

*Beulah Hill, overlooking the source of the Effra. It became a fashionable spa in the early nineteenth century – on 2 July 1834, 3000 people were present at a fête champêtre – but by 1851 it had, according to* The Times *of 4 June, 'fallen into a languid and deserted condition'.*

earth excavated during the enclosing of the Effra), and continues to Vauxhall, crossing South Lambeth Road at Cox's Bridge ('Cokkesbougge' as it was called in 340 when the Abbot of Westminster was sent a bill for its repairs) and across Nine Elms Lane, to enter the Thames between New Covent Garden and Vauxhall Bridge.

## FALCON BROOK

Most westerly of south London's rivers is Falcon Brook. West of Falcon Brook, south London's rivers are either open, like the Wandle and Beverley Brook, or partly open, like the Graveney, which flows into the Wandle. Originally called the Hildaburna, Falcon Brook rises near Tooting Common and flows between Clapham and Wandsworth Commons, entering the Thames at Battersea. (The name 'Falcon' was not adopted until the seventeenth century, when the Lords of Battersea Manor were the St Johns, whose crest was a falcon rising.)

Beyond Clapham Junction, opposite Falcon Grove, the river divides, making Battersea an island. The main branch goes west, meandering through York Gardens and entering the Thames at Battersea Creek, a few hundred yards upstream from Westland Heliport. The other runs north-east under Falcon Park and along the line of the Victoria to Clapham Junction railway line, past Battersea Dogs' Home to New Covent Garden, where it joins an artificial watercourse, The Ditch, at Nine Elms, which separated the parishes of Lambeth and Battersea, falling into the Thames just downstream from Battersea Power Station.

## HACKNEY BROOK

London's one buried river which does not directly enter the Thames. Hackney Brook, runs from Hornsey, through Highbury, Stoke Newington and Hackney, to the River Lea. Its name is Danish in origin: the 'Hack' of Hackney derived from Haca, a Danish nobleman who once owned the river, and the 'ey' meaning island. Today its valley is occupied by London's high-level interceptory sewer.

The brook rises on the slopes of Crouch Hill and flows south-east across Seven Sisters Road, Isledon Road and the mainline from King's Cross Station along Gillespie Road, past Arsenal Football Stadium. It then runs down Riversdale Road to Clissold Park, and continues east around the tombs, temples and fallen angels of Abney Park Cemetery (a poor man's Highgate), then through Clapton to Hackney Downs, Mare Street and Morning Lane.

At Morning Lane it is joined by the waters of an old well. William Robinson described its demise in the late nineteenth century.

> Some years ago there was a spring of pure water near the old churchyard and Morning Lane, to which the inhabitants used to resort for water. This well has been upwards for a century enclosed within a square brick-and-

tile building, with a doorway entrance. In the year 1837, for want of proper attention, the old building, or well-house, was found to be in a very dilapidated state, and instead of repairing it the churchwardens of that day thought it would be cheaper to pull it down and set up an iron pump, which, by impregnating the water with the quality of iron, has rendered the water once so celebrated almost useless.

The brook continues down Morning Lane, along Wick Street, and, passing close to the northern corner of Victoria Park, goes under the A102 to Iceland Road, where it joins the slow and turgid River Lea.

## LOST RIVERS

There are several lost rivers under London referred to by London's chroniclers but now impossible to trace. As well as the Old Bourne, which Stow says flowed into the Fleet at Holborn Viaduct, there is the Shoreditch, the Cranbourne and the Langbourne.

The Shoreditch, called either after the Anglo-Saxon name for sewer ('shore') or after the neurotic mistress of Edward IV, Elizabeth Shore (who was supposed to have lived beside it), was alleged to run from Shoreditch across Aldgate High Street to the Thames at the Tower.

The Cranbourne was said to run from Leicester Square to the Thames just below Aldwych, and was named after Viscount Cranbourne, heir to the Marquess of Salisbury.

The Langbourne was, according to Stow,

a great stream breaking out of the ground in Fenchurch Street, which ran with a swift course, west, through that street, athwart Gra [Gracechurch] Street and down Lombard Street, to the west end of St Mary Wolnothes church, and then turning the course down Shareborne Lane, so termed of sharing or dividing, it brake into divers rills or rillets to the river of Thames: of this bourn that ward took the name, and is till this day called Langborne ward. This bourn also is long since stopped up at the head, and the rest of the course filled up and paved over, so that no sign thereof remaineth more than the name aforesaid.

The Shoreditch, it would appear from the map, was a confusion with the City Ditch, which ran along its supposed route and provided the moat around the Tower of London. The Cranbourne might have been an illicit sewer built by Richard Frith, the builder who developed Soho, and who has one street named after him. The Langbourne either never existed (since Stow's course takes it uphill) or was one of mediaeval London's primitive sewers. Considering that Shareborne Lane was often nicknamed Shitbourne Lane, a mediaeval sewer seems its more likely role.

Whatever the truth, these rivers are now lost beneath us. And lost with them is another London, which will never reappear. Yet there is still a memory of it, in those springs and streams beneath London that can still be traced, ''mid glistening pebbles gliding playfully', even though their waters no longer run sweet.

53

# 3 The Bowels of the Earth

The sweaty brickwork of the tunnel was closing in on us, the hot and humid smell of detergent contrasting with the cold water all around. With every step, the dull, turbid screen of mist parted to allow us through. Shafts of light from our torches, picking out the sweating highlights of geometrical lines of bricks, created their own claustrophobic *son et lumière*; with every move we made, vast, distorted shadows transformed us into Phantoms of the Opera.

We were wading through the tunnel in single file. Cold, greyish water, flowing eastwards at knee-height, pushed against the backs of our waders, urging us on. We could not walk upright: the egg-shaped tunnel was only five feet high. We moved cramped in a stoop, mirroring the distortion of our shadows on the brickwork.

After a while the man at the head of the file turned around.

'Keep in your place,' he said. 'And if you get lost, then don't start doing anything clever like trying to find us. Just stay where you are. We'll find you.'

The man who had spoken was the Ganger, the head of a team of five flushers, who spend their working hours cleansing the bowels of London. The others said nothing; they weren't expected to. He was the natural leader, the one to whom the rest of the gang looked for approval. He rarely opened his mouth. He had no need of words. A little beyond the hump of middle age, he knew the intricate maze of London's underworld as well as his hand. He needed maps no more than words.

Like the rest of his gang, he had on heavy waders that came up to his waist. Beneath them, he wore thick, thigh-length woollen socks, like leg-warmers. Above the waders and the leg-warmers, he was garbed in a blue jacket, kept in place by belt and safety harness.

He turned again, the beam from his powerful torch temporarily blinding the file of men behind him.

'They always send visitors down ones like this.' He paused for a while to let the words sink in. He looked round and philosophically shook his head. 'They're not all like this. You should see some of 'em under the City. They're mediaeval: they don't show 'em to visitors.'

His words, spoken almost in a whisper, echoed down the tunnel and came back to us. We nodded and moved on in the darkness: an unearthly darkness, like the blackness of a child's nightmare. No one said another word.

We waded through the middle of a stream, the contours of the tunnel bringing us back mid-stream whenever we veered off course. Although the tunnel we trudged through was egg-shaped, the sewer bed was flat, covered by a layer of sediment that felt like sand and shingle; our boots sank into it with every step.

*Opposite:*
*The sewer at Upper Thames Street. 'You should see some of 'em under the City. They're mediaeval. They don't show 'em to visitors.'*

'That's what we call muck, down 'ere,' the Ganger said, giving the sediment a soft kick. 'It collects and blocks everything. Our job's shovelling it up. Fancy it? Gotta watch it, though, even if you're only walking. It's full of little pockets of gas. That's why we 'ave 'em breathing apparatuses.' He caught the eye of the man behind him. 'Kills the rats and eels, don't it? Painless, kind of euphanasia.'

He was sending us up. 'You do get 'em.' He was being serious now. 'Not 'ere. In the locals and branches, where they're all crumbling. It's bloody disgusting in some of 'em older ones. They don't take visitors

*A team of flushers, led by their Ganger – descendants of mediaeval London's gong-fermors.*

down the sewers with rats in 'em.'

'What's it like working here?'

'What's it like?' He smiled ironically. 'It's lovely. You know what a man-entry sewer is? It's three feet. Just think of that. For a start there's a foot of water and detritus. And if you don't know what detritus means, it means shit. The sewer's probably old – over a hundred years – and the bricks are crumbling. In the big ones you can drop the water gates, and work in the dry. But you can't do that in the smaller sewers. There ain't no gates. When you're in 'em,

56

you've either got to shovel up the muck or rebuild the walls. You've got this trolley which you've got to push over the rubble, and it's got a couple of skips on it. You fill up the skips, and push the trolley to the nearest manhole. Then the skips get winched up, unloaded and sent down again. You spend more time pushing the bleeding trolley than shovelling up the muck.'

As he spoke, a frog, sitting on a broken pile of brickwork, stared, croaked and stared again.

'Nice, ain't 'e? By tomorrow, the rats'll 'ave got 'im.'

He went on. 'It's 'ardly an 'ealth farm down 'ere. You've 'eard of Weil's Disease? You get it from rat's piss. It gets into cuts and scratches and ends up in your brain. You get compensation for that. But what's more common is 'epititus, and there ain't no compensation for that. Then there's the chemicals, too. Normally factories report when they send something down. But of course they don't tell us what they're not supposed to. You're working down there and suddenly a whole load of ammonia 'its your lungs.'

*Flushers going down below. Harness, safety light and, above all, back-up van and two-way radio, are essential to their survival underground.*

Our journey under London had begun at a manhole cover near Clapham North Underground station. In a small blue and white van, parked by the side of the road, we changed our clothes between gulps of strong sweet tea. The van was equipped with a shower, a kitchenette and a two-way radio – its most vital piece of equipment, which kept continuous contact with the flushers as they explored the labyrinth of sewers below. From inside the van, the driver received regular weather forecasts, which, for the men below, could prove to be the difference between life and death. London's sewers combine storm water and waste water; a sudden rainstorm can flood sewers, sending a tidal wave towards the Thames, sweeping all before it. Before radios were standard issue, the moment a rainstorm began, the driver gave the warning by raising the nearest manhole cover some six inches and letting it drop, its echo reverberating down the tunnels below.

'That's when you get the 'ell out of it,' the Ganger told us. 'Because if you don't, there ain't nothing but your life-line to save you.'

We looked at our life-lines warily, like cautious sky-divers inspecting their parachutes.

We trooped out of the van and descended into the manhole down a small circular shaft with iron rings driven into its sides. After some twenty feet, we found ourselves on a concrete landing, where another shaft descended further still. Before going down the second shaft, the Ganger slowly lowered a spiral safety lamp to check for gases: carburetted hydrogen (which explodes), sulphurated hydrogen (the product of putrid decomposition), and carbonic acid (which miners call choke-damp). If any of the gases are present, the safety lamp goes out. And while they are down below, the flushers all carry small strips of chemically-treated paper that change colour when gases build up to danger point.

57

*Above:*
*The middle-level, southern interceptory sewer at Charlton diverts London's wastes and waters eastwards into the low-level interceptory sewer and thence to treatment plants at Beckton and Plumstead.*

*Right:*
*'Suddenly, without warning, the tunnel opened. We found ourselves in a cavernous chamber, twenty feet high, crowded with pillars, arches and buttresses, like a cathedral undercroft. . .'*

*Below:*
*A storm-outlet sewer draws off the water pouring over the weir.*

'That's another time when you get the 'ell out of it,' he said.

We looked at his face. It was quite serious. He was not sending us up this time.

He brought up the lamp, nodded to his companions, and started the descent down the second shaft for another twenty feet, until we reached a small crypt, which at a gentle slope, led to the sewer itself. Our eyes, accustoming themselves to the contrasts of torchlight and darkness, cast around. It was like confronting the Styx, the river of Hades.

We waded on silently. We had already travelled a quarter of a mile before the ganger turned and warned us not to get lost. Already the dark, never-ending tunnel, lit only by the torches that each of us carried, was becoming monotonous. Another quarter of a mile. The brickwork of the tunnel seemed to hem us in. The continuous stoop strained the muscles at the back of our necks and between our shoulder blades.

Suddenly, without warning, the tunnel opened. We found ourselves in a cavernous chamber, twenty feet high, crowded with pillars, arches and buttresses, like a cathedral undercroft. To our right, a series of tunnels at different angles brought in main and local sewer tributaries. To our left was a weir, twenty feet across, over which, in a rainstorm, the rising water flows, down to a chamber at lower level. From there it pours into storm-flow sewers (most of which incorporate London's underground rivers), and out into the Thames.

This is the great middle-level, southern interceptory sewer, one of a series of subterranean waterways flowing beneath London from west to east, parallel to the River, drawing off the wastes of London as they surge down towards the Thames, and carrying them eastwards to the vast sewage treatment plants at Beckton, north of the River, and Plumstead, south of the River.

The men who had led us there belonged to one of the oldest professions in London, stretching back 800 years to the 'gong-fermors', or rakers, who cleansed mediaeval London's cess-pits. Unlike today's flushers, the gong-fermors were highly paid, earning as much as £2 a job in the fourteenth century. It could also be highly dangerous work. Two men were asphyxiated trying to retrieve a barrel of wine that had fallen into a cess-pit, and in 1326 one gong-fermor, Richard the Raker, fell into his own cess-pit and drowned 'monstrously in his own excrement'.

It was not until the reign of Henry III, when the population had outstripped this primitive system of gong-fermoring, that London really began to reek. To deal with the problem, the king built the first water pipes in the capital; constructed, improved and maintained its first public conveniences since the Romans; and, using flowing water, dug its first underground drainage system, under the Palace of Westminster. (These public latrines could be dangerous places. In 1290 one John de Alyndon was mugged and murdered in a public lavatory on London Wall, while in 1312 'a certain man of Cheap Ward, while coming by night from a common privy in London Wall through Ironmonger Lane, met another man with whom he quarrelled, so that one of them was killed'.)

Building and maintaining London's public lavatories in the following century was an expensive business. To build a latrine on London Bridge in 1383 cost £11 (a year's wages for a skilled man), while the wages of a public lavatory cleaner were as much as seven pence a night. The most expensive, and the most spectacular, example was at the east end of Cheap Street and drained into the Walbrook. It required the excavation of 139 loads of earth, and boasted stone seats.

Although Henry III was in many ways London's first great sanitary reformer, he over-reached himself. Infuriated by what they saw as

*The job of the sewer worker, entirely manual, has remained virtually unchanged for centuries: scrubbing walls, shovelling muck, examining length after length of sewer.*

reckless public extravagance, London's ratepayers revolted, first driving the King out of the city, then bringing him back in chains following his defeat – a lesson to over-zealous local government officials and sanitary reformers.

For the next five centuries the history of London's drainage can be read as one long litany of complaint from long-suffering, slowly suffocating citizens.

A whiff of mediaeval London comes down to us from a complaint made to the Assizes of Nuisance in 1328 by William Sprot, that his neighbours, William and Adam Mere, had let their 'cloaca' overflow his wall. It recurs in 1347, when two men were before the Assizes accused of piping their 'odours' into their neighbour's cellar, the crime undetected until the cellar overflowed.*

Ten years later, in 1357, Parliament passed its first sanitary act, requiring the Chancellor that the University 'remove from the streets and lanes of the town all swine and all dirt, dung, filth . . . and cause the streets and lanes to be kept clean'. A second act, passed in 1383, ordered those with latrines over the Walbrook to pay the Lord Chamberlain two shillings a year for cleaning the river. A third, enacted in 1388, made it illegal to 'corrupt or pollute ditches, rivers, water and' – surely the first ever clean-air provision – 'the air of London and elsewhere'. A fourth, in 1477, prohibited the making of any 'priveye or seye' over the Walbrook or any other town ditch.

Alas, it was too little too late. The bowels of mediaeval London had become well and truly constipated.

The next major attempt to cleanse underground London was in the reign of Henry VIII, with the passing of the Bill of Sewers in 1531. The Act created Commissions of Sewers, described the 'oaths and other qualifications' of their members, and empowered them to 'survey walls, streams, ditches, banks, gutters, sewers, gates, bridges. . . trenches, mills, milldams, ponds, locks, flood-gates . . . and other impediments' and to 'correct, repair, or amend them'.

The Commission of Sewers was not the only innovation in the field of sanitation during the sixteenth century: two centuries before its time, and forgotten after its first flush of youth, came the water closet.

The inventor was Sir John Harington, a cousin of Queen Elizabeth. He built two water closets, one for himself on his Kelston estate, and the other for the Queen at Hatfield House. He also wrote a book about them: *The Metamorphosis of Ajax, A New Discourse on a Stale Subject* (1596),

---

* The problem persisted for three centuries. Samuel Pepys, writing from the aptly named Seething Lane on 20 October 1660, complained: 'Going down to my cellar. . . I put my foot into a great heap of turds, by which I find that Mr Turners house of office is full and comes into my cellar, which doth trouble me, but I will have it helped.'
He also suffered that other perennial hazard, the flying chamber pot. On 30 April he recorded: 'At night home and up to the leads, but were, contrary to expectation, driven down again with a stinke, by Sir W Pen's shying of a shitten pot in their house of office close by, which do trouble me, for fear it do hereafter annoy me.'

which, appropriately enough, the Queen kept on a chain in her Hatfield lavatory. A copy of Harington's manuscript prepared for his printer is in the British Museum, while the original manuscript, written in his secretary's hand, can be found at Arundel Castle.

In his book, Harington, having mentioned in passing that Richard III had planned the murder of the Princes in the Tower while sitting on his pot, moves to his own innovation: 'Wherein by a tripartite method is plainly, openly, and demonstratively, declared, explaned, and elequidated, by pen, plot and precept, how unsaverie places be made sweet, noysome places made wholesome, filthie places made cleanly.' Many puns later, he reaches the heart of the matter:

> In the privie that annoys you, first cause a Cisterne containing a barrel or upward, to be placed either behind the seat, or in any place, either in the room, or above it, from whence the water may by a small pype of leade of an inch be conveyed under the seate in the hinder part thereof (not quite out of sight) to which pype you must have a locke or a washer to yeald water with some pretie strength, when you would let it in.
> Next make a vessel of an ovall form, as broad at the bottome as at the top, 11 foote deep, one foot broad, XVI inches long, place this verie close to your seate, like the pot of a close stoole . . .
> Item, that Children or busie folke, disorder it not, or open the sluce, with putting their hands, without a key, you should have a little button, or scallop shell, to bind it downe with a vice pinne, so as without the key it will not be opened . . .
> If water be plentie, the oftener it is used and opened, the sweeter; but if it be scant, once a day is inough, for a need, though twentie persons should use it.

Harington's invention never caught on. The ways of all flesh still led to the cess-pit, and in the cess-pit gathered a new breed of men – the saltpetremen. During Elizabeth's wars against Spain, it was discovered that nitrogen from excreta could be used in the manufacture of gunpowder. The arrival of the saltpetremen followed hard on the discovery. The government, short of gunpowder, decreed that saltpetremen could enter any house and dig up the excreta. To Parliament, this stank of tyranny. As one Member fumed in 1601:

> They digge in doves cotes when the doves are nesting; cast up malting floor when the malt be green, in bedchambers, in sick rooms, not even sparing women in childbirth, yea even in God's house, the Church.

Not even all the Queen's saltpetremen could dig up and cleanse all of London's cess-pits in their search for profit. They scarcely scratched the surface of the problem. The American historian, Ernest Sabine, commented in the 1930s:

> Whatever contamination resulted to the waters of the numerous city wells, the cesspool system continued, in fact came into more common use,

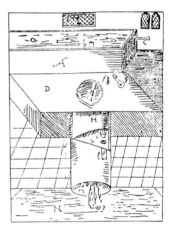

*The water closet was invented by Sir John Harington to banish 'noysome smells and odours'. Although, in* The Metamorphosis of Ajax *(1596), he gave precise descriptive and diagrammatic instructions for its design and installation, the idea was not taken up commercially until 200 years later.*

partly, no doubt, because of the ever-growing public opinion against the discharge of privy filth into the streams, ditches, and open sewers of a city growing ever more densely populated.

The Statute of the Streets (1633) strengthened the primitive laws of the fourteenth and fifteenth centuries by forbidding 'widrawes' in public under penalty of twenty shillings, while the Acts of Common Council (1671) prohibited the building of 'Houses of Easement' over drains and sewers without a licence from the Commissioners of Sewers. A fine of twenty shillings per month was to be levied for as long as the offence continued after a warning from the Commissioners.

The state of London between these two acts can be gauged from a book by John Evelyn, *Fumifugium* (1661), a diatribe against pollution, in which the diarist, royalist and pamphleteer, who later became one

*An eighteenth-century advertisement 'for emptying Bog-Houses, Drains and Cesspools, with the utmost Expedition'. Joseph Waller was a relatively prosperous nightman, with his own horse, cart and assistants; his less fortunate brethren were reduced to a bucket slung between two poles (see page 65).*

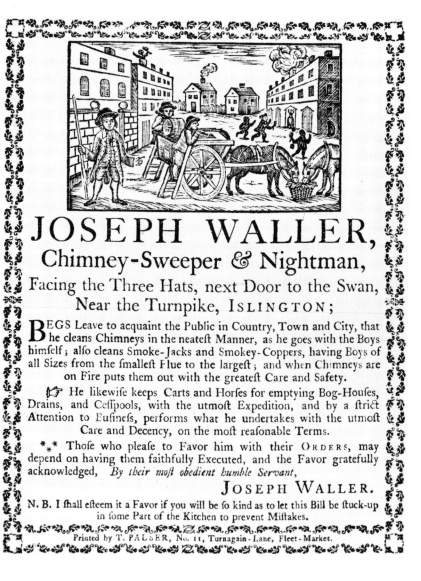

# JOSEPH WALLER,
## Chimney-Sweeper & Nightman,
### Facing the Three Hats, next Door to the Swan, Near the Turnpike, ISLINGTON;

BEGS Leave to acquaint the Public in Country, Town and City, that he cleans Chimneys in the neateſt Manner, as he goes with the Boys himſelf; alſo cleans Smoke-Jacks and Smokey-Coppers, having Boys of all Sizes from the ſmalleſt Flue to the largeſt; and when Chimneys are on Fire puts them out with the greateſt Care and Safety.

☞ He likewiſe keeps Carts and Horſes for emptying Bog-Houſes, Drains, and Ceſspools, with the utmoſt Expedition, and by a ſtrict Attention to Buſineſs, performs what he undertakes with the utmoſt Care and Decency, on the moſt reaſonable Terms.

\*\*\* Thoſe who pleaſe to Favor him with their ORDERS, may depend on having them faithfully Executed, and the Favor gratefully acknowledged, *By their moſt obedient humble Servant,*

### JOSEPH WALLER.

N. B. I ſhall eſteem it a Favor if you will be ſo kind as to let this Bill be ſtuck-up in ſome Part of the Kitchen to prevent Miſtakes.

Printed by T. PALSER, No. 11, Turnagain-Lane, Fleet-Market.

Abbildung der Statt LONDON, sambt dem erschröcklichen brandt daselbsten, so 4 tagen lange gewehrt hatt. A: 1666. im 7bris.

| | | | | |
|---|---|---|---|---|
| 1. Yorke house. | 5. Somerset house. | 9. Baynards cast. | 13. Guild hall | 17. St Petrus. |
| 2. Durham house. | 6. Arundel house. | 10. St Andre in Holb. | 14. St Lorentz Poultney. | 18. St Duston in the East. |
| 3. New exchainge. | 7. Essex house. | 11. St Pawls Church. | 15. the Royal exchainge. | 19. Alhallows harking. |
| 4. Savoy. | 8. Temple. | 12. Boo Church. | 16. St Michael. | 20. Costum house. |

of London's Commissioners of Sewers, describes a journey from Whitehall to Fleet Street. 'The ground under my feet', he complains with poetic licence, 'was so hot as made me not only sweat, but even burnt the soles of my shoes and put me all over in a sweat.' He saw 'the lead ironworks, plate and melted – the fountains dried up and ruined, whilst the very waters remained boiling; the viragos of subterranean cellars, wells and dungeons formerly warehouses still burning in stench and dark clouds of smoke like Hell.' He concludes: 'The City of London resembles the face rather of Mount Etna than an Assembly of Rational Creatures.'

Five years after Evelyn's journey, the Fire of London took hold of the City. In four days, the greater part of the 'Square Mile' was burnt down. The conflagration began in Pudding Lane on a Sunday morning, 2 September 1666, and lasted until the following Wednesday. 'The bellowing winds', recounts a contemporary, 'drove the flames forward as their noise was like a thousand chariots beating together upon the stones.'

Yet, scarcely had the fire been extinguished than projects for a new Baroque London, more magnificent even than Paris or Rome, began to emerge.

Evelyn's plans (*London Redivivum*), outlined for Wren 'within two or three days of the Incendium', envisaged not only a new city arising of

*The Fire of London, a cleansing instrument, was also a cleansing opportunity missed. The city's 200,000 cess-pits persisted, and persistently overflowed, until Bazalgette's revolutionary system of interceptory sewers was adopted in the nineteenth century.*

63

'far greater beauty, commodiousness and magnificence' than the old one, but an underground city to service it, based on a 'subterranean plan of all the vaults, cellars, and arched Meanders yet remaining, thereby to consider how they may fall out, and accommodate to new erection, what were fit to be filled and dammed up, and what to be reserved.' But Evelyn's plans, like Wren's, were rejected, defeated by London's confused and complicated system of landowning titles.

Although the Fire acted as a cleansing agent, London, rebuilt as it was without any overall plan, soon became polluted again. The arching-over of the Fleet and the building of the London Bridge sewer around the Walbrook kept pollution at a bearable level in the eighteenth century, but by 1810 most of London's one million

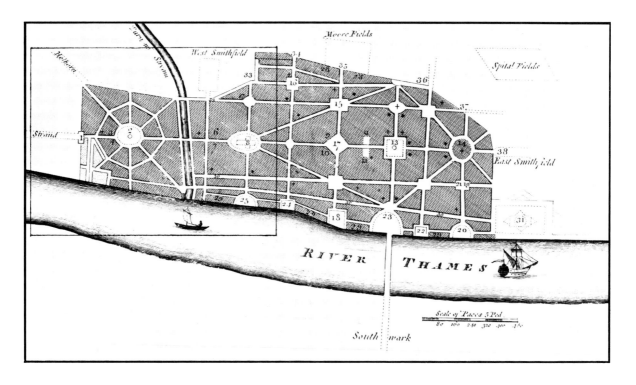

*John Evelyn's plan for London after the Great Fire. It included a subterranean network of services but was never adopted.*

population was still served by some 200,000 cess-pits.

By the beginning of the nineteenth century, London's pollution was intolerable. What made it so was the popularisation of the water closet, invented, as we have seen, two hundred years earlier. The first patented water closet – built by Alexander Cummings, a watchmaker of Bond Street in 1775 – had all the essentials save one: the exit of the soil pan was closed by a sluice valve, which had to be opened each time it was flushed. In 1778, Joseph Bramah connected the flush handle to the sluice valve, so that everything happened in one movement. He made 6000 of these water closets.

At the turn of the century came the next great step forward, with the 'Hopper Closet'. It incorporated a powerful flush and an 'S' bend in

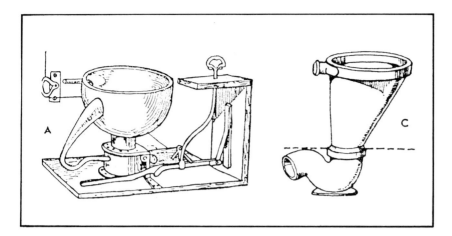

*Bramah's water closet (far left) had the flush handle connected to the sluice valve, while Hopper's incorporated an S-bend, which allowed a pool of water to remain in the basin.*

the soil pipe, which allowed a pool of water to remain in the basin, replaced at each flush. Hopper produced two types, the 'Castle' and the 'Cottage'. The modern WC, as amended by Thomas Crapper, is still largely Hopper's design.

Before Hopper, Londoners had had to make do with chamber pots, the contents of which were thrown out of the window with the warning shout 'Gardy-loo'('Gardez l'eau'), which, like Thomas Crapper later, brought a new word into the English language. The arrival of the water closet was a giant step forward for personal hygiene and two steps backward for public sanitation. The snag was that its water and waste went straight into existing cess-pits, which overflowed into the street sewers (originally designed for rainwater), and contaminated the city before emptying themselves into the Thames.

The labyrinth of primitive and overloaded nineteenth-century London sewers bred its own race of troglodytes: the toshers. Just as London's grubbers made a living by scratching in the gutters, and mudlarks by gleaning lumps of coal from the Thames silt, so toshers made theirs by scouring the sewers:

*Sewer workers of the nineteenth century: nightmen, rat-catcher and 'tosher'.*

Many persons enter the sewer openings on the banks of the Thames at low

tide, armed with sticks to defend themselves from rats . . . and carry a lantern to light the dreary passages, they wander for miles under the crowded streets, in search of such waifs as are carried there from above. A more dismal pursuit can scarcely be conceived . . . Many venturers have been struck down in such a dismal pilgrimage, to be heard no more; many have fallen suddenly choked, sunk bodily in the treacherous slime, become a prey of swarms of voracious rats, or being overwhelmed by a sudden increase of the polluted stream. (Archer: *Vestiges of Old London*, Part III)

Toshers considered themselves a superior breed, a proletarian élite. According to contemporary descriptions, they wore long greasy coats with huge pockets, canvas trousers and slops of shoes suitable for tramping in the mud. Knowledge of the tides and of the maze of sewers beneath London was essential. Some never re-emerged, 'their lights extinguished by the noisome vapours – till faint and overpowered they dropped down and died upon the spot.' (Mayhew)

It was not unusual for toshers to spend eighteen hours at a time in the sewers. For mutual protection they worked in gangs of three or four. Their profession was illegal, so they took care to dowse their lights when passing under ventilation grids or manhole covers. The tosher's haul – his 'tosh' – ranged from pennies to gold sovereigns; his dream was to find a 'tosheroon', coins of copper and silver fused, over centuries, into a ball.

Eventually the authorities decided to inhibit access to the sewers. During the 1840s, strong brick walls and iron gates that opened and closed with the tides were erected along the Thames entrances. Thus this race of underground men, like the old coin of the realm, the half-crown, known as the 'tosheroon', disappeared.

After a series of major cholera outbreaks, sanitation reform became a *cause célèbre*, Benjamin Disraeli's slogan *Sanitas Sanitatum* becoming the popular motto of the moment. In 1848 the seven separate local government authorities responsible for London's sewage were brought together in a Consolidated Commission of Sewers. Robert Stephenson was one of the Commissioners, and Charles Dickens' brother Alfred one of the Commission's inspectors. The first task the Commissioners set themselves was a survey, underground and overground, of the whole of London – John Evelyn's dream was finally to become a reality. With new, etched, copper-plate maps, five feet to a mile, the Commission set out to rebuild London's antiquated sewage system and rid the capital of its 200,000 cess-pits. Spurred on by the Victorian reformer Edwin Chadwick, the Commission flushed every one of London's 369 sewers. Since no one realised that cholera was water-borne, flushing made London even more unhealthy, turning the Thames – into which all sewers flowed – into a putrid, disease-ridden, tidal sewer.

To reinforce the urgent need for action, London was plagued by an appalling smell in 1858, just ten years after the founding of the Commission. The smell, or 'Great Stink' as it was called, was so overwhelming that the windows of the House of Commons were draped in curtains soaked in chloride of lime, and members debated whether to move upstream to Hampton Court. There were plans to evacuate the Law Courts to Oxford and St Albans. Traffic on the Thames came to a halt as paddle steamers churned up the sewage-laden river ('*Aqua mortis*') into stinking eddies.

The source of the stink was not far to seek, if one contemporary description is typical:

> A sewer from the Westminster Workhouse, which was of all shapes and sizes, was in so wretched a condition that the leveller could scarcely work for the thick scum that covered the glasses of the spirit-level a few minutes after being wiped . . . A chamber is reached about 30 feet in length, from

*An open sewer running underneath a lodging house in Fish Lane, Holborn, in about 1840. Before it was realised that cholera was water-borne, sewers were allowed to flow directly into the Thames, which itself became a gigantic sewer.*

*The Bow Common open sewer at Limehouse. The condition of these City sewers was one of the major sources of disease, death and, of course, the 'Great Stink'.*

the roof of which hangings of putrid matter like stalactites descend three feet in length. At the end of the chamber, the sewer passes under the public privies, the ceilings of which can be seen from it. Beyond this it is not possible to go . . . The deposits have been found to comprise all the ingredients from the breweries, gasworks, and the several chemical and mineral factories; dead dogs, cats, kittens and rats: offal from the slaughter houses . . . On 12th January we were nearly losing a whole party by choke damp, the last man being dragged out on his back (through two feet of black foetid deposits) in a state of insensibility . . . There is so much rottenness and decay that there is no security for the sewers standing from day to day, and to flush them for the removal of their 'most loathsome deposits' might be to bring some of them down altogether.

(T McLaughlin: *Coprophilia*)

The crisis was such that the House of Commons set up a Select Committee to report on the Stink and find a means of reducing it. One ingenious witness, Mr Samuel Gurney, proposed to seal the ends of the sewers and lead the gas by means of pipes to chosen high points, where it would be fired and allowed to burn harmlessly. The Commons Committee was so impressed by Gurney's zeal that they gave permission for a pipe to be built from the brand-new Victoria Street sewer to the top of Big Ben, from where its fumes, it was hoped, would drift harmlessly away in the wind. Only last-minute advice from a professional engineer prevented Big Ben from being blown up and the Houses of Parliament from crumbling in an almighty explosion of gases. Eventually, heavy rain broke the hot and humid summer. The Great Stink came to an end.

The Commission of Sewers – scrapped in 1855, almost before it had started its work – had been replaced by an entirely new body, the Metropolitan Board of Works, forerunner of the London County Council and the later Greater London Council. The Board was not founded, as might have been expected, to tackle the horrifying conditions of working-class housing, so savagely and truthfully described by Henry Mayhew and Edwin Chadwick. Nor was it expected to lay down principles of city planning or a rational road plan. Still less to coordinate a transport or communications system for the metropolitan sprawl. Its task was to come to grips with London's greatest evil: the notoriously defective sewage system.

I was determined on the merciful abatement of the epidemic that ravaged the Metropolis, to turn my attention to the state of this vast city, I knew that unless great and speedy radical changes in the constitution of its local affairs were effected, it was utterly impossible to expect that these affairs would be well conducted.

(Sir Benjamin Hall, the first Commissioner of Works)

The Board of Works was not short of suggestions. Indeed, the idea of interceptory sewers was first put forward in 1834 by John Martin – painter of such biblical scenes as *Belshazzar's Feast* – in his pamphlet *On rescuing the Thames from every species of pollution* – *for the improvement of*

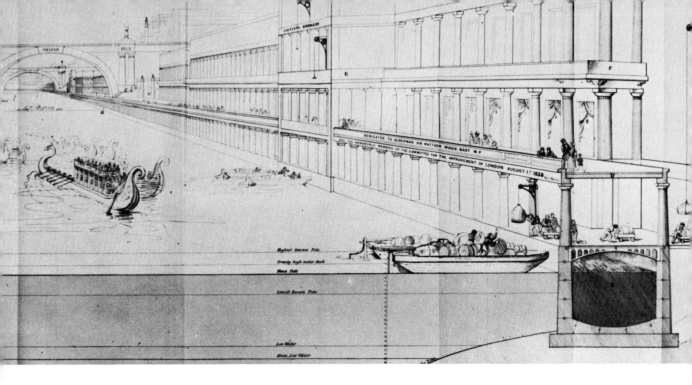

the Wharfage — the establishment of the public works — and for other objects of Public Utility and Importance.

Martin planned to channel all pollution and filth within the London district away from the Thames, so that 'the water shall become as unobjectionable as a noble River in its natural state ever offered to man'. To accomplish this, there were to be two main sewers, twenty feet wide: on the north bank of the Thames from Millbank to the Tower, terminating with the Regent's Canal at the eastern end of Commercial Road; and on the south bank from Vauxhall to Rotherhithe, terminating at the Surrey Canal.

At the terminal points Martin proposed to install two huge receptacles for converting the sewage into manure, as currently practised 'in China'. Martin planned further to ventilate his sewers at each end with enormous fires which, creating draughts, would extract the vapours and purify them with the flames.

The sewers were to be below high-water mark, with an upper floor of wharfs, fronted by a classical colonnade, with a promenade to encourage the 'working population to indulge in the healthy exercise of walking' on Sundays.

The Victorian establishment became fascinated by Martin's idea of turning waste into profit, and in 1848 two public companies were formed for this purpose. One proposed to collect the sewage of Westminster and Pimlico and convey it by deep underground channel to the market gardens around Hammersmith, where a steam engine was to distribute the liquid manure. The other company had an equally felicitous plan — to gather up the sewage of the Effra, Earl's Sluice and the Peck, dry it out, and sell it in a solid state.

In 1857, the Government ordered the two leading government

*John Martin, visionary painter and practical reformer, produced a stream of pamphlets for reforming the sewer system. This plan envisaged sewers below the high-water mark, with an upper floor of wharfs, fronted by a classical colonnade, with a promenade to encourage the 'working population to indulge in the healthy exercise of walking' on Sundays.*

**BY HIS MAJESTY'S LETTERS PATENT.**

1820.

*Urate and Poudrette Manures.*

# ANTIMEPHITIC COMPANY.

*Agriculture.*

## HEALTH, CLEANLINESS AND ECONOMY.

All Letters addressed to the Company must be Post Paid.

London, *December 23.*

*Albany Cottage Factory, Albany Place, Kent Road.*

*Sir,*

Deeply impressed, as we are, with a conviction of the vast advantages, which the recent discovery in France of the new Manure, denominated URATE, must ensure to the Agriculture of this Country, we hasten to transmit you a pamphlet, just published, on that most important subject.

It is the Report to the Royal and Central Agricultural Society of France, made by Mr. Héricart de Thury, in the name of the Committee of Manure. It contains a judicious and profound analysis of the fertilizing properties of URINE in its various states, and particularly points out the results to be expected from the employment of URATE as Manure. The Tables of experiments, we feel confident, will be found too minute and clear, not to prove Satisfactory to the Agriculturists of this, and every other enlightened Country, in the World.

We have the Honour to be,
Sir,
Your most Obedient
and most humble Servants.
For Self & Partners.

*Tho Wassé*

To Everard Brande Esq.re Apothecary to the King and Royal family chemists, Messrs Hoffman and Will, to investigate the practicality of converting waste into manure. In their report, they estimated that London's waste nearly equalled the entire guano import to Britain, but ended up by rejecting the idea.

> We have been taunted with the superior wisdom of the despised Chinese, who have no elaborate underground sewerage system, and who, instead of carrying away their floods of sewerage wealth into the sea by tunnels built at the cost of millions of money, gather it every morning by public servant with more regularity than our dust is called for by the contractors, and take it away to nourish agriculture. Our reply to these taunts is, that people (adopting the vulgar superstition) who are as numerous as ants, and who have to live in boats because the land is too crowded to hold them with any comfort, must be often at their wits' end to procure food, and are, therefore, no models for a well-to-do civilised nation to copy.

The creation of the Metropolitan Board of Works produced over 140 different schemes for 'the merciful abatement of the epidemic that ravaged the Metropolis'. One gentleman proposed furnishing each house with a hermetically sealed tank, to be collected each week by drays and taken by rail into the country to be sold. Others suggested floating cisterns of sewage, to be towed out to sea, their contents either sold at convenient ports, or dumped into the water when no one was looking. A woman (the only one amongst the 140) suggested sewers running like the spokes of a wheel from central London into the country, where it could be sold in little shops. One project even envisaged atmospheric tubes on either side of the Thames, beginning somewhere in the House of Parliament, whose members' waste could then be sucked in a great vacuum to the east end of London, where the poor and inarticulate, who were unable to protest, resided.

Ingenious and imaginative these plans may have been; they were all rejected. Instead, in 1859, the Metropolitan Board of Works accepted the scheme of their own engineer, Joseph Bazalgette, son of a Royal Naval Officer of French extraction. It was Bazalgette – whose bronze bust can be seen near Hungerford Bridge on the Thames Embankment – who adopted Martin's system of intercepting the rivers and the main sewers before they reached the River.

Bazalgette's scheme, built between 1859 and 1865, had three main interceptory sewers running north of the Thames – the high-level interceptory sewer, the middle-level interceptory sewer running under Oxford Street, and the low-level interceptory sewer, which is integrated in Bazalgette's Thames Embankment – and three others, still in use today, running south of the Thames. In addition, Bazalgette designed a series of weirs, mostly on the courses of London's underground rivers. When, because of exceptional rainfall, the waters swelled beyond the capacity of the interceptory sewers, the water was to flow over the weirs into 'storm relief sewers' carrying it into the Thames.

*Joseph Bazalgette, the chief architect of underground London, joined the Metropolitan Commission of Sewers in 1847, becoming engineer-in-chief. He was knighted in 1875 and elected President of the Institute of Civil Engineers in 1884.*

*Above:*
*Machinery for opening the emergency storm gates leading from the Fleet Sewer into the Thames.*

*Below:*
*Bazalgette's map of main interceptory sewers. The work, undertaken on behalf of the Metropolitan Board of Works, was started in 1859 and took six years.*

Modestly and factually, Bazalgette described his proposed scheme in a paper read to the Institute of Civil Engineers in 1865, the year the work was completed. The interceptory sewers, he told his audience, would be egg-shaped. Thus the lower the water level the faster the flow and the more effective the scouring.

There are altogether almost 100 miles of Bazalgette's interceptory sewers, built between 1859 and 1865, carrying off the contents of some 450 miles of main sewers, which are themselves fed by some 13,000 miles of smaller local sewers – swallowing, treating and eventually disgorging the half million gallons of waste passing through the bowels of London each day.

The principle behind this uninterrupted flow of water, chemicals, refuse, detritus and excreta is simple: gravity. From the small local sewers, no more than two or three feet in diameter, that lie under London's streets, the waste is fed into fast-flowing main sewers, which run down to the Thames, many of them built along the lines of London's lost rivers. From these 700 miles of main sewers, the wastes are drawn off into the interceptory sewers.

Five of these interceptory sewers (three of them built by Bazalgette, two thirty years later) lie north of the Thames, three to the south. Each begins on the western side of London, with a tunnel no more than four feet high, gradually widening, as it takes in its underground tributaries, to a height of eleven feet.

On the north side of the Thames, the high-level interceptory sewer

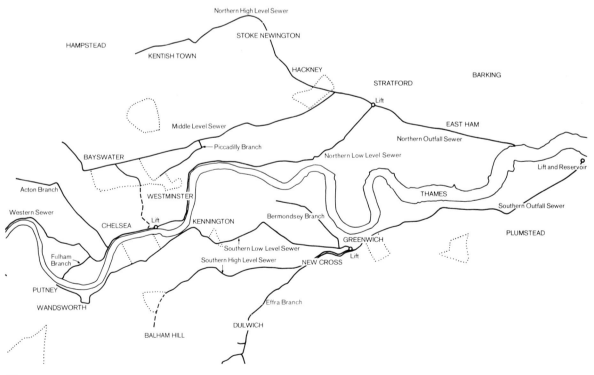

begins on Hampstead Hill, taking in the waters of the Fleet, crosses Highgate Road near Kentish Town, then traverses Holloway Road and Highbury Hill (at Drayton Park) to Stoke Newington, and then, swallowing the Hackney Brook, follows the route of the brook to Victoria Park, where it crosses the River Lea, and continues to Abbey Mills Pumping Station in Stratford.

Below the high-level interceptory sewer lie two middle-level interceptory sewers. One begins close by Kilburn and runs under Edgware Road and along Euston Road, past King's Cross, and under Pentonville Road and southern Islington, joining the high-level interceptory sewer under Hackney. The second runs from Kensal Green, under Bayswater, along Oxford Street, parallel with the Central Line. From Oxford Street, this second middle-level interceptory sewer continues under Theobalds Road and Clerkenwell Road, then along Old Street and the old Roman Road at Bethnal Green, crossing the River Lea at Old Ford and running side by side with the high-level interceptory sewer to Abbey Mills Pumping Station.

Below the two middle-level interceptory sewers lie two low-level sewers. One, flushed from its source by Stamford Brook, runs from close by Ravenscourt Park, under Hammersmith and Kensington, along Brompton Road, Piccadilly, the Strand and Aldwych, then under the City and Aldgate to Abbey Mills. The second is probably the most magnificent of all. Beginning at Hammersmith, where it

*Above:*
*The Penstock Chamber, the portcullis of the sewers, cuts off or diverts the flow.*

*Below:*
*Not everyone was satisfied with Bazalgette's work. A cartoon in* The Hornet *of 1870 complained of his lack of foresight in failing to provide storm outlets from the outset.*

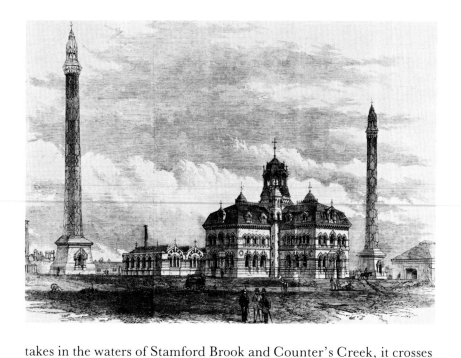

*Abbey Mills Pumping Station, 'one of the most magnificent examples of ''Venetian Gothic'' industrial architecture in Britain'.*

*Work on the northern outfall sewer, running across Plaistow and East Ham marshes to Beckton, was started in 1861.*

takes in the waters of Stamford Brook and Counter's Creek, it crosses Fulham, along a line parallel to Dawes Road, and then runs under King's Road to Cheyne Walk. From Cheyne Walk, it becomes an integral part of the Thames Embankment. Hugging the banks of the Thames, it continues under Chelsea Embankment (where it picks up what is left of the River Westbourne) to the Thames Water Authority's Western Pumping Station by Chelsea Bridge, where, in order to provide sufficient gradient for smooth flow, its waters are raised sixteen feet. From the Western Pumping Station it continues under Grosvenor Road, Millbank and the Houses of Parliament, and on

inside Bazalgette's Victoria Embankment, Blackfriars and Cannon Street to Tower Hill. From Tower Hill it leaves the Thames and swings north-east under Whitechapel and Stepney to Bow, from where it crosses the River Lea, to Abbey Mills. There the combined waters of the two low-level interceptory sewers are pumped up some thirty-six feet to arrive at the same level as the high- and middle-level interceptory sewers.

Abbey Mills Pumping Station is one of the most splendid examples of 'Venetian Gothic' industrial architecture in Britain. Built between 1865 and 1868 by Joseph Bazalgette, it originally housed eight enormous Cornish Beam engine pumps, which have now been replaced by electrically-operated pumps. With wrought-iron staircases and decorative cast-iron columns, the station is a cathedral of industrial archaeology.

From Abbey Mills, the combined effluents are taken up in the northern outfall sewer, which runs in a concrete embankment, now a public walkway, across the marshes of Plaistow and East Ham to the

*The construction of the Crossness sewage treatment works at Beckton, at the confluence of the Thames and Barking Creek.*

acres of sewage treatment works at Beckton, lying at the confluence of the River Thames and Barking Creek. (The Beckton Works, when they were built in 1865, were revealingly described in an architectural magazine, *The Builder*, as 'Medieval with Byzantine and Norman features'.)

South of the River are three major interceptory sewers. Of these, the high-level interceptory sewer, known as the Effra sewer, is the most interesting. It starts at Herne Hill, flushed by the waters of the Effra. There it abandons the River Effra's route and turns eastward under Peckham and New Cross to Deptford Pumping Station, just off Greenwich High Road. Below the Effra sewer lies the middle-level interceptory sewer, which starts on Balham Hill and runs under Clapham High Street, then winds its way under Stockwell and Brixton, where it is joined by the waters of the high-level interceptory sewer and continues through Camberwell to Deptford. The low-level interceptory sewer runs from Putney, through Battersea, Vauxhall

and under the Old Kent Road and Bermondsey to Deptford Pumping Station, where its waters are raised twenty feet to the level of the other two interceptory sewers. From Deptford, the combined waters are taken in the southern outfall sewer through Woolwich and over Erith Marshes to the sewage treatment works at Plumstead.

Constructing the interceptory system was a stupendous undertaking, involving 318 million bricks, 880,000 cubic yards of concrete and mortar, and the excavation of three and a half million cubic yards of earth. The price of bricks in London rose by fifty per cent while it was being constructed. Considering that the system was built during the wettest summer and coldest winter recorded in the nineteenth century, it was a remarkable achievement.

Since then the system has been extended. Further interceptory sewers were built in the latter half of the nineteenth century and some in the early years of this century, but no new interceptory sewers have been built under London since 1913.

Bazalgette's system is now over 100 years old, while most of the main sewers which run into it are over 150 years old. They are beginning to wear out. To rebuild the entire system would cost billions

*Top:*
*Beckton under construction in 1865.*

*Above:*
*The works, 'mediaeval with Byzantine and Norman features', were opened by the Prince of Wales.*

76

of pounds. Instead, the Thames Water Authority, which is responsible for London's sewers through the Metropolitan Public Health Division, has opted for piecemeal repair and renovation. Slowly, over the next decade, stretches of sewer under London will be given new life. They will be sealed and reinforced, chemically and structurally. To save billions being spent in a generation's time, millions have to be spent now. Unfortunately, modern renovation techniques for sewers are capital- not labour-intensive – an investment programme which is scarcely likely to find favour with the politicians. Yet renovation is essential to prevent a recurrence of the Great Stink in the twenty-first century.

'The tools of the trade for a surveying drainage engineer', wrote Eric Reed, previously Director of Operations for the Thames Water Authority, 'used to be a mirror, a light and the ability to bend down and look backwards between his legs.'

What has revolutionised the tools of the drainage engineer is the application of closed-circuit television. Of London's thousands of miles of sewers, less than five per cent are larger than three feet in diameter. This five per cent, which includes Bazalgette's interceptory

*A sectional view of the tunnels from Wick Lane, near Old Ford (top), gives a good impression of the building techniques employed – seen again (above), in a completed sewer at Bermondsey.*

sewers and the main sewers using London's underground rivers to feed into them, are the least serious part of the problem. Large enough for men to work in them (just), they can be inspected, repointed and repaired. The greater problem is the ninety-five per cent of the smaller sewers and drains, which are largely the responsibility of the borough councils. Until the development of closed-circuit television, these were an unknown quantity. From time to time they collapsed or became blocked; their repair (which meant digging holes in the ground) was expensive, time-consuming and disruptive. The application of closed-circuit television as a means of survey has enabled all of London's sewers to be inspected systematically. By the mid-1990s, the entire labyrinth will have been recorded on video film. The video camera's means of transport (a halfway house between a radio-controlled boat and a hovercraft) has itself opened up new possibilities for the repair of smaller sewers, while the vehicle has been adapted to carry miniature excavators, grouting material and hydraulic cutters – an infinitely cheaper and less disruptive process than digging down to the sewers from the surface.

If closed-circuit television has now identified the extent of London's sewage sclerosis, what is the solution? There are, in fact, several, depending on the size of the sewer, the extent of the damage and the ecological conditions of the subterranean environment. One of the commonest methods used is called 'slip lining', whereby a new pipe of either high- or medium-density polyethylene is threaded through the existing sewer. The space between the old sewer and the new lining is then grouted to form a whole. Another method, suitable only for the larger, man-entry sewers, is to reline them with tailor-made panel segments of polyester resin concrete or alkali-resistant glass fibre. A third method, called 'Seerseal', is to move the closed-circuit television's 'hovercraft' along the sewer, mounted with a pair of sprayers containing chemicals which, when mixed together, form a hard skin. The 'hovercraft', with the video camera on it, takes up its position, and the sprayers, monitored by the camera, direct the chemicals onto the walls of the sewer, forming a waterproof membrane.

Other methods include the use of high-pressure water jetting or compressed air jetting (first to clear debris, then to make holes in the new lining for the sewer's 'root and branch' side connections); the use of miniature percussion tunnelling machines (with names like 'telemole' and the even smaller 'telemouse') to clear blockages and dig new sewers without disturbing the soil above; and the adaptation of nylon-reinforced PVC fabrics.

But the most interesting method is one developed in Oxford in 1970. A vast membrane of polyurethane – resembling a hot air balloon or a contraceptive – is sealed over the opening of the sewer and high-pressure water is fed through, turning it inside out and forcing it through the sewer until inversion is complete. The high-pressure water is then taken out and replaced by hot water so that the lining sets against the sewer's structure.

The man behind the renovation of London's sewers is Graham Cox, who took over from Eric Reed as Thames Water's Director of Operations in the early 1980s. Ex-Royal Engineer, ex-para, amateur historian and twentieth-century Bazalgette, Cox is tackling the problems of renovation with such energy and enthusiasm that he could almost be said to possess a hydraulic brain. He has written:

> In London, the Victorians were the first to attack the drainage of a conurbation by a major scheme. Although they had no previous facts on which to base their calculations, they bequeathed to London a system of good sewers of immense capacity. Should not this generation, 100 years later, attempt to leave behind it at least a system which is adequate?

Cox himself feels that the Oxford method is one of the most effective – 'although I prefer the word "sock" to "contraceptive",' he says with a smile. Sock or contraceptive, it is all the same; together with the other methods it will – if the money can be found – save twenty-first-century London from an outbreak of nineteenth-century cholera. The Victorians would have been fascinated.

*An aerial view of the Crossness works at Beckton. Barking Creek on the right, the Thames in the foreground.*

# 4 Patterns of Pipes

In the Thames Embankment, directly above Bazalgette's low-level interceptory sewer, but running below the level of the Thames, is a little-known tunnel. It runs from the Houses of Parliament (with an entrance door at the base of Boadicea's statue by Westminster Bridge), beneath Hungerford, Waterloo and Blackfriars Bridges, and then turns north-east, just where the River Fleet rolls its tribute of dead dogs to the Thames, under Queen Victoria Street, almost touching Mansion House Underground station, as far as the Bank of England.

Built with the same perfect brickwork as the interceptory sewer beneath it, but arched rather than circular, the tunnel is about six feet high. It was designed by Bazalgette to carry the cast-iron pipes of water, gas and hydraulic power. Dark and forbidding, its brickwork sweating and dripping down either side, the smell of the River seeps into the tunnel, giving the impression of being an antechamber of the Thames. The tunnel echoes with the sound of footsteps, of traffic above and of flowing water below, while every hundred yards or so the darkness is broken by shafts of sunlight coming through the pavement gratings.

The cast-iron pipes, flanked by lines of British Telecom cables, range in diameter from thirty-six-inch gas pipes to twelve-inch hydraulic power pipes. Coupled by either cast-lead-filled sockets, flange-joints or bored-socket-and-spigot joints, the pipes, like the tunnel, or subway, are a monument to the cast-iron age of subterranean London.

Bazalgette's tunnel within the Embankment is not the only one of its kind in London. There are altogether eleven and a half miles of such service subways under the City, Dockland and the West End. You can spot them at pavement level by the long, wide rectangular grids at regular intervals, through which the heavy cast-iron pipes are lowered from street level. The oldest was built under Garrick Street in 1861. The most modern – a circular tunnel unmarked by any grid – was built under Oxford Street to divert subterranean services when Oxford Circus Underground station was being modernised in 1968.

The heart of the system lies under Piccadilly Circus. From there, the system of subways fans out under Piccadilly, Trafalgar Square, Shaftesbury Avenue, Regent Street, Charing Cross Road and Holborn. Most are just below street level, marked with the names of the streets above for easy identification. But under Piccadilly Circus itself, the network sinks far deeper. There the subway drops forty feet down into a circular, cast-iron tunnel, built in the 1920s to divert services during the modernisation of Piccadilly Circus Underground station. With shafts leading up and down, branches leading out on one

*Opposite:*
Ce qu'il y a sous le pavé de Londres – *the pipes under London laid bare in a nineteenth-century French illustration.*

81

side and the other, Piccadilly has a second, subterranean circus, hardly known, yet as essential to central London as the vast roundabout above.

These subways are the only 'service subways' under London, built to house gas and water pipes in a rational pattern. Elsewhere, London's pipes make do with trenches in the ground as London has had to do since the Middle Ages.

The first water pipe mains in mediaeval London were bored elm trunks, eight inches in diameter, tapered at one end to fit into one another. The earliest gas pipes in the 1800s were also made of bored elm trunks, provoking complaints by the water companies that their disease-infested and polluted water pipes were being contaminated by gas. From bored elm pipes, both water and gas mains went through the same transition: first to earthenware, then to cast-iron. Indeed, the first cast-iron mains of the Gas, Light and Coke Company were bought second-hand from the York Building and West Middlesex Water Companies. These cast-iron pipes ranged from two to forty-eight inches in diameter, the heavier ones needing hoists to lay them into position. They were tested for strength by sustaining a 300-foot column of water, while skilled workmen were supposed to check them for faults by tapping them with a hammer.

Only in the smaller pipes leading from the mains in the street to the houses on either side was there any notable difference. The water companies continued to use lead, as they had since the Middle Ages. The early gas companies, on the other hand, used army-surplus musket barrels, in cheap supply after the Napoleonic Wars, modified to screw into each other by the London gunsmith James Russell. Since then musket barrels have been replaced by cast-iron, cast-iron by spun-iron, and spun-iron by flexible plastic tubes. The old muskets are

*In the eighteenth-century watercolour (right), wooden pipes (also photographed above) cross the Fleet.*

82

still remembered, however, in the name that the gas industry gives to the tiny pipe leading from the mains to the meter: the 'barrel'.

## WATER PIPES

The water pipes that serve London today (over 8000 miles of mains between two and sixty inches in diameter) at present mostly flow eastwards. From the River Thames, just upstream from Teddington (Tide-end-town) Lock, water is drawn into huge reservoirs, all linked by a tunnel eight feet four inches in diameter, from where it is slowly filtered through layers of sand before being piped eastward beneath the city. Over seventy per cent of London's water comes from the reservoirs at Surbiton, Ashford Common, Hampton, Kempton Park and Walton-on-Thames.

Only one series of water pipes has been laid against this eastwardly flow: the pipes that run west from the River Lea's reservoirs at Coppermills, on the eastern side of London, which replaced the old Lea Bridge Waterworks in 1972. For some time, the Lea provided London with seventeen per cent of her water, mostly in east London. But the Lea proved inadequate. So a concrete, segmented water tunnel, eight feet four inches in diameter, was built by the engineers Sir William Halcrow and Partners in 1955, running from Hampton in the west deep under London to bring adequate water to the Lea Valley.

Originally, mediaeval London, bounded by the Walbrook in the east and the Fleet in the west, drew its 'sweet and fresh' waters from John Stow's springs and streams. It was not until the thirteenth century, by which time the Fleet and Walbrook had degenerated into sewers, that London began to dry up.

In 1236, Stow records,

> the citezens were forced to seek waters abroad: therefore some, at the request of King Henry III, in the twenty-first year of his reign, were, for the profit of the City and good of the whole realm, thither repairing; to wit, for the poor to drink, and the rich to dress their meat, granted to the citezens and their successors, by one Gilbert de Sandford, with liberty to convey water from the town of Tyburn by pipes of lead into the City.

The Great Conduit, as it was called, which conveyed the water from the Tyburn to the City, followed the route of Oxford Street, Holborn and Cheapside, and was financed by French merchants from Amiens, Nele and Corby, who wanted to break into the London wool markets. From this west-east conduit water was distributed north and south in underground, bored-elm pipes, with quills of lead running off into the houses of the well-to-do. When Edward I returned from the Holy Land in 1274 'the Conduit in Chepe ran all day with red and white wine'. And in *Henry VI Part II* Shakespeare mocks at poor Jack Cade and his peasant rebels: 'Here, sitting upon London-stone, I charge and command that at the city's cost, the pissing conduit run nothing

*Lead quills, and later, pipes, carried water to the houses of the rich; the poor had to make do with water carriers, on foot or on horse.*

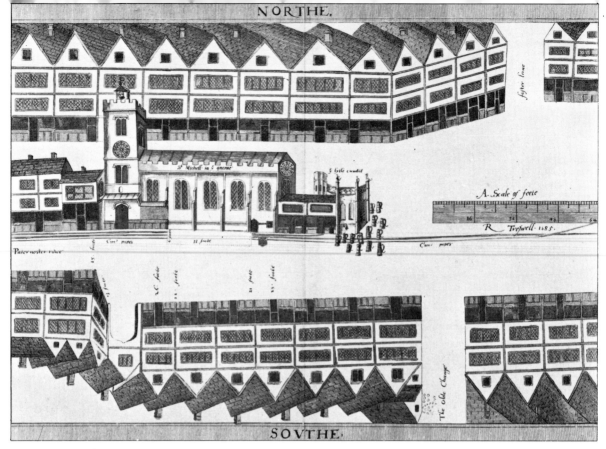

SOVTHE.

but claret wine this first year of our reign.'

As London grew, so more conduits were built, while the City Prison (the Tunne in Cornhill) was turned into London's first underground reservoir. There was a Little Conduit near St Paul's; a conduit was built from Highbury to Cripplegate (which, as late as 1811, could still be seen opposite 14 Highbury Place); another was built at the southern end of Upper Street, from a spring in White Conduit Street, which was not destroyed until the Regent's Canal was cut in the early nineteenth century. A conduit built by Sir William Lamb opposite Great Ormond Street is still remembered in Lamb's Conduit Street, while in the centre of the City the Standard Conduit at Cornhill became the point of measurement for all milestones to London, some of which are still inscribed 'from the Standard in Cornhill'. John Stow wrote:

> These conduits used in former times yearly to be visited, but particularly on the 18th of September 1562, the Lord Mayor Harper, eldermen and wardens to the twelve companies, rid to the conduit's head, for to see them after the old custom. And afore dinner they hunted the hare and killed her and thence to dinner at the head of the conduit. There were good number entertained with good cheer by the Lord Chamberlain; after dinner they went to hunting the fox . . . and thence the Lord Mayor, with all his company, rode through London to his palace in Lombard Street.

Many of these conduits were destroyed in the Great Fire of 1666, but their days had already been numbered by Elizabethan and

Jacobean improvements to London's water supply. Stow recorded:

> The greater part of them do still continue where first erected, but some, by reason of the great quantity of ground they took up, standing in the midst of the City, were a great hinderence, not only to foot passengers but to porters, coaches and cars, and were . . . taken down and removed to places more convenient.

New sources of water for London began to be found and new storage systems created: waterworks at London Bridge, reservoirs at Hampstead Ponds; and the excavation of the New River. The first water pump on London Bridge was built in 1552 by a Dutchman, Peter Moris, and was quickly followed by a second wheel pump built by an Englishman, Bevis Bulmar. The pumps were worked by huge waterwheels built into the arches of London Bridge, capable of raising water at the rate of 216 gallons per minute – 'a most artificial forcier', John Stow called it. Until then all water supply in London had been based on gravitation.

Another scheme to increase Elizabethan London's water supply was the excavating and damming of the source of the Fleet to make Hampstead Ponds. Two hundred years later Highgate Ponds and the ponds of the Vale of Health also became reservoirs.

But Moris's wheel and the creating of Hampstead Ponds were

*Opposite, above:*
*The pipe of the Little Conduit ran alongside St Paul's. The wooden buckets were collected by the water carriers, who belonged to one of London's most powerful mediaeval guilds.*

*Opposite below:*
*A seventeenth-century pump in the yard of the Leathersellers' Hall near Bishopsgate. On public holidays the maiden's breasts flowed with wine.*

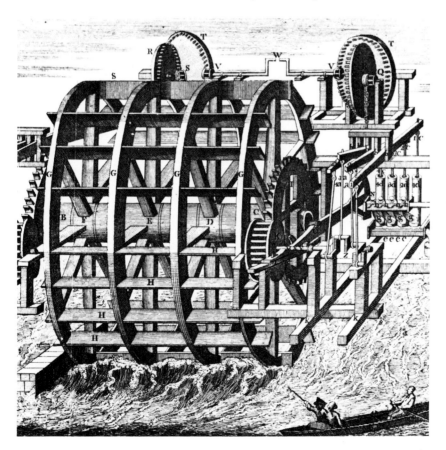

*Above:*
*The first waterworks in London were built by Peter Moris on London Bridge in 1552.*

*Left:*
*London Bridge Waterworks, not Peter Moris's, but a later one by George Sorocold, built in the early eighteenth century, and able to rise and fall with the tide.*

*Top:*
*The source of the Fleet was*
*dammed in the seventeenth*
*century to create a reservoir,*
*Hampstead Ponds.*

*Above:*
*The source of the New River:*
*Chadwell Springs.*

insufficient for the growing needs of London, which, by 1600, had surpassed Venice as the largest city in the world. In 1609, desperate for water, Parliament empowered a Welsh jeweller, Hugh Middleton, to finance and build a canal thirty miles long from the springs of Amwell and Chadwell in Hertfordshire to London. Middleton, clever, ambitious, rich and quite without engineering experience, threw himself into the task; and into the wells of Amwell and Chadwell he poured all his wealth. He wrote to a friend:

> The difficulty of preserving a level surface is great, for the depth of the trench in some places descended a full thirty feet, if not more, whereas in other places it required a spriteful art again to mount it over a valley in a trough between a couple of hills, and the trough all the ground very deep and rising a height above twenty-three feet.

The canal, which ended at New River Head, was completed in 1612. Originally it terminated at the Round Pond, just off Rosebery Avenue, site of the present headquarters of the Thames Water Authority. Hollingshead called the New River 'one of the most beautiful of artificial rivers . . . serving the highest parts of London in their lower rooms and the lower parts of London in their higher rooms'. It continued to serve London from the New River Head in Clerkenwell for 200 years.

In 1856, when a new pumping station was built, in the style of a mediaeval castle, at Stoke Newington, the last mile of the New River was put underground. Its final stages in the open can now be seen in

THE NEW RIVER WORKS, STOKE NEWINGTON : THE ENGINE-HOUSE AND RESERVOIRS.

*Top and above:*
*The canal ended at the New*
*River Head pumping station,*
*built in 1609 by Hugh*
*Middleton.*

*Left:*
*A view of the new pumping*
*station built at Stoke Newington*
*in 1830.*

The state of London's water in the nineteenth century invited a barrage of criticism from social reformers and satirists alike.

Above:
'The Silent Highwayman', a cartoon drawn by Tenniel for Punch in 1858.

Opposite:
'Monster Soup' – a 'Microcosm dedicated to the London Water Companies' (above); and 'Source of the Southwark Waterworks', pleading 'Give us clean water', of 1827 (below).

Finsbury Park, where it makes a half-circle to the east, under Seven Sisters Road Bridge, to the pumping station on Green Lanes, while the covered section running through Islington has been made into a garden walk, the 'Green Finger'.

With the development of the steam pump in the eighteenth century came new opportunities to draw water from the Thames. But improvement in quantity was not matched by improvement in quality. Tobias Smollett wrote in the eighteenth century:

If I drink water I must quaff the mawkish contents of an open aqueduct, exposed to all manner of defilement, or swallow what comes from the River Thames, impregnated by all the filth of London and Westminster – human excrement is the least offensive part of the concrete which is composed of all the drugs, minerals, and poisons used in mechanics and manufacture enriched with the putrifying carcasses of beasts and men; and mixed with the scourings of all the washtubs, kennels and common sewers within the bills of mortality.

By the late eighteenth century, London was dominated by eight water companies – the Chelsea, West Middlesex and Grand Junction Companies in west London, the New River Company in north London, the East London Waterworks in east London, and the Southwark and Vauxhall, Lambeth and Kent Companies in south London.

Despite high death rates, fortunes were made out of the supply of poisonous waters. Eight private companies supplied London. Some streets had three separate pipe lines with three sets of labourers, selected for their belligerence, all looking after the interests of their separate companies. Plumbers made fortunes by persuading customers to change from one supply to another, and streets were virtually closed to traffic as they were torn open to allow connections to be transferred.

(J C Wylie: *The Wastes of Civilization*)

Realising that cut-throat competition would be ruinous, the companies came together in 1811 and divided London between them. The half-century of monopoly that followed proved as dangerous to Londoners as the half-century of competition that had preceded it. There was no incentive for the companies to improve their supply, while the poorer districts of London, where there was no profit to be made, were ignored completely.

In 1827, a pamphleteer, 'The Dolphin', wrote:

The water taken up from the River Thames between Chelsea Hospital and London Bridge, for the use of the inhabitants of the Metropolis, being charged with the contents of more than 130 public common sewers, the drainings from the dung-hills and lay-stalls, the refuse of hospitals, slaughter-houses, colour, lead gas and soap works, drug-mills, and manufactures, and with all sorts of decomposed animal and vegetable substances, rendering the said water offensive and destructive to health, ought no longer to be taken up by any of the Companies from so foul a source.

89

In the same decade that London's notorious sewage system was finally overhauled, the eight water companies, who had made millions out of the supply to Londoners of unwholesome water, were curbed by Parliament. The Metropolis Water Act of 1852 appointed a London Water Examiner and ordered the companies: first to cover all the reservoirs within five miles of St Paul's; second to filter all their water through sand beds; third to remove their source of intake to above Teddington Weir. The results were immediate. In Lambeth the death rate, which had been 130 per thousand before the Lambeth Water Company moved up-river, dropped to 37 per thousand.

One thing that disappeared with the water companies was the old Cornish Beam Engine, that beautiful and unforgettable giant, which pumped up the vile fluids of the Thames in the first half of the nineteenth century. The action of these engines, with their two great arms – their beams – resembles that of a village pump, one arm plunging down, the other sucking up. Five of these engines still exist, and you can see them at the Kew Bridge Engine Museum, by Kew Station, the old Grand Junction Pump House, with the water tower above it.

It was another half-century before the water companies were taken into public ownership, but the 1852 Act had broken their power for good. There were still many improvements to be made. Until late in the nineteenth century the water companies turned on the water in each area for a limited time each day only. The poorer the district, the shorter the period. The result was what London's first Water Examiner, Sir Francis Bolton, called 'that domestic abomination – the water cistern, where the purest water is often liable to contamination from the dirty and neglected state of the cistern itself'.

Doctor Horace Jefferson, resident medical officer for London Fever Hospital, wrote of the poorer quarters of London:

> Those houses best supplied have each a butt holding about eighty gallons, into which flows from a stand-pipe for about ten minutes to half an hour each day, and is supposed to supply the wants of twenty persons for cooking, the washing of their person, house and linen, and for the rinsing down of the water closet at such times as may appear to suit the caprice of every one of the inmates. At other places larger butts, but in relation to the number of persons proportionally smaller, supply a whole court of ten or more three-roomed houses which have no backyard and a population of 150 persons – members of thirty different families. On Sundays even this supply is absent, the water of the day before is gone, and in many houses that for the Sunday cooking has to be borrowed from neighbours who may have provided themselves with a larger butt, who are more provident, or more dirty.

'The radical remedy for this state of things', announced Bolton, 'would be the immediate adoption of the system of constant supply.' This the water companies refused, however, to do. They claimed that it would be too expensive, and that the mains were not large enough. The Metropolitan Board of Works replied by trying to take over the companies in 1878, but was defeated by the companies' lobbying power. The newly-formed London County Council tried again in 1889 and 1891. Each time they, too, were defeated. They retaliated by waging a guerrilla war against the companies, refusing to cooperate with them and preventing them from digging up the roads. Finally, in 1900, a Royal Commission recommended the take-over of the companies and the creation of a Metropolitan Water Board for London. The Act was passed in 1902.

The 8000 miles of pipes, two to sixty inches in diameter, that London inherited from the water companies – a series of daddy-long-leg limbs stretching eastward from the reservoirs of west London – are still with us. But over the years they have proved inadequate. Put simply, in a drought, the more westerly the residential district, the more constant the water; the further you go east, the drier it gets.

To offset this shortage in the east, the Metropolitan Water Board built their raw water main in 1955, running for nineteen miles deep under London, linking the western reservoirs with the Coppermills reservoirs in the north-east. Using a siphon to create the initial flow, it runs from Hampton in a north-east direction under Richmond, Barnes (where it crosses beneath the River), Kensington and Camden to the Stoke Newington Pumping Station, and from there to the reservoirs of the River Lea, hard-pressed each summer. All along the way are intermediary shafts, which either link up with the pumping stations at Stoke Newington and Lockwood (in Walthamstow) or are maintained for emergency fire-fighting. And hardly a Londoner knows it is there.

On 1 April 1974, the Metropolitan Water Board was replaced by the Metropolitan Division of the Thames Water Authority, responsible for six million consumers. With the new title came a new concept: the ring water main.

The ring water main will be a tunnel eight feet four inches in diameter, built of pre-cast concrete segments. It will girdle London on the high ground, and the water will flow by force of gravity to consumers in the Thames Valley. Already the southern part – from the Thameside reservoirs beyond Teddington to Merton Abbey Pumping Station – has been built. The next, eastern stage, to be completed gradually over the next decade, will link Merton Abbey, via Honor Oak, with the Lea Valley reservoirs. The completed semi-circle will then form an extended 'bow' with the raw water main. The last stage – unlikely to be finished until the 1990s – will be to form the northern and western semi-circles. When the circle is complete, the whole pattern of water pipes beneath London will have been transformed: the effect on the city will be long-lasting. 'A tunnel ring main, constructed in the Metropolitan area,' wrote Eric Reed of Thames Water in 1979, 'is likely to determine the method of operation of the water supply system for the next one hundred years at least.'

## THE LONDON HYDRAULIC POWER COMPANY

Beneath London, as unknown to most Londoners as the raw and ring water mains, are another set of water pipes, now 'thrown dead' or dried up – the pipes of the London Hydraulic Power Company. Yet in their day they provided the greatest lifting power under Victorian London. The network of pipes extended from Limehouse in the east to Earl's Court Exhibition in the west, from Euston Road and Pentonville Road in the north to Lambeth, Southwark and Rotherhithe in the south. The hydraulic pipes cross the Thames at five points: over the River on Vauxhall, Waterloo and Southwark Bridges, and under the River in the Tower Subway and in the duct under the carriageway in the Rotherhithe Tunnel. You can still see the square manholes with 'LHP' written on them, set in the pavement in front of each of the buildings they used to serve.

The principle behind hydraulic power, adopted by William Murdock, Resident Engineer of Boulton and Watt in Cornwall, hardly differed from that used by the Romans at their warehouse in Ostia. Raw (untreated) water was pumped at a pressure of 400 pounds per square inch through the miles of pipes running beneath London, and was used to raise and lower cranes, operate lifts, West End theatre safety curtains, wagon hoists, even hat-blocking presses. So powerful was the force in these pipes that a safety official of the London Hydraulic Power Company had to be present at every public procession in the centre of London as a precaution against a bursting main, which could blow out a great cavity in the road.

The great pressure in the pipes was forced by five pumping stations: at Bessborough Gardens (Pimlico), Blackfriars Bridge, Albion Docks (Rotherhithe) and London Docks (Wapping Wall) on the Thames, and at the City Road Basin (Islington) on the Grand Union Canal. By statute the Company could extract twenty-five million gallons a week from these pumping stations, which were originally steam-driven but converted after the War to electricity.

Founded in 1871, the Company survived for just over a hundred years, the last representative of that great breed of Victorian private enterprises perversely enjoying statutory protection. Throughout the late nineteenth and early twentieth centuries, the network of pipes grew. By 1927, the heyday of hydraulic power, there were 184 miles of mains beneath London. Apart from the dozen experimental miles in steel, the entire system is in its original cast-iron pipes, treated with an anti-corrosive and wrapped in hessian.

The development of electric power and the devastation of the War (261 mains were broken during the Blitz) took its toll on the London Hydraulic Power Company. The decline of London Docks and the demolition of hundreds of Edwardian mansions, all of which had hydraulic lifts, brought about the death of hydraulic power. By 1971, a hundred years after the Company started, only fifteen million gallons were being extracted each week.

By the mid-1970s, the London Hydraulic Power Company had ceased to operate. It was bought by a consortium, including Trident and Rothschild, in 1981. Its pipes may be dry, but it is unlikely that they will remain empty for long. Subterranean estate is valuable property. Already the Greater London Council and New Scotland Yard are linked by a cable running through the hydraulic mains, and

*Left:*
*An hydraulic devil at St Katharine's Docks. These vast cranes were mounted on wheels, so that they could be moved along the quay from one ship to another.*

*Above:*
*Joseph Bramah's hydraulic press, patented in 1795, was originally installed in the Tower of London to print maps for the army.*

soon the pipes may run cable for cable television. Thus old pipes, like John Stow's old rivers, assume new roles: cast-iron conduits for coaxial cables.

## GAS PIPES

*Frederick Albrecht Winzer was born in Brunswick in 1763 and educated in Paris. He displayed his first gas light at the Lyceum in September 1804. It consisted of 'a long flexible tube suspended from the ceiling, communicating at the end with a burner, designed with much taste, being a cupid grasping a torch with one hand and holding the tube with the other'. Winzer died in poverty in Paris in 1830, and was buried at the Père Lachaise Cemetery, but a monument has been erected to his memory in Kensal Green Cemetery, with the inscription: 'At evening time it shall be light' (Zach XIV, 7).*

Gas was almost entirely a nineteenth-century phenomenon. The first street lighting by gas started in the 1800s, and the decline of the industry was under way by the 1890s. Of course gas had been in use by man long before the 1800s: in 500 BC the Chinese were using natural gas, piped in bamboo tubes, to evaporate salt at Szechwan.

The first appearance of man-made gas was in 1688, the Year of the Glorious Revolution. The Reverend John Clayton, Rector of Crofton near Wakefield, recorded:

> I got some coal and distilled it in a Retort in an open Fire. At first there came out only Phlegm, afterwards a black Oil, and then, likewise, a Spirit arose which . . . caught Fire at the Flame of the Candle, and continued burning with Violence as it issued out . . . I have kept this spirit a considerable time in bladders, and tho' it appear'd as if they were only with Air, yet if I let it forth and lit it with a Match or candle it would continue burning till all was spent.

So gas could burn – but it was over a hundred years before anyone found a use for it.

The man responsible for bringing gas pipes to the sub-surface of London was Frederick Albrecht Winzer (1763-1830), an attractive charlatan who, as well as being a foreigner, possessed the unlucky attribute of placing more faith in others than they placed in him. He was in Paris when a Frenchman called Le Bon, who had been brought up by charcoal burners near Joinville, was experimenting with gas from wood. Failing to cull the secret of Le Bon's method, Winzer nonetheless grasped the essentials and made his way to England. He arrived in 1803. His first mistake was to try to be too English. He changed his name from 'Winzer' to 'Winsor', which only served to betray his ignorance of the English.

Le Bon's experiments (cut short when he was murdered – for no apparent motive – on the Champs Elysées in 1804) were also noted by Gregory Watt, son of James Watt of Boulton and Watt. Hearing of Le Bon, Boulton and Watt set William Murdock, well-known, as we have seen, as a hydraulic engineer, to developing gas. Murdock chose as his assistant Samuel Clegg. Clegg, who had studied under the physicist John Dalton, later left Boulton and Watt to become Chief Engineer to the Gas Light and Coke Company, which had been set up by Winsor, who had first tried to steal Le Bon's method. It was like *La Ronde*.

While Murdock was concentrating on the lighting of factories and large buildings, each of which would have its own gasworks, just as houses today have their own central heating systems, Winsor – even though he knew little about the chemistry of gas – saw the potential of a central gasworks supplying consumers by pipes laid under the street.

He understood publicity, too, and on the King's birthday in 1805 ran a small pipe along Pall Mall from Carlton House, now the site of the Carlton Club, and lit the whole street. The *Monthly Magazine* did full justice to his public relations flair.

> The inflammable gas, which is quite transparent or invisible, began to flow into the pipes soon after eight o'clock, and a lamplighter or a person with a small wax taper (the evening being quite serene) appeared and lighted the gas issuing from each burner in succession. The light produced from these gas lamps was clear, bright and colourless, and from the success of this considerable experiment hopes may now be entertained that this long-talked-of mode of lighting our streets may at length be realised. The Mall continued crowded with spectators until nearly twelve o'clock, and they seemed much amused and delighted by this novel exhibition.

Winsor set up a company, the New Patriotic Imperial and National Light and Heat Company, offering fifteen shillings' interest on every five pounds invested. It failed. In 1812, he tried again with the more modest-sounding Gas Light and Coke Company, 'for lighting the Cities of London and Westminster and the Borough of Southwark'. (That was all there was to central London at the time.)

The Company prospered, although Winsor was dropped from it

*Bottom:*
*'A Peep at the Gas Lights in Pall Mall' – a Rowlandson cartoon of 1805 inspired by Winzer's consummate publicity exercise.*

*Below:*
*Samuel Clegg's gas works, constructed in the Strand in 1812 to light Ackermann's Repository of Fine Arts.*

*Hot-air balloons, like Montgolfier's 'Eagle', seen ascending here in 1864 from Cremorne Gardens, a public pleasure park off Cheyne Walk (above), and street lighting (below, on the Embankment), were two of the popular uses for gas in the nineteenth century.*

with an annuity of £600 (which was later also dropped). It achieved royal recognition in 1814 when a request came from the Palace to light up a pagoda designed by the Prince of Wales to celebrate the somewhat premature 'final victory' against Napoleon. The pagoda was built, the mains were laid. The gas was tested and Clegg, the engineer in charge, ordered the pressure to be raised. The fireworks speckled the sky and then the speckles slowly floated down earthwards and pagodawards. There was a loud bang and the Prince of Wales' pagoda joined the second round of fireworks which were now speckling the sky. Shame-faced, the Government transported the pagoda to Woolwich, where it became a Royal Artillery Museum.

Some welcomed the setback. W H Wollaston scoffed: 'They may as well light London with a slice of the moon.' Sir Humphrey Davy reckoned that a mound of earth as large as Primrose Hill would be needed to hold the gas down. The Earl of Harewood doubted whether *any* encouragement to manufacture would be advantageous to the country.

But the Company grew, and by the year of Waterloo had over 122 miles of mains. The diameter of the mains grew too, from 16 inches in 1820, to 36 inches in 1850, to 48 inches in 1870.

The popularity of hot-air ballooning gave an additional boost to the new gas industry. Two balloonists, Graham and Green, who gave displays at Sadler's Wells Theatre, were given special rates by the Gas Light and Coke Company. Wisely, however, a request by a Mr Smithers in August 1824 for a free filling 'for his intended ascent in an elegant balloon to the glorious cause of the suffering Greeks' was refused. Mr Smithers' elegant balloon failed to get off the ground. The special problems of attaching underground mains to very large gas balloons occurs again and again in the history of the gas industry. In the end, a special main, reserved exclusively for balloonists, was laid from Fulham Gasworks to Hurlingham.

Balloonists proved the least of the gas company's problems. So vile was the pollution from the gasworks that the Commissioners of Sewers refused to allow the gas wastes into their sewers. The Gas Light and Coke Company had to dig their own sewer from the Peter Street Gasworks to the Thames, and to employ one Henry Ruegg, at a guinea a week, 'to attend in the neighbourhood of these works in order to ascertain and register any offensive smells which he may observe in his perambulation'.

Ruegg was not the only unlikely-sounding name to find a place in the roll-call of the new subterranean industry. A man called Samuel Lay was employed to superintend the laying of gas pipes; a Joseph Bagster was registered as the Gas Light and Coke Company's 'Collector of Desperate Debts'; while the inventor of the 'incandescent' gaslight had the unfortunate name of Frankenstein.

The names may have been colourful, but the attitude of the industry was thoroughly pedestrian. In 1820 the Gas Light and Coke Company deplored the action of Mr Hicks of *The Times*, who had adapted a burner 'to boil water for the men's tea'. By 1851 this had all changed. The Great Exhibition included a gas-heated bath. 'It is a useful and economic application of that material, and will enable hot baths to be used extensively in the houses of the middle classes,' reported the *Illustrated London News*.

One of the main problems confronting the industry was how to store the gas once it had been made. The earliest gas-holders were brewer's vats, a large number of which were bought second-hand from the Golden Lane Brewery Group. But they were insufficient, and by 1815 Winsor was scouring London for treacle barrels, rum casks and porter puncheons.

The first large gas-holders, designed by Clegg, were built at Brick Lane, Curtain Road, Peter Street and Horseferry Road. It was Clegg, too, who designed the telescopic gas-holder. The principle was simple: an inverted iron bell rose up and down in a circular tank filled with gas, and sealed at the bottom with water, while the pressure of the iron bell forced the gas into the pipes.

As the gasworks got larger, so their demand for coal grew, drawing them to the banks of the Thames, alongside the waterworks. Coal came up the River on barges and was loaded into vast ovens, or retorts, for baking. There the coal softened to give a thick brown smoke which was converted into gas.

The largest gas-holder built in the nineteenth century was at Beckton on the Thames marshland at Galleon's Reach; it was opened in 1868. The painting by W L Wyllie in 1880 gives the place a romantic, end-of-the-world aura with Turneresque water reflections and Conradian clouds. This is more than a little artistic licence. Its siting was fortunate for Londoners, however. It was the Gas Light and Coke Company's third choice. Their first was the site of the old Chelsea Waterworks, now Victoria Station; their second the redundant Millbank Prison, now the Tate Gallery.

The oldest gas-holder to have survived is the No 2 holder at Fulham, built in 1830, the year that Winsor died in poverty in Paris. It is 100 feet in diameter and holds a quarter of a million cubic feet of gas. Like the Horseferry Road gas-holder, it was sunk into a deep excavation so as not to dominate the skyline of the Thames like the later gas-holders and power stations.

With the growing demand for gas, new companies had sprung up throughout the nineteenth century: the City of London Gas Light and Coke Company in 1817, the Imperial Gas Company in 1821, soon joined by the Independent, Equitable, South Metropolitan, London, Commercial and Western.

The streets of London became an obstacle course. The pavements were the responsibility of the parish authorities – an excellent system

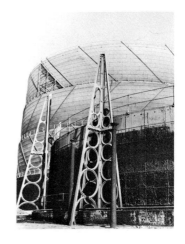

*Above:*
*Gas-holders sprang up around London. The Fulham gas-holder of 1830 (top), is the oldest to survive.*

*Below:*
*The coal from which the gas derived was delivered from the collieries by barge: the East Greenwich jetty of the South Metropolitan Gas Company in 1924.*

97

*The advent of gas added another layer to the pipes criss-crossing London. Civil war among the rival companies disrupted still further laying of the mains.*

in John Stow's days, but unworkable in a city where one main might pass through ten separate parishes. There were pitched battles between the workmen of the rival companies, who were forever fracturing and tapping each other's mains. As early as 1821, the gas companies had followed the example of the water industry and agreed to a division of London.

From then on the companies were authorised to dig up their own territory only, cutting up the thoroughfares with their narrow trenches and wrecking the streets with their shallow and badly laid pipes. This happy and chaotic state continued until 1873, when the first steamroller took to the roads of London and systematically flattened every gas pipe in its path. From then on, gas pipes had to be laid deeper and with more care – which meant more expensively.

Few of the new companies lasted long, and by the 1870s most of them had been swallowed up by the Gas Light and Coke Company; the Equitable in 1871, the Western in 1872, the Imperial and Independent in 1876. The man responsible for this virtual monopoly of gas in London was John Orwell Phillips, Company Secretary of the Gas Light and Coke Company, who liked to be known as the 'Bismarck of Gas'. (This streak of eccentricity in the industry continued right up until nationalisation. One of the last directors of the Company, William Lyle Galbraith, wrote his internal memos in Ancient Greek.)

*Beckton gas works in 1881: the interior of No 9 retort house.*

As early as 1848, fears of monopoly among consumers, local authorities and public-spirited busybodies, had found a champion in Charles Pearson, Solicitor to the City of London, a believer in the benefits of garden suburbs for the working class, the advocate of a number of imaginative measures in the field of penal reform, and the unsuccessful contender of a large number of bye-elections.

To break the monopoly of the gas companies, Pearson, who regarded himself as an advanced liberal, had proposed an original idea for ownership of gas mains and gas pipes. They would be owned by cooperatives of consumers, who would be able to link up with any company offering them gas at free market prices through a 'Gas Market', linked to all of London through a spaghetti of mains: conjuring up a vision of a giant gas marketplace with the bidders of rival gas companies raising and lowering their prices as they themselves rose and fell on their telescopic gas-holders.

In his great public work, Pearson had been ably assisted by another pleasant, quirky Victorian: Alexander Angus Croll, ex-superintendent of the Brick Lane Gasworks, who was convinced that his past employers had 'stolen' his gas purification invention. In fact, they had rejected it as totally impracticable.

Pearson and Croll had taken their campaign to the people, holding

*The gasworks near Regent's Park: industrial architecture dignified by T H Shepherd c 1827. They 'are an immense pile of buildings in the parish of St Pancras, in the road leading to Kentish Town, and have a degree of architectural beauty arising from their intrinsic magnitude, the simplicity of their component parts, and the imposing grandeur of the two large columnar chimneys that surmount the roofs'.*

99

ill-attended meetings nightly and pressing for either the introduction of Pearson's 'Gas Markets' or for the gas companies to be taken over by the Commissioners of Sewers. This last public-spirited suggestion had been heartily endorsed by the Commissioners themselves. Then Pearson had changed his mind, redirecting his attention to founding the Great Central Gas Consumers' Company, in which the consumers were to have been the shareholders. Croll offered to run the Company, provided it used his purification process. Pearson, who knew nothing about gas, happily accepted. The Commissioners of Sewers were less enthusiastic, but in December 1849 Pearson's company was given permission to dig up the streets and lay pipes.

The company's trunk main was to have run from Bow Common to the City. In fact it never got past Bow Bridge. The Commercial Gas Company, which – like the other companies – saw Pearson's scheme as a threat, already had a main running along one side of the bridge. The night before Pearson's pipes were due to reach the bridge, the Commercial laid a pipe ten inches in diameter along the other side. The Trustees of the Middlesex and Essex Roads were in the pay of the Commercial; the parish authorities were in the pay of the Great Central. The parish beadle ordered the Commercial to remove their new pipe. The 200 Commercial workmen who had gathered started to build a barricade on the bridge. The Great Central liberally provided free gin for the Commercial workmen, and then stormed the barricade with 200 of their own workmen.

This was too much for Charles Pearson. He called a truce and arranged a peace parley on neutral ground in Norwood Cemetery. He agreed to let his Great Central Consumers' Gas Company be taken over by the Gas Light and Coke Company. Thus his anti-monopolist project ended up strengthening the very monopolists whom he had originally tried to curb.

The Gas Light and Coke Company now dominated London. For their workers there was a twelve-hour day and a seven-day week, as well as 'punctual and steady attendance during Xmas week'. A major strike in 1872 was broken by the Bismarckian Phillips, who dismissed all the strikers on the grounds that they were 'unworthy' of the Company.

. Twelve-hour days and seven-day weeks were not the only social battlegrounds for the nineteenth-century gas companies. In 1819, during the Reform Riots, the Foot Guards were stationed at Horseferry Road, and in 1830, when there was a threat that 'evilly disposed persons' might break into the works, the management stayed at their posts all night with muskets. Troops were stationed there again in the great Chartist demonstrations of 1848, when there was a possibility that the Horseferry Road works would be taken over by revolutionaries and the Houses of Parliament plunged into darkness. That same year, Professor Michael Faraday was investigating the

*Opposite:*
*The South Lambeth Gasworks at Nine Elms, engraved by Gustave Doré in 1872. Employees of the Gas Light and Coke Company worked a twelve-hour day and a seven-day week; strikes were met with instant dismissal.*

100

possibility of lighting the Houses of Parliament with primitive napalm.

After 1867 there were new threats to the gas companies. On 17 December 1867 Fenian terrorists exploded a mine against the wall of Clerkenwell Prison and blew up a gas main. A few weeks later, in January 1868, an informer passed on information about a plot to blow up the Horseferry Road and Curtain Road gasworks. The buildings were searched and a barrel of gunpowder found hidden by the Curtain Road gas-holder. The Gas Light and Coke Company promptly instructed all its Irish workers to sign an Address of Loyalty to the Queen. They duly signed.

There were accidental explosions to contend with as well. In 1815 the Gas Light and Coke Company ordered from Joseph Bramah 'an extinguishing engine of the largest power'. The first explosion

*Above:*
*Nine Elms Gasworks, where the largest gas explosion in nineteenth-century London occurred in 1865. Eleven men died.*

*Right: A gas explosion in the Tottenham Court Road which left the sewers beneath the street exposed.*

recorded – after the unfortunate incident involving the Prince of Wales' pagoda – was in 1822, when a wine merchant investigated a leak with a lighted candle. The second occurred in 1824, when 'an inexperienced person [sent] to examine a defect' lit a candle, resulting in a large hole in Westminster Bridge Road.

The largest gas explosion in nineteenth-century London was at the Nine Elms Gasworks, Battersea Road, on 31 October 1865. A million cubic feet of gas exploded and eleven workmen were killed.

> These who saw the explosion describe it as one vast upheaving of flame shooting high in the air, with a burst which shook everything around. People nearly a mile off were thrown violently down, and persons who were in houses in streets adjacent to the works received some severe burns from the heat of the flames. The flames indeed, mounted so high that even though it was the middle of the day they guided firemen to the scene from long distances. (*Illustrated London News* 4 Nov 1865)

As the monopoly of the gas companies grew, so did the calls for public ownership. And as the calls increased in tempo with the turning of the century, the gas industry declined. By the 1920s, the gas companies were complaining that local municipalities and boroughs with their own electricity generating plants were discriminating against the gas companies on the new council estates. A sign of the times came in 1937 when the old Horseferry Road gas-holder was demolished and rebuilt as a subterranean government citadel. The demolition was watched by an old man who had been a tea boy sixty years earlier for the navvies who had excavated and built it.

Nationalisation, when it came in 1948, seemed only to confirm the industry's decline. Since London was dominated by one large company, the Gas Light and Coke Company, nothing changed very much structurally – except that London was divided between North Thames and South-Eastern Gas. The company, having already witnessed the nationalisation of coal, electricity and transport, accepted the new order of things; the last governor of the Gas Light and Coke Company, Michael Milne-Watson, became chairman of North Thames Gas.

*Before North Sea gas could be put through the pipes, the old gas had to be flushed out. It was 'flared off', the flare changing its colour when the process was complete.*

The discovery of natural gas in the North Sea off Holland at Slochteren on 14 August 1959, followed as it was by the discovery of three enormous fields off the Norfolk coast, gave the gas industry a new lease of life. But coal and natural gas are very different from each other. Natural gas will not burn properly in 'town' gas appliances without adaptation. North Sea gas has twice the calorific value of 'town' gas and needs twice as much air to burn efficiently. The holes that draw in the air and the holes that let out the gas have to be enlarged. Committed by the summer of 1966, the Gas Council found itself having to modify every single gas appliance in the country: a total of thirty-five million appliances in over thirteen million homes and workplaces. In London the conversion began in April 1968 and was not completed until August 1976. Nor was conversion of public lighting in central London an easy task. There were 2000 gas street lamps to be converted, not least some highly decorative wrought-iron Victorian ones at Friary Court just inside St James's Palace; indeed, North Thames Gas still employs lamp-lighters for the 109 gas lamps in the Inner and Middle Temples.

With conversion the whole character of London's gas has changed. There is a new national grid, and a ring gas main girdles London. The great gasworks beside the Thames are now abandoned. But the pipes they served are still being used.

# 5 Tunnels under the Thames

Walk into Wapping Underground Station – on the north bank of the Thames – the gentle curves of its pagoda entrance hemmed in by crumbling warehouses straight out of a Doré drawing, and buy a ticket to Rotherhithe on the south bank of the River. Make your way down the circular staircase of the great shaft, now embracing a modern lift. The shaft, fifty feet in diameter and eighty feet deep, is no ordinary shaft. Men died digging it. At the bottom of the shaft, step onto the platform. At the end of the platform is a long dark tunnel. It is no ordinary tunnel. 'The very walls were in a cold sweat,' wrote *The Times* when it opened in 1843. They still are. The air in the tunnel is foetid and dank, and from its depths comes the constant churning of water pumps. There is an illuminated sign to train drivers: 'Men working at pumphouse at other end of tunnel. Whistle.' Close by is another sign, a plaque with the inscription:

> The tunnel which runs under the Thames from this station was the first tunnel for public traffic to be driven beneath a river.

The 400-metre-long Wapping-to-Rotherhithe tunnel, built by Marc Isambard Brunel at a cost of ten lives and £614,000, was not, of course, the first tunnel to be dug under water – the Babylonians built a tunnel under the Euphrates and the Romans built one under Marseilles harbour. But it is the first modern tunnel, and the first to be dug under the Thames.

Two attempts had already been made, and had failed. The first was in 1798, when an enterprising engineer, Ralph Dodd, announced that he would build 'a grand uninterrupted line of communication in the south-east part of the Kingdom', a tunnel under the Thames between Gravesend and Tilbury. It would 'be constructed wholly with keystones; therefore the greater the pressure the stronger will be the work,' explained *The Times* on 21 July 1798. 'The expense of this stupendous undertaking is estimated at so low as £15,955.' The great day came. The tunnel ran into quicksand and out of money.

A second attempt was made in 1802 by Cornish engineers Robert Vazie and Richard Trevithick (the inventor of the first steam-propelled wagon): it almost succeeded. Initially, the tunnel advanced through clay (the easiest material to tunnel through) at a rate of 120 feet a week. Half-way across, the workmen were slowed down by quicksand 'as fine as flour'. On 26 January 1808, within 120 feet of the other bank, the Thames broke in. The tunnel was cleared, work continued, and on 2 February, Trevithick was able to write: 'We are beyond low water mark on the north side of the drift. If we have no further delays, we shall hole up to the surface in ten or twelve days.' That day the Thames broke in again. The Thames water bailiff

*Opposite:*
*The twin entrances to Brunel's Thames Tunnel, stretching under the River. Edward Lear heard its praises sung in Italy; the Khedive of Egypt wanted his own version built under the Nile; but to Londoners it became 'The Great Bore'.*

*Brunel's revolutionary tunnelling shield, based on his observation in prison of* teredo navalis, *the common shipworm.*

ordered all work to stop, and the Thames Navigation Committee, who were financing the project, refused to provide more money. 'Though we cannot presume to set limits in the ingenuity of other men,' they wrote, 'we must confess that, under the circumstances which have been so clearly represented to us, we consider that an underground tunnel which would be useful to the public and beneficial to the adventurers, is impractical.'

Brunel's Wapping-to-Rotherhithe alignment was chosen for geographical and economic reasons. Rotherhithe, on the south bank, was a district of flourishing industry, packed with mills, wharfs, factories and people. The docks on the north bank – St Katharine's, the London and the West India – took in huge quantities of foreign goods, some of which had to make the four-mile journey by road via London Bridge, the nearest river crossing. In the 1820s, some 4000 carts and wagons crossed London Bridge daily, while 350 Thames watermen ferried 3700 people across the river each day. The proposed Wapping-Rotherhithe Tunnel was designed to shorten the journey for wheeled traffic and to reduce the number of ferry boats milling about on the River: an important early exercise in transport planning.

Brunel, a royalist exile from Revolutionary France, came to England via America, where he had built the first major canal in the New World, the Lake Champlain-Hudson Waterway. He arrived in England in 1797 and made a fortune manufacturing pulleys for the navy and boots for the army. However, the end of the Napoleonic Wars brought bankruptcy, and it was in a debtor's prison that Brunel was first to observe the activities of *teredo navalis*, the common shipworm.

*Teredo navalis* is a natural tunneller. Digging with two shells on either side of its head, it eats into the ship's timbers, passing the shredded wood through its body as excreta to form a brittle lining which strengthens and protects its new-found burrow. Brunel's idea, patented in 1818 on his release from prison, was to build a vast shipworm: an iron cylinder, with corkscrew blades twice the size of a man, to be propelled forward by hydraulic jacks, while the sides of the tunnel were to be reinforced by bricks as the cylinder advanced. Unable to find a motor strong enough to turn the blade, Brunel was forced to abandon this embryonic drum-digger.

Undaunted, he kept the cylinder, but replaced the blades with a honeycomb of thirty-four separate cells, each faced with an oak plank. Working in alternate cells, the miners removed the planks, hacked out four and a half inches of tunnel face, and replaced the planks, jacking them forward to the new position; they then repeated the process in the adjoining cell. So Brunel's primitive shield advanced, while teams of masons and bricklayers lined the tunnel behind it.

Brunel was never short of advice. One man, John Johnson, Secretary of the Benevolent Institution of Smiths, suggested laying the

*Above:*
*A cross-section of the Thames Tunnel, sent in a minutely-detailed report to the Russian Court at St Petersburg.*


*Below left:*
*A contemporary lithograph of the construction of the tunnel.*

*Below right:*
*The shield in action. 'Working in alternate cells, the miners removed the planks, hacked out four and a half inches of tunnel face, and replaced the planks, jacking them forward to the new position; they then repeated the process in the adjoining cell'. (The endpapers of this book also illustrate the operation of the shield.)*

tunnel in a vast trench across the Thames within a dried-up coffer-dam. If this wasn't practical, he went on, the tunnel could be built out of a series of twenty-eight-foot-long diving bells, lowered into the Thames with workmen inside, who would bolt the bells together, cut openings in their sides and thus form the tunnel: the very engineering principle used 150 years later for the building of the Rotterdam Sub-Aqua Railway and the Bay Area Rapid Transit underneath San Francisco Bay.

Work began on the Wapping shaft of Brunel's tunnel at one o'clock on 2 March 1825. To the applause of 'many persons of respectability', including a Red Indian chief, Little Carpenter, Brunel cemented the first brick with an engraved silver trowel. On 12 July, the tunnel claimed its first casualty: a ganger named Painter fell down the shaft while drunk and killed himself.

The shaft was built of brick and ringed with steel. Brunel built it on the surface and gradually sank it down to the required depth under its own weight. By 28 November, the shaft – the same shaft you walk down to Wapping Underground station today – was in position, and Brunel's honeycomb shield gradually squelched forward. But on 26

The tunnel claimed many lives during the eighteen years of its construction. Workers (left), examine the shaft after a flood. The contemporary press (below), initially laudatory, soon began to view the operation with derision.

THE TUNNEL!!! or another BUBBLE BURST!

January 1826, when the tunnel had advanced only fourteen feet, the Thames broke in. Setback followed setback: there were constant seepages; there was a gas explosion; the tunnellers developed boils, stomach pains, nausea and diarrhoea. A miner named Francis Riley became delirious and died, and his death was followed by financial crisis.

In February, work restarted, and by March the tunnel was halfway across the Thames. One month later, Brunel's resident engineer collapsed from overwork. The only person with sufficient experience to take over was Brunel's eighteen-year-old midget son, Isambard Kingdom. In August, he was joined by Richard Beamish, a humourless, Anglo-Irish, ex-Guard's officer-turned-engineer. The tunnel had advanced 200 feet. To save money, the directors decided to cut the men's wages. To raise money they opened the tunnel to the public at a shilling a time, and society ladies were lowered into it in an armchair attached to pulleys.

*Isambard Kingdom Brunel.*

The Thames Tunnel was rapidly becoming a national Aunt Sally. *The Times*, having heralded it as a 'great national enterprise', now called it 'the Great Bore'. (But abuse at home did not prevent admiration abroad: the Khedive of Egypt invited Brunel to build a tunnel under the Nile.) 'Some public singers went into the tunnel and gave a very good entertainment,' Marc Brunel wrote in his diary on 11 April 1827. 'It was somewhat gratifying, but with the anxiety I now feel, the pleasure was checked by the reflection that perhaps in a few days the place may be full of water.' There was a tunnel waltz, and even a musical spectacle, 'The Thames Tunnel, or Harlequin Excavator', with a cast including Father Thames, an Ancient Flounder and a Thames Waterman, who sang of being 'an enemy to bridges and tunnels below the Thames'.

Brunel had good reason to be anxious. The miners were finding china, wood and coal in the higher cells of the shield. The tunnel was dangerously close to the river-bed.

On 21 April, in a makeshift diving bell weighing 8000 pounds, Isambard Brunel and his assistant, William Gravatt, descended into the Thames. On the river-bed, directly above the tunnel, they found what they were looking for – a deep depression. Isambard climbed into it and pushed an iron rod into the bed. From inside the tunnel a miner pushed the rod back, thus establishing the proximity of the tunnel face to the river-bed. Four days later they made a second descent. *The Times* correspondent described the diving bell, 'lowered amidst the anxious anticipation of the surrounding visitors. The usual signs were given and promptly answered, and after remaining for about twenty minutes under the water, and completing their inspection, the subaqueous adventurers returned.' They then packed the depression with bags filled with clay, and tunnelling continued.

Cuts proposed to the men's wages posed an equally dangerous

threat to the tunnel. There was growing discontent. On 1 May, *The Times* reported the miners striking 'amid scenes of riot and confusion'. The strike lasted three days, during which the tunnel slowly filled with water and the shield rusted. 'These men have presumed on their success and their great endowment of animal courage,' wrote Beamish. 'It is only another proof of the impossibility of placing reliance upon vulgar minds though somewhat elevated above the herd.'

A week after the collapse of the strike, the tunnel gave way. The face 'became alive', as Beamish noted, and the Thames poured in. One workman, Richardson, was drowned and another died of fever and dysentery before the tunnel was cleared again. Marc Brunel suffered a paralytic stroke, but, lying in his bed, he ordered a pulley to be constructed from the shaft to his bedroom so that he could inspect specimens of soil encountered during excavation.

That September, Marc Brunel, on his feet but moving with difficulty, decided to celebrate the resumption of the tunnelling. He organised a banquet inside the tunnel for the 130 miners and bricklayers, and for forty distinguished guests. The band of the Coldstream Guards (Beamish's old regiment) played *Der Freischütz*. Toasts were offered to the Dukes of York, Clarence and Wellington, as well as to the King. Then, spontaneously, a workman stood up and offered his own toast, 'To Our Tools'. The men raised their picks and shovels, their cheers, according to *The Times*, 'resounding with surprising effect throughout the whole length of the subterranean or, rather, subaqueous edifice'.

On 28 January 1828, the Thames burst in again. The entire tunnel was filled in fifteen minutes. Two men died, but Isambard, carried by the force of the water up the shaft of what is now Wapping underground station, escaped with his life. 'Before it was known who

*A diving bell was lowered into the Thames in April 1827 to investigate a deep depression in the river bed.*

*Below:*
*A drawing by I K Brunel shows him stepping from the bell onto the shield.*

*Bottom:*
*The diving bell descends, watched by a curious and excited crowd. The boatload of clay-filled sacks pierced with hazel rods was used to pack out the depression.*

*A banquet given in the tunnel to encourage both the workers and the outside world: the music was operatic; the toast, 'To Our Tools'.*

was lost and who was saved, the wives and relatives of the workmen rushed in, and added to the confusion and distress of the scene by their wild gestures and exclamations,' according to one eye-witness.

By May, the debris was cleared, but tunnelling had halted. The Company had run out of money. The tunnel face was covered over with a mirror and visitors were again brought down at a shilling a time. Priestley's *Navigable Rivers and Canals*, published in 1831, contains a melancholy little obituary of the Thames Tunnel: 'At Rotherhithe there is a tunnel which has been cut under and about half way across the river, but has been stopped, not only by the water getting through, but by lack of funds.'

In 1835, the government stepped in, provided the money, and tunnelling was resumed. The following January, freed of financial shackles, the tunnellers soon found themselves faced with a new danger: foul-smelling soil, impregnated by gases, described by the new assistant engineer, Thomas Page, as 'vomiting flames of fire which burnt with a roaring noise'. There were cave-ins, too – one veteran miner, Garland, suffocated to death under the wet sand. Conditions got steadily worse. Marc Brunel's diary for May 1838 tells a terrible tale:

16 May:      Inflammable gas. Men complain v. much.
26 May:      Heywood died this morning. Two more on the sick list. Page is evidently sinking very fast . . . Inspected the Shield. Not much water there, but the air is excessively offensive . . . It affects the eyes. I feel much debility after having been some time below.
28 May:      Bowyer died today or yesterday. A good man.

On 4 April 1840, fifteen years after the first brick had been laid, the tunnel was complete. It was finally opened by Queen Victoria on 27 January 1843: Marc Brunel received a knighthood and the Thames watermen flew black flags in protest.

The fame of the Thames Tunnel spread throughout the world. When Edward Lear reached a remote monastery in Calabria, he found that the Abbot had informed his monks:

England is a very small place although thickly inhabited. It is altogether about the third of the size of the City of Rome . . . The whole place is divided into two equal parts by an arm of the sea, under which is a great tunnel so that it is all like one piece of dry land. Ah! Che Celebre Tunnel!

Without the money to construct carriage ramps, the only way in or out of the tunnel was by two vertical shafts. Although 50,000 people passed through in the first twenty-four hours, it quickly lost its charm, and was taken over by whores and 'tunnel thieves', a new class of criminal who hid in its arches and mugged passers-by beneath the

*The tunnel was opened by Queen Victoria on 27 January 1843. 'Marc Brunel received a knighthood and the Thames watermen flew black flags in protest.'*

Thames. There was even a suggestion of turning the tunnel into a pipe for conveying south London's sewage to the north bank.

Nathaniel Hawthorne, then American Consul in Liverpool, described a visit he made in 1855:

*Opposite:*
*A bird's eye view of the entrance shaft of the Thames Tunnel.*

> . . . an arched corridor of apparently interminable length, gloomily lighted with jets of gas at regular intervals . . . an admirable prison . . . There are people who spend their lives there, seldom or never, I presume, seeing any daylight, except perhaps a little in the morning. All along the extent of this corridor, in little alcoves, there are stalls or shops, kept principally by women, who, as you approach, are seen through the dusk offering for sale . . . multifarious trumpery . . . So far as any present use is concerned, the Tunnel is an entire failure.

In 1869, twenty-six years after the tunnel opened, it was taken over by the East London Railway, which ran trains to Brighton through it. Finally, it found a role: transferred to the London Underground system at the end of the century, it now forms part of the Metropolitan Line between Wapping and Rotherhithe.

The economic failure of Brunel's tunnel had a sobering effect on London's enthusiasm for digging under the Thames. It was not until the year that the East London Railway Company took over the Rotherhithe tunnel that a passageway under the Thames was tried again. The scheme was put forward by Peter Barlow, an engineer who had cut his teeth building the Metropolitan Railway. Aware of Brunel's difficulties, no contractor tendered an offer. Then a South-African-born, twenty-six-year-old engineer, James Henry Greathead, offered to undertake the work himself.

Greathead's plan for building a tunnel from Tower Hill to Vine Lane (off Tooley Street) was revolutionary – revolutionary by virtue of its speed and cost of execution. Not only was the estimate for the construction a mere £16,000, compared with Brunel's £614,000, but he also guaranteed to complete the tunnel in less than a year – Brunel's had taken fifteen years.

To build the tunnel, he designed his own tunnelling machine: the Greathead Shield. It worked on the same principle as Brunel's, but was more sophisticated. If not revolutionary, it was certainly brilliantly evolutionary. The front end of his shield consisted of a circular iron ring divided into seven segments, in which the tunnellers worked under compressed air. Behind this working area was a watertight bulkhead, which would be closed with planks to stop 'running ground' (sand) or 'flowing ground' (water, quicksand, etc). The shield was six feet seven inches in diameter and held three workmen at a time. Brunel's shield had weighed 120 tons; Greathead's weighed only two and a half. As the shield advanced on hydraulic rams, eighteen-inch, cast-iron sections of tubing were inserted, forming a lining behind the shield in much the same way as Brunel's shipworm. In the space left between the excavated tunnel and the cast-

*Above:*
*Commemorative engraved roundels of the construction and completion of the tunnel.*

115

*The shield designed by James Henry Greathead to dig the Tower Subway: cost and time were a fraction of Brunel's.*

iron segments, workmen packed grouting, which they inserted with hand syringes.

The Greathead Shield moved steadily forward, working day and night, four and a half feet every twenty-four hours. The tunnel was completed in just ten months.

The Tower Hill entrance was on Crown land. The tunnellers were made to pay dearly for the privilege. *The Times* commented:

> The site of the tunnel works on Tower Hill does not attract much notice. It is a little boarded space about the size of a kitchen with a small steam crane in the centre. They could not afford more for the Government – either disapproving of the idea or believing that such a luxury as tunnel building ought to be well paid for – charges at the rate of £150,000 an acre plus a fine of £10 a yard for tunneling under Crown ground and £3 a yard for tunneling under their side of the river. In all the Government took about a tenth of the Company's modest capital.

To make matters worse, the tunnellers found a bag containing 300 silver coins from the reign of Henry III. These too, as treasure trove,

went to the Crown.

The tunnel – named Tower Subway – was opened in 1870, complete with a twelve-passenger cable car service. The fare was twopence first class, a penny second class. The subway proved financially no more viable than Brunel's tunnel. Its cable-cars were taken out and the tunnel became a walkway – highly successful at that, with over a million pedestrians a year passing through it until Tower Bridge removed its *raison d'être* in 1894. Abandoned, it was bought by the London Hydraulic Power Company as a conduit for their high-pressure water mains. It thus gained the distinction of being the only privately-owned tunnel under the Thames. With the demise of hydraulic power, the tunnel today carries water mains for the Thames Water Authority. Tomorrow it may carry cables for cable television.

You can still see the entrances to the Tower Subway: a shabby pillar-box on Tower Hill and another on Vine Lane. From its entrances, spiral staircases lead down the shaft to the tunnel. It is dark and gloomy, with lines of water pipes flanking a small narrow passage. The tunnel lining consists of eighteen-inch, cast-iron segments stretching like the ribs of a huge whale, gently dipping down to the centre, then rising up again on the other side.

The Tower Subway unleashed a spate of subterranean speculation. 'In time', enthused a contemporary, Walter Thornbury, 'there will be subways at Gravesend, Woolwich and Greenwich.' There was a scheme for a pneumatic railway from Whitehall to Waterloo. Greathead's partner, Peter Barlow, suggested installing 'omnibus

*The Tower Subway: advancing the shield; putting the castings; carriage interior; the entrance on Tower Hill.*

117

subways', eight feet in diameter, equipped with twelve-seater
carriages and propelled by gravity. Because of the rise and fall of the
surface, there would be three sets of subways at different depths; the
carriages, complete with passengers, were to be raised from one level
to another by hydraulic lifts.

Greathead himself did not stop at his shield. On 29 September 1887,
he patented one of the world's first tunnelling machines. According to
the patent, it had a central rotary cutter with rotating arms to break
down the spoil. Its drawback was that its central shaft left insufficient
room to clear the debris. It was never built.

In a second patent, filed on 4 January 1889, he had solved the
problem of the mounting spoil. It was a solution that was to prove
prophetic. An airlock and an outlet pipe were positioned immediately
behind the cutter. High-pressure water would wash the spoil away
through the pipe.

Neither machine got beyond the drawing board. London's first
underground tunnelling machine was built by Greathead's rival, John
Price. Used in the 1897 excavation of the Central Line deep-level tube
between Shepherd's Bush and Marble Arch, it had a conical rotating
cutter head and four radiating arms, which raked the debris and

scooped it into a chute to be funnelled into skips. The machine was electrically powered and operated independently of the shield, which was propelled forward by hydraulic rams. The central shaft still proved an obstacle to the removal of debris, and, as well as being unable to turn corners, the machine tended to deviate in the direction in which the machine's cutters were rotating.

Gradually, over the years, these faults were eliminated. The power was shifted from a central shaft to peripheral drive. A second set of rotary arms was added – both rotating at one and a half revolutions per minute in opposite directions, to break up the spoil and keep the machine on course. The machine was integrated with the shield. All these improvements took time to perfect. Within a few years of his first machine, Price built an improved model. It was used to tunnel the West End branch of the Northern Line and reached a speed of 180 feet per week.

Over the next fifty years, Price's machine evolved into the modern drum-digger. The first model was built by Kinnear Moodie and Arthur Foster, and used in 1955 to bore the tunnel for the raw water main, which passes under the Thames at Barnes. The drum-digger consists of two drums, an outer one with a cutting edge and an inner one with cutting teeth, each rotating every fifteen seconds. The teeth cut into the clay and, via a hopper, guide the spoil onto a conveyor belt for disposal. The drum is pushed forward by hydraulic rams operating under a pressure of 2000 pounds per square inch, which can be individually controlled to 'steer' the digger.

The machine has its drawbacks, however. Like other mechanical diggers, it can only be used in one stratum, clay: once the tunnel goes beyond clay, it is useless, and the workmen have to revert to using a basic Greathead Shield, hand-excavating with pneumatic spades. This method was used, for instance, to dig the section of the Victoria Line which runs under the Thames between Pimlico and Vauxhall. Still the problem remains of debris blocking the machine. The more it finds itself in 'running' or 'flowing' ground, the more the face of the digger has to be closed, and the quicker it blocks. In 'running' ground, the face sometimes can be frozen with chemicals; in 'flowing' ground, there is no obvious answer – the chemicals tend simply to wash away.

Stable soil means that the digger can be dispensed with altogether and a mechanical excavator built into the shield. The excavator tears away the clay and sends it either into skips or onto a conveyor belt. In less stable soil, engineers have to fall back on Greathead: to that almost forgotten patent in which he had suggested using high-pressure water to wash debris away down a thick pipe. Until then the only method of tunnelling in unstable conditions under the Thames had been by using compressed air. Inevitably, the more unstable the soil, the greater the chance of blow-outs. Besides, there remains the problem of how to get

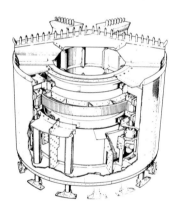

*Top:*
*John Price's underground tunnelling machine; still limited in the removal of debris and the turning of corners.*

*Centre:*
*The conveyor belt of a Price machine.*

*Above:*
*A cut-away view of the Kinnear Moodie drum-digger.*

119

the debris out of the bulkhead without the compressed air escaping.

Two major landslides in 1950, one at Surte in Sweden, the other at Knockshinnoch in Ireland, pointed the way to a solution. In both cases the soil was clay, similar to that known as 'bentonite'. Scientists observed in both cases that the clay, having absorbed large amounts of water, swelled up and suddenly transformed itself into liquid form when subjected to a chemically-inspired shock. With stabilisation, the process could be reversed.

When the Fleet Line (later called the Jubilee Line) was on the drawing board, a trial Bentonite Tunnelling Machine, based on the phenomenon observed by the tunnellers in the Swedish and Irish landslides, was built by Robert L Priestley Ltd. The new line was planned to run east from Charing Cross and under the Thames Estuary, crossing the River at six points – it was to pass through all the subterranean obstacles encountered by Brunel over a century earlier.

The company began by driving an experimental length of tunnel under New Cross. The machine, delivered to the New Cross site on 12 December 1971, consisted of a cylindrical mechanised shield with a steel bulkhead immediately behind it. Bentonite slurry was pumped into the bulkhead against the face of the tunnel, the shock transforming the face into liquid form while the bentonite slurry continued to support the face. The liquid debris was then pumped out of the bulkhead and up to ground level, where the process was reversed and the bentonite separated from the debris. The bentonite was then recycled throughout the whole system.

*A Bentonite Tunnelling Machine, tested for the first time under New Cross in 1971.*

The New Cross tunnel, 472 feet of it, is still there, although the Fleet Line extension to Thamesmead was never built. The Bentonite Tunnelling Machine itself has gone on to other things: digging a sewer under Warrington.

The bentonite process is just as applicable to smaller tunnels. It has changed the nature of mini- and micro-tunnelling. Until the use of bentonite, the only effective miniature tunnellers were 'percussion moles', which punched their way through the earth. Small in diameter, they were unable to remove debris. Now, miniature bentonite tunnelling machines, like the Japanese Telemole and Telemouse – to which guidance systems can be attached – dispose of the waste soil and avoid the disruption and inefficiency of trenching, which meant that ninety-five per cent of the excavated earth had to be put back into the ground again.

The decades that followed the building of the Tower Subway produced another great tunnelling engineer, Dalrymple-Hay, who built the Waterloo-to-City Underground railway (which runs diagonally under the Thames almost beneath Blackfriars station), and modified Greathead's Shield by giving it a cutting 'hood'. He became tunnelling consultant to the London Passenger Transport Board in the

1930s. A contemporary of Greathead, he was, by then, a very old man. He had a firm belief in his own immortality, so it was with some difficulty that the London Passenger Transport Board persuaded him to appoint a partner who would eventually take over.

The man Dalrymple-Hay nominated was William Halcrow – a subterranean genius fit to rank alongside Greathead and Brunel. Virtually every tunnel built under London since the 1930s has been built by him: the Post Office Railway, the Whitehall tunnel system, the deep-level air-raid shelters, the Post Office cable tunnels, the Victoria Line, the Jubilee Line, the raw water main. Halcrow and his firm (Sir William Halcrow and Partners) designed the lot.

Halcrow was responsible for introducing a number of developments in tunnel linings and tunnelling machines. Faced with a shortage of cast-iron during the war, he turned to pre-cast concrete and designed concrete lining segments with concave and convex ends, so that they fitted together like keystones. Ten years later, he took his tunnel-lining methods another step foward. Behind the tunnelling machine but within the shield, he used hydraulic jacks to force the concrete segments directly against the sides of the excavated tunnel, expanding them into position against the clay. Not only did the process eliminate the time-consuming business of grouting, but it also made the whole stronger. The lining was called 'Donseg'; it was used in the raw water main, and, later, in the tunnels of the Victoria Line.

In the century since Greathead's Shield, each technological advance has resulted in a new wave of tunnelling beneath London: railway tunnels, road tunnels, foot tunnels, cable tunnels, and water tunnels. Together they create an intricate network beneath us. But, unlike Brunel's and Greathead's original schemes, these new tunnels are not confined to the River. Rather are they part of larger systems under London, much of which we above ground know very little about.

Although London has comparatively few bridges, compared with, say, Paris, she can boast of more tunnels under her capital river than any other city in the world. From Hammersmith Bridge to the Thames Estuary there are over twenty tunnels under the Thames.

The first tunnel you encounter, going downstream from Hammersmith Bridge, is the Thames Water Authority's raw water main, which runs under the River from the West Middlesex Water Works reservoir in Barnes to the waste ground next to the Riverside Theatre in Hammersmith.

At Battersea Power Station there are two more tunnels. Both have become virtual fossils since the power station ceased to operate. The first one carried electricity cables across the Thames, and it still holds some cables in it. With its meccano-like brackets for holding the cables on either side of the small walkway in the centre, it is already on the way to being a prize piece of industrial archaeology. The tunnel goes slowly down to a dip in the middle of the River, then slowly rises again,

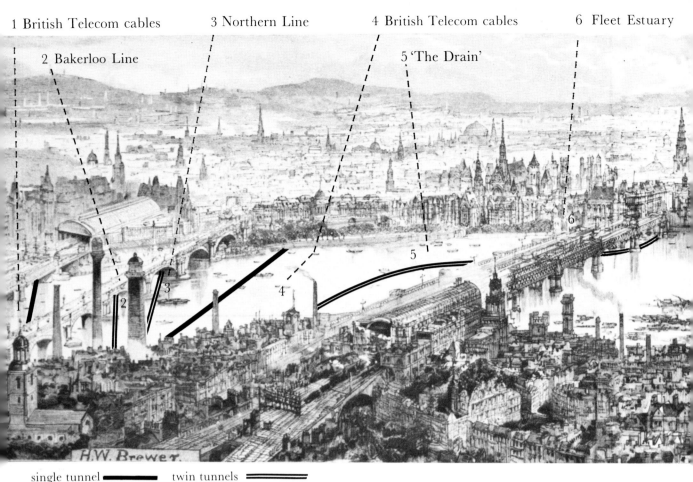

1 British Telecom cables  3 Northern Line  4 British Telecom cables  6 Fleet Estuary

2 Bakerloo Line  5 'The Drain'

H.W. Brewer.

single tunnel ━━━━  twin tunnels ═══

*An 1890 view of London by Brewer updates the famous Visscher view of the Jacobean city. Superimposed on Brewer – the 'crowd of tunnels between Hungerford and Blackfriars Bridges'.*

so the banks of cables create an optical illusion, suggesting that everything is slightly out of key with reality.

The second tunnel running under the Thames from Battersea is unique. When the power station was functioning, it carried untreated Thames water, heated to boiling point in the power station, under the River to Dolphin Square and the Churchill Gardens Estate, supplying the flats with central heating before discharging the water back into the Thames. The great boilers of the power station are now cold, and the blocks of flats have their own heating systems. The tunnel lies empty and dry, awaiting a new role.

Below Battersea Power Station, just before you reach Vauxhall Bridge, are London's newest tunnels under the Thames: the twin tunnels of the Victoria Line between Vauxhall and Pimlico underground stations, built in 1968.

Between Hungerford and Blackfriars bridges, the River is crowded with tunnels. There are four sets of twin underground tunnels running north from Waterloo under the River, all four of them built in the wave of tunnelling that followed the Tower Subway: the West End branch of the Northern Line between Waterloo and the Embankment, the Bakerloo Line between Waterloo and the Embankment, British Rail's own underground railway, the Waterloo-City Line (known as

LONDON:1890

7

'the Drain' by those who use it), and the disused 'Charing Cross Loop', once part of the Northern Line.

Much deeper than these four twin underground tunnels run two Post Office tunnels. One runs north-west, from the 'Rampart' telephone exchange at Colombo House near Waterloo to Trafalgar Square Post Office, passing under the Thames a little downstream from Hungerford Bridge. The other runs north-east from Colombo House to the 'Citadel' exchange in Faraday House, crossing under the Thames at an angle just below Blackfriars Bridge. These two tunnels under the River link up with both the government's deep-level tunnels under Whitehall and the twelve miles of Post Office cable tunnels stretching east to west across London.

Downstream from the crowd of tunnels between Hungerford and Blackfriars bridges, there is the twin tunnel running under the Thames at an oblique angle, which once carried the Northern Line from London Bridge Station to King William Street, and is now abandoned. It was followed by Greathead's Tower Subway, running almost under HMS Belfast. Beyond Greathead's tunnel lies Brunel's original Thames Tunnel from Wapping to Rotherhithe.

Below Brunel's tunnel is the Rotherhithe Road Tunnel, running from Stepney to Rotherhithe. Built between 1904 and 1908 at a cost of

LONDON:1890

8

*The Rotherhithe Road Tunnel, which runs from Stepney to Rotherhithe, under construction.*

£½m – the second road tunnel under the Thames – it is decorated by tens of thousands of bland and characterless white tiles, broken by the occasional pretentious piece of granite. Its dreary uniformity and self-consciously grand approaches, between Cable Street and Limehouse Basin in the north, and Jamaica Road and Surrey Docks in the south, marked the end of the post-Greathead era of tunnelling beneath Victorian and Edwardian London.

Below the Rotherhithe Road Tunnel, the Thames meanders, first on a southern bend around the Isle of Dogs, then on a northern bend around Greenwich Marshes. Between Greenwich and the Isle of Dogs are two tunnels. The first, hardly used now, carries a few cables from the remains of Deptford Power Station to the Isle of Dogs. The second is a pedestrian tunnel, built in 1902: the Greenwich Foot Tunnel. The entrance, on the north bank, almost hidden in the shrubbery of Island Gardens, resembles a pagoda-shaped public convenience crowned with a glass dome. A poster on the pagoda's wall displays the London County Council's bye-laws of 1903:

> No person may enter the tunnel in a state of intoxication . . . No person shall spit on or upon the tunnel or its approaches, stairs, lift, passages, or other means of ingress or egress thereto or therefrom.

Inside the entrance, a circular staircase spirals round a lift shaft,

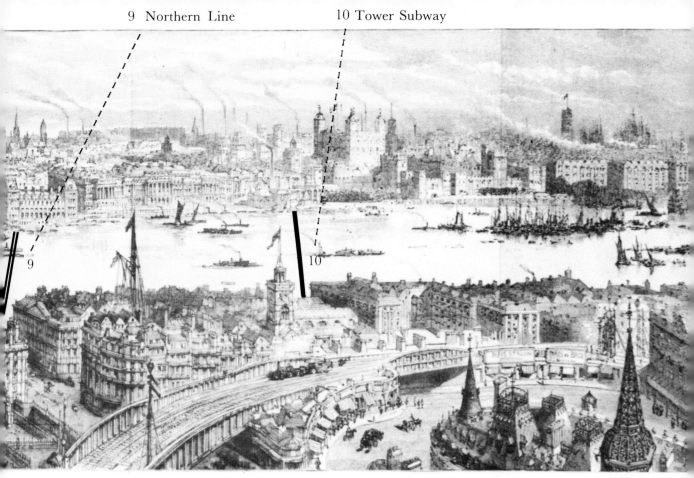

9

10

single tunnel ▬▬▬        twin tunnels ═══

served by a mahogany-veneered Edwardian lift complete with two sets of gates, like a pre-War Underground station lift. At the bottom of the shaft, the lines of off-white glazed tiles dip down to mid-stream, then rise again to another Edwardian lift that emerges on the surface cheek-by-jowl with the gigantic Cutty Sark on one side and the miniscule Gypsy Moth on the other.

On the northern bend of the River are two more tunnels. The northbound, upstream tunnel, the original Blackwall Tunnel, built between 1889 and 1897, was the first road tunnel to be excavated under the Thames; the south-bound tunnel, a little downstream, built between 1965 and 1967, with a marked improvement in off-white tiles, is the latest, if not the last.

The first Blackwall Tunnel, designed by Lord Cowdray, who had just built the Hudson Tunnel in New York, used a million off-white tiles. With its monumental approaches (the A102) it was, in its time, the largest subaqueous tunnel in the world. It took seven years to build, and when it was opened by the Prince of Wales in 1897 was hailed as a celebration of Imperial splendour and British genius. The engineer responsible for the working of the tunnel, Alexander Binnie, chief engineer to the London County Council, was more modest. He wrote in the *London Magazine* of 13 May that same year:

*Downstream from the 'crowd of tunnels' on the previous pages are three more tunnels – the best-known of which is Greathead's Tower Subway. Brunel's tunnel, along with several others, lies outside the scope of Brewer's picture, closer to the mouth of the River.*

125

Holland Tringham

We must not forget that credit is due to the men who have gone before: to that remarkable genius, the elder Brunel, who conceived the idea of the Shield, although he himself was unable to use it; to Bramah, to whom we are indebted above all others for the hydraulic press; and to Dundonald, who, in 1830, invented the mode of tunneling under compressed air, without which the Blackwall Tunnel could not have been constructed.

Downstream from the Blackwall tunnel are the most easterly tunnels under the Thames: the Woolwich Foot Tunnel, a London Electricity Board tunnel carrying cables between the ruins of Barking Power Station and Thamesmead, and London's newest tunnels under the Thames, two service tunnels carrying cables under the Thames Barrier across Woolwich Reach.

The Woolwich Foot Tunnel, like its Greenwich counterpart, is served by old lifts and runs from two LCC pagodas, one by Ferry Approach in south Woolwich, the other by the British Rail station in north Woolwich. It is lined with the standard off-white tiles, but they have become defaced by thousands of scraps of graffiti, whose multi-coloured messages defiantly challenge the dull monotony of public convenience architecture. 'Adventures in colour', someone has written over a National Front logo. Letters from the Underworld.

*Opposite:*
*A contemporary view of the Greenwich Foot Tunnel of 1902.*

*Above:*
*Sir Alexander Binnie, born in 1839, started his career as a civil engineer in India, and became chief engineer of the LCC. He built the Nagpore Water Works, Blackwall Tunnel, Bradford Waterworks and Barking Road Bridge.*

*Left:*
*The reverse of a medal struck and presented to the Prince of Wales at the opening of the Blackwall Tunnel.*

127

# 6 Trains Underground

L'*Enfant du Métro* is the story of a little girl, born on the Paris Underground, who remains there searching for her lost parents. She pictures for herself the world above by drawing on the mystical names of the stations she sees signposted below: Babylone, Etoile, Pyramides.

A child lost in London's Underground could similarly conjure up visions of an entire world. There would be earls at Earl's Court, kings at King's Cross, sheep at Shepherd's Bush, acrobats at Piccadilly Circus, Gabriel at The Angel and a minor deity at The Temple. Nor would London's child want for a world to explore. She would have 82 miles of tube tunnel to wander through, over 100 Underground stations to visit, fresh air to breathe from 130 giant ventilation fans, a constant temperature of 73° Fahrenheit to enjoy, and 300 London Transport police to help her find her parents.

It is highly unlikely, however, that she could spend very long in the London Underground unnoticed. She would never be alone. In the daytime her world would be shared by one and three-quarter million passengers; at night with the signals crews, maintenance teams, engineering gangs, billboard men and cleaners who take over the stations and tunnels.

But the Underground at night can be a terrifying place. Even more terrifying if the small girl were to encounter what the London Transport night crews call the 'Asbestos Train', which resembles a vast, vacuum-operated snow-plough, and travels very slowly – less than a mile an hour – through the tunnels, sucking up rubbish. Officially that is its only function. It does have another role, however. For over fifty years, London Transport's engine brakes have been lined with asbestos.* The asbestos content of the brake lining is less than five per cent, but each time a brake is applied, tiny particles of asbestos are released into the atmosphere. Over the years, a film has built up on the tunnel lining, which – each time the air is disturbed by a train – is blown from the walls into the faces of the passengers waiting on the platforms. Soon a new Swedish brake lining which does not use asbestos will be available, but for some years yet the systematic vacuuming of the tunnels – removing the asbestos along with the rubbish – must go on, preferably at night, when as few people as possible know about it.

Night is a time of frantic activity in the Underground. The lights are all on, giving the tunnels depth and contours. There is a twenty-four-hour staff canteen at Baker Street. Electrically-operated shunters, called battery trains, go by, pulling anything from rails to cables, even escalators. Maintenance crews wear bright orange dungarees, which glow in the artificial light.

*Opposite:*
*The Metropolitan Railway – the world's first underground railway – at the entrance to the Clerkenwell Tunnel, in the valley of the Fleet.*

* Since the early 1980s the brake linings used have been asbestos free.

If the little girl managed to escape the attention of London Transport's police, she would probably be found by that esoteric body of workers in the Underground: the fluffers. The fluffers are a small corps of stalwart ladies who work in the tunnels in the small hours, after the last train has left and before the first one comes in. The fluffer's job is to do just that – dust the fluff. The air in the tunnels is mostly warm and dry. Friction on the live rails, caused by the pick-up shoes, attracts dust, which in time forms a thick crust. So when the current is turned off, the ladies go to work with their feather dusters. The earth-mothers of the London Underground would certainly 'fluff out' the reluctant and bewildered stowaway.

The story of London's first underground railway, the Metropolitan, begins in 1843 with none other than our old friend from the days of the Gas Market, Charles Pearson.

A solution to London's traffic problem was desperately needed. The population of the city had doubled in forty years. A quarter of a million people entered London each day to work, travelling on foot, by river steamer, by coach and omnibus. Traffic control by semaphore, lights, bells and whistles had been tried and had failed. There had even been a plan for gas-lit subway streets for horse-drawn traffic, vetoed by the police as a 'lurking place for thieves, or their means of escape'.

Pearson's vision was of an underground railway which would link all the main-line railway termini in London. In 1843, he began his

*The building of the Underground was meant to alleviate London's endemic traffic problems, but these two views of Ludgate Hill (with the London, Chatham and Dover Railway in the background) – in an engraving by Doré of 1872 and a photograph taken twenty years later – show that nothing had changed.*

advocacy in *An Address to the Electors of Lambeth*. His bye-election campaign, like his previous efforts, was a failure, but his scheme to run trains in drains turned out to be his monument. Henry Mayhew wrote tolerantly of his schemes:

> We knew him well, and while discussing our joint schemes for utilisation of convict labour, have often smiled at the earnestness with which he advocated his project for girdling London round with one long drain-like tunnel and sending people like so many parcels in a pneumatic tube, from one end of the metropolis to the other.

Pearson envisaged that 'the line for the greater part of the distance will run beneath the surface of the roadway through a spacious archway. It will be thoroughly lighted and ventilated.' The railway was to run from Paddington, through Euston, St Pancras and King's Cross, to Farringdon; it would wipe out the squalid streets of the Fleet Valley, replacing them by colonies of suburban workers' villages with easy access to central London via underground railway.

Next year *Punch*, which had closely followed Pearson's career, satirised his plans:

> We understand that a survey has already been made and that many of the inhabitants along the line have expressed their readiness to place their coal cellars at the disposal of the company. It is believed that much expense may be saved by taking advantage of areas, kitchens and coal holes already made, through which the trains may run without much inconvenience to

*To the originator of the Metropolitan Line, Charles Pearson, it was a simple matter of diverting the slum-dwellers of Fleet Street to garden suburbs. To the Rev William Denton it was all too clearly a plan to 'pass only through inferior property', destroying 'the abodes of the powerless and the poor'. Either way it would 'avoid the properties of those whose opposition is to be dreaded – the great employers of labour'.*

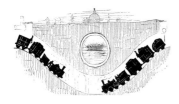

Punch, *of course, had a field day: 'Our modern projectors having exhausted the old world of railways above ground, have invented a new world of a subterranean kind . . . This is a magnificent notion for relieving any particularly over-crowded pocket from its oppressive burden . . .'*

*Nos 23 and 24 Leinster Gardens, Paddington, from the front (above) and the rear (right). Only the painted windows and the lack of letter boxes betray the houses for what they are: facades built to hide the engines of the Metropolitan Line as they let off steam behind and below.*

the owners, by making a judicious arrangement of the time-table. It will certainly be awkward if a family should be waiting for a scuttle of coals, and should not be able to get it until after the train has gone by; but a little domestic foresight, seconded by railway punctuality, will obviate all annoyances of this kind. Those who are disposed to sink a little capital cannot do better than bury it under the metropolis . . .

Pearson's main problem was finding an engine suitable for use underground. The users' problem was managing to breathe. Ordinary steam engines would not do: passengers and crew would suffocate. At first, Pearson thought of using stationary engines and hauling the trains by windlassed cables. When this proved impracticable, he suggested powering the railway by atmospheric pressure. The Metropolitan Line's engineer, Sir John Fowler (whose portrait by Millais has a tunnel and plans for the Metropolitan as its

background), then devised a smokeless engine powered by red-hot bricks under the boiler. 'Fowler's Ghost', it made only one run.

Finally, an engine was built diverting the smoke and steam into a tank behind the engine by means of a ducted exhaust. The smoke and steam were to be released when trains emerged from tunnels; hence one curious relic of this underground steam age, the dummy pair of houses still in existence as 23 and 24 Leinster Gardens, W2. Identical to adjoining houses, their facades consist in reality of nothing more than a five-foot wall. To complete the disguise, artificial windows and doors were built into the walls, behind and below which the old Metropolitan engines let off steam.

Pearson spent the next fourteen years trying to raise capital for his venture. Finally, after £300,000 had been subscribed by the Great Western Railway, the Great Northern Railway and the City of

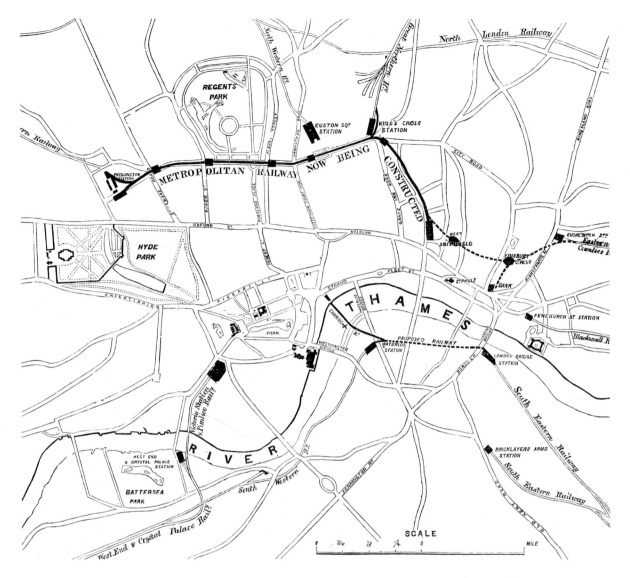

London Corporation, the first shaft was sunk in Euston Square in 1860. John Hollingshead describes the scene:

*A contemporary map showing the first stage of the Metropolitan Railway from Paddington to Farringdon, and its projected extension to the City.*

> A few wooden houses on wheels first make their appearance and squat like Punch and Judy shows at the side of the gutter. A few wagons next arrive, well loaded with timber and planks, and accompanied by a number of gravel-coloured men with pickaxes and shovels. In a day and a night, or a little more, a few hundred yards of roadway are enclosed, and a strange quiet reigns for a time, in consequence of the carriage traffic being diverted . . . The calm of the main thoroughfare is soon disturbed by the arrival of steam engines, horses, carpenters and troops of navvies within the enclosure. The sound of pickaxes, spades and hammers, puffing of steam, and murmur of voices begin: never to cease, day or night.

Huge timber structures spring up at intervals along the centre of the road, where spots for opening shaft holes are marked out, and it is not

133

many hours before iron buckets are at work, dragging up the heart of the roadway. This rubbish is carted off on a tramway as quickly as possible and tilted down a gaping pit, with a noise like distant thunder, to be carried away into the country along the underground branch railway already completed.

The projected line looked simple on paper: Paddington to Euston Road and the Fleet Valley to the City. But it meant diverting the Westbourne, the Tyburn and Fleet, together with gas pipes, water mains and sewers, all of which stood in its way. Along Euston Road the land was unstable sand and gravel which had to be drained; only outside the City, at Mount Pleasant, where a tunnel was necessary, did the Metropolitan Line strike clay. The greatest obstacle was the Fleet. The least – in Victorian eyes at any rate – was the thousands of poor people who lived in the Fleet Valley. The new railway displaced 12,000 of them from 1000 homes. Sign of the times – not a single vocal complaint. Mount Pleasant apart, the line was built by the cut-and-cover method, which meant digging huge trenches in the road, laying the line, arching over the trenches and rebuilding the road above.

The whole operation took three years. There were constant lawsuits and claims for compensation from aggrieved property owners. The

*The cut-and-cover method of construction involved tearing up many of London's major roads over a three-year period.*

*Opposite:*
*The first stages of the Metropolitan Line, at King's Cross (above); work in progress at Blackfriars, on the District, London's second underground railway (below).*

*Below:*
*The building of the now-abandoned line between St Pancras and Smithfield, British Rail's subterranean goods depot, linked to the Metropolitan, closed down after the War.*

Metropolitan Company complained that they were papering over cracks with five pound notes. Meanwhile, accidents took their human toll. In May 1860, a drunken train-driver overshot the platform at King's Cross and careered into the Metropolitan Line diggings. On 1 November, an engine shunting out wagons of spoil blew up, killing the driver, the stoker and a passing cabman – whose head was severed by the engine's chimney. Human disasters were matched by construction calamities: on 5 November, a water main in Farringdon Street burst, flooding the cutting; the following May, after several days of creakings, the northern side of Euston Road caved in; on 2 April 1862, the Fleet Sewer burst in on the diggings. Arnold Bennett later described the disaster:

> The terrific scaffolding of beams was flung like firewood into the air and fell with awful crashes. The populace screamed at the thought of workmen entombed and massacred. A silence! . . . The whole bottom of the excavation moved in one mass. The crown of the arch of the mighty Fleet Sewer had broken.

Eventually the line opened on 9 January 1863 – twenty years after Pearson first campaigned for its creation – with free rides and a grand banquet for 700 Victorian notables. There were two absentees – Lord Palmerston, who excused himself stating that he was anxious to remain above ground for as long as possible, and Charles Pearson himself, who had died six months earlier. The Metropolitan Railway had been his project: he had conceived it, created it, worked for it and been ridiculed for it. Yet when the Metropolitan Company had offered him

*Opposite:*
The building of the Metropolitan Line in the Fleet Valley loosened and destabilised the soil along the course of the old river. The bursting of the Fleet Sewer was the most dramatic of the accidents that marred the construction of the line. Arnold Bennett watched as the 'whole bottom of the excavation moved in one mass'.

*Above:*
The 'mighty Fleet Sewer', whose 'terrific scaffolding of beams', according to Bennett, 'was flung like firewood into the air and fell with awful crashes.'

*Left:*
Seven hundred people attended the banquet to celebrate the opening of the line.

137

a reward, he refused it. 'I am the servant of the Corporation of London; they are my masters, and are entitled to all my time and service. If you have any return to make you must make it to them.'

On 10 January, the line was opened to the public:

### Public Opening of the Metropolitan Railway

On Saturday, from as early an hour as six o'clock in the morning until late at night, trains filled with people were running at short intervals of time between Paddington and Farringdon Street. It soon became apparent that the locomotive power and rolling stock at the disposal of the company was by no means in proportion to the requirements of the opening day. From eight o'clock every station became crowded with intending travellers, who

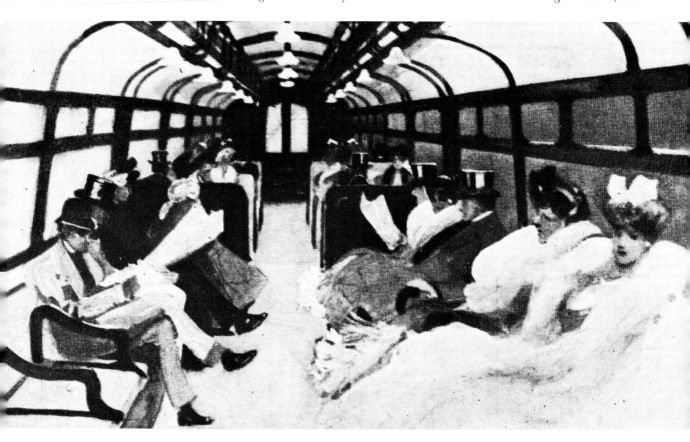

*Passengers on the Underground tended to divide into two classes: working men took the 'twopenny tube' in the early morning, while the middle class followed some hours later.*

were admitted in sections, but poor were the chances of a place to those who ventured to take tickets at any mid-way station, the occupants being, with but very rare exceptions, long-distance or terminus passengers. However, the crowding at King's Cross was immense. This station is certainly the finest on the line, throwing even the termini into the shade. Here the constant cry as the trains arrive of 'No room!' appears to have a very depressing effect upon those assembled. Between eleven and twelve at this station, and continuously for the space of an hour and a half, the money-takers refused to take money for passengers between King's Cross and Farringdon Street but they issued tickets between that station and Paddington, and many whose destinations were Citywards, determined to ride on the railway on its first day of opening, took tickets for the opposite direction in order to secure places for the return journey.

(Daily Telegraph, 12 January 1863)

Pearson dreamt that his railway would sweep London's slums away and replace them with garden suburbs. 'I have seen the advantage', he said, 'to my own class. Sixpence takes us by omnibus backwards and forwards; the poor man has not sixpence to give; he has no leisure to walk, and no money to ride; he is chained to his scene of labour and there he must stay.'

The slums were indeed swept away – but as yet there were to be no

garden suburbs. In 1861, while the Metropolitan Line was still being built, the Rev William Denton, vicar of St Bartholomew's in Cripplegate, published his *Observations on the Displacement of the Poor by Metropolitan Railways and Other Public Improvements.*

> The special lure of the capitalist is that the line will pass only through inferior property, that is through a densely peopled district, and will destroy the abode of the powerless and the poor, whilst it will avoid the properties of those whose opposition is to be dreaded – the great employers of labour.

In the years of expansion that followed, the poor found a new

*An engraving of the Metropolitan by Gustave Doré. The workers welcomed it: 'If a man gets home tired after his day's labour he is inclined to be quarrelsome with his missus and children . . . while if he gets a ride home . . . he is as pleasant a fellow again over his supper.'*

champion in Thomas Hughes, MP for Lambeth, who told the Commons:

> If the House does not insist on proper terms being made with the poor, metropolitan companies will become a greater social tyranny such as ten years ago none of us would have believed we could ever submit to. And not only will it be a tyranny, but a tyranny without prestige, tradition or picturesque. Already grievous injury has been inflicted on vast numbers of the humbler classes who have been turned out of their holdings . . . And this is done and great blots are put on the map of the metropolis that a man might be able to get from one side of the town to the other in five minutes' less time.

Henry Mayhew, however, saw the new railway as beneficial. In *The Shops and Companies of London* (1865) he describes a journey on the Metropolitan Line. Most of the passengers he spoke to said that cheap fares were a great benefit to the working man. One labourer from Notting Hill told him that he would have had to walk six miles to and from work each day if it were not for the underground railway. There was only one man who was suspicious of the new railways, a carpenter. 'He was one of those strange growling and grumbling characters so often met with among the working class.' He failed to perceive the advantage of paying a shilling a week on fares when he was paying the same rent in Paddington as in Clerkenwell.

> 'Come, come, mate', another passenger interrupted. 'Fair's fair. Just think of what these here trains save you at night after your work's over. If a man gets home tired after his day's labour he is inclined to be quarrelsome with his missus and the children, and this leads to all kinds of noises, and ends in him going off to the pub for a little bit of quiet; while if he gets a ride home, and has a good rest after he has knocked off for the day, I can tell you he is as pleasant a fellow again over his supper.'

*Two of the schemes submitted to the Select Committee of Metropolitan Communications in 1855: Sir Joseph Paxton's 'Great Victorian Way or Grand Girdle Railway and Boulevard under Glass' (right), and William Moseley's 'Crystal Way', an atmospheric railway enclosed in glass, which was to run from Cheapside to Oxford Circus. Neither was adopted.*

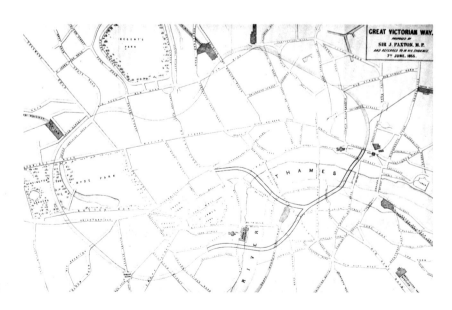

The success of the Metropolitan Line, coming as it did in the middle of the Victorian railway boom, produced a flood of more-or-less zany ideas on how the new form of transport should be developed. There were schemes to drain and lay a line in the Regent's Canal; to pull trains by cables operated by windmills; to build a ten-mile, circular railway covered in glass; to build an atmospheric railway powered by air pressure; and to build a railway line alongside the Thames.

The circular railway, set within its splendid greenhouse, almost happened. It was planned by Sir James Paxton, who, doffing his hat to the Queen, called it the Great Victoria Way. His Crystal Palace was already connected to the station of the same name by a tunnel designed and built by him. The railway was to be enclosed within an arcade of glass, fronted by shops, footpaths and even chapels. The trains would run on atmospheric pressure. 'I think', opined Paxton, 'this would make London the grandest city in the world.'

Paxton's Great Victoria Way, like the idea of powering trains by atmospheric pressure, was one of those unproductive culs-de-sac in the nineteenth century's march of progress. One railway using atmospheric pressure was actually built: the London-Croydon-Epsom Railway, which ran along the dried-up bed of the Surrey Canal. Three stationary engines forced high-pressure air into a fifteen-inch pipe with a continuous valve, covered by a leather flap, encased in beeswax and tallow. But the beeswax melted in summer and the leather flaps hardened and cracked in winter, while every season brought rats seeking shelter in the pipe. The idea was abandoned.

The idea of an atmospheric railway tunnelled deeply under London was the brainchild of Frederick Bramwell, President of the Institute of Mechanical Engineers. It was to run through London clay from Hyde Park to the Bank. The idea was only abandoned after the experience

*One pneumatic railway was built, in 1864 – to connect the low-level and high-level stations at Crystal Palace.*

141

*Sir Joseph Bazalgette had power of decision over the fanciful schemes put forward by railway enthusiasts. Of fifty-three proposed, he accepted one: the District Line.*

of Croydon's atmospheric rats.

*Punch*, as usual, entered the lists:

> As the contemplated railway must in several places be carried through the side and the centre of a street, it will be necessary for the gas and water companies to be approached so they may all cooperate in this great national Work. If the atmospheric principle should be adopted, arrangements could perhaps be introduced to obtain the use of the principal main belonging to the waterworks as a continuous valve.

The chief opponent of the many hare-brained schemes was Sir Joseph Bazalgette, engineer of the Metropolitan Board of Works and chief architect of underground London. He counted fifty-three different railway schemes for London and rejected them all – except one for a railway running alongside the Thames, to be called the District Line. It should run parallel to the Metropolitan Line, Bazalgette said, and be built as an integral part of the proposed Thames Embankment. At either end, the District Line was to curve northwards, the Metropolitan Line southwards and the two were to link up to form the Circle Line.

The Metropolitan Company made a bid for the new line, but the contract was given to the Metropolitan District Railway. Competition ensured that the Circle Line was not completed for twenty years.

The building of the District Line began on 29 June 1865 with the Westminster-South Kensington section. For a year, 2000 workmen, 200 horses and 58 engines dug their way underground. On 23 August 1866, the directors of the District Railway inspected the line. Starting at Westminster, where the brickwork and arches had been completed, through Broadway where rows of houses were being torn down, by tunnel under Victoria, where the remains of the Westbourne and the Five Fields Swamp had flooded the works, to Earl's Court, where two vast kilns produced fifty million bricks a day from the excavated clay, the directors rumbled underground, until they arrived at Paddington for celebratory luncheon at the Great Western Hotel.

In spite of one of the contractors going bankrupt, the Westminster-South Kensington section (and the link with the Metropolitan Line in West London) was ready by Christmas Eve 1868. But to the Embankment section there were continuous delays. Bazalgette, unable to wait any longer, built his Embankment without the District Line. *The Times* fumed on 18 April 1869:

> It is at least two years since the company announced their intention of proceeding with their works immediately. There is nothing whatsoever in the way of engineering or mechanical difficulty which might have prevented the railway going on with its works as the Embankment was formed, and it does seem too bad that we must now wait for the slow completion of this stupendous work only to see it pulled down to pieces again.

By 1870, the District Line had reached Mansion House, less than a mile from the Metropolitan Line at Tower Hill. Yet it was to be

*Left:*
*Bazalgette intended the District Line to be incorporated into the Embankment from the outset. Delays to the line meant that the Embankment was built first, only to be torn up again a few years later when the District Line finally put in an appearance.*

*Below:*
*The twin tunnels of the District Line at South Kensington.*

*Above:*
*The two arch-enemies who*
*dominated London's*
*Underground in its early days*
*– James Staats Forbes of the*
*District Railway (left), and Sir*
*Edward Watkin of the*
*Metropolitan Railway (right).*

another thirteen years before they were joined.

Two personalities dominated the conflict between the two rival lines: James Staats Forbes, chairman of the District Railway, and Sir Edward Watkin, who took over the Metropolitan Railway in 1872. Forbes, veteran of the London Chatham and Dover Railway, and the man reputed to have saved the British-owned Dutch and Rhenish Railway from bankruptcy, ruled the District Railway for thirty years.

> He had the genius for the propagation of railways, for scenting new avenues for connections and train services. He propounded his ideas with such vigour as to carry his shareholders with him regardless of whether his ventures were likely to be profitable or not.
>
> (O S Nock: *Underground Railways of the World*)

Watkin, who ruled the Metropolitan, was one of the most remarkable railway giants of the nineteenth century. Born in Salford in 1819, he became a director of the Manchester Athenaeum in his twenties, a director of the Trent Valley Railway, London and North-Western Railway and Manchester Sheffield and Lincolnshire Railway in his thirties, and president of the Great Railway of Canada in his

*High Street Kensington, one of the stations on the Circle Line. Forbes and Watkins, whose rivalry had delayed the completion of the project for fourteen years, were unwilling fellow-travellers on the first journey.*

forties. He built the Athens-Piraeus Railway, and tried to build the Channel Tunnel. His underlings hated him; his rivals despised him; his shareholders applauded him.

> In personality he was the very opposite of Forbes: a dour, hard-working promoter and financier, quite lacking in the light-headed touches that made Forbes' most fantastical flights of bunkum seem plausible. (*Ibid*)

The two men were old opponents from the days when Watkin had been a director of the South-Eastern Railway – rival to Forbes' London Chatham and Dover. They hated each other.

The Metropolitan and District Lines were linked in the west, but there was no connection to the east. Even in the west, the link was confused and complicated, with High Street Kensington and Gloucester Road being jointly owned properties, but South Kensington, well within the District Railway's sphere of influence, being owned solely by the Metropolitan Railway. Faced with a Metropolitan station astride his line, Forbes promptly knocked down thirty new houses in Pelham Street to make way for a rival station at South Kensington – without parliamentary approval. In September

1884, public opinion and government pressure finally forced resolution. The lines were linked, in spite of the two men, and, for the first and last time in their lives, Forbes and Watkin were forced to sit side by side on the first train round the Circle Line.

What was the Circle Line like in those early days? An article in *The English Illustrated Magazine* in the early 1890s describes the round trip:

In a short time, our train rushed into the station, and a moment later we had boarded the engine. I was accommodated with a position near the left-hand tank, whence I could get an uninterrupted view ahead: but it had its drawbacks as the water in that tank was hot. No time is wasted at stations on the Underground, and a minute later the train was off – off into the black wall ahead with the shrieking of ten thousand demons rising above the thunder of the wheels. The sensation was altogether like the inhalation of gas preparatory to having a tooth drawn. I would have given a good deal to have waited just a minute or so longer. Visions of accidents, collisions, and crumbling tunnels floated through my mind; a fierce wind took away my breath, and innumerable blacks filled my eyes. I crouched low and held on like grim death to the little rail near me . . .

I looked ahead. Far off in the distance was a small square-shaped hole, seemingly high up in the air, and from it came four silver threads palpitating like gossamers in the morning breeze. Larger and larger grew the hole, the threads became rails, and the hole a station. Blackfriars, with rays of golden sunlight piercing through the gloom.

Off again, a fierce light now trailing out behind us from the open furnace door, lighting up the fireman as he shovelled more coal into the furnace, throwing great shadows into the air, and revealing overhead a low creamy roof with black lines upon it that seemed to chase and follow us. Ever and anon the guard's face could be dimly seen at his window, more like a ghost than a man; while in the glass of the look-out holes were reflected the forms of the engine men like spirits of the tunnel mocking us from the black pit into which we were plunging . . .

The road now began to go uphill and at the same time the air grew more foul. From King's Cross to Edgware Road the ventilation is defective, and the atmosphere is on par with the ''tween decks, forrud' of a modern ironclad in bad weather, and that is saying a good deal. By the time we reached Gower Street I was coughing and spluttering like a boy with his first cigar.

'It is a little unpleasant when you ain't used to it:' said the driver, with the composure born of long usage, 'but you ought to come here on a hot summer day to get the real thing!'. . .

The ventilation holes in the tunnel roof about this part give a beautiful effect of light streaking into darkness; especially one before Edgware Road is reached, where the silver column of light fell on a green signal lamp, set low on the permanent way . . .

We shot once more into St. James' Park, 70 minutes after leaving it.

Ventilation, or rather difficulty of providing it, continued to be the main brake on the development of London's Underground. Until an alternative form of locomotion could be invented, no tube could be properly ventilated, and passengers would continue to be irked by the discomfort of this mode of transport – or, worse, come to fear it.

Not least of their fears was suffocation. The 'sewer' railways of the original, steam-driven Metropolitan and District Lines were nothing if not smoky: the explorer underground could be forgiven for mistaking London's Inner Circle for one of Dante's lesser circles. The problem was how to ventilate tunnels without causing discomfort to passengers or creating a nuisance on the surface. Attempts to build smokeless locomotives were unsuccessful, and until the development of electric traction the designers had to make do with air-holes, which joined the many other orifices, grating covers, manholes and valves dotting the crowded streets of London.

The Royal Commission set up as far back as 1846 to investigate railway proposals for the capital had been much concerned with this problem. The Commissioners had cross-examined Charles Pearson about his plans for letting air into the Underground. Was there not a danger of mass suffocation? Pearson's solution had been simple – the insertion of air-holes at regular intervals to allow the smoke and asphyxiating air to escape. 'How do you propose to prevent articles being thrown down the holes and obstructing the railways?' the Commissioners had asked. Pearson dismissed the objection, saying that the usual method of suppressing mischievous activities would be invoked: the penalties of the law.

The first tunnelling engineers did not take ventilation very seriously. They had persuaded themselves that the piston action of the locomotives alone would be sufficient to circulate the air, especially in a confined tunnel. Changing over to electric traction at the turn of the century did something to reduce pollution; but in the deep-level tubes, where there could be no air-holes, the exhausts of the engines, combined with the smell of concentrated humanity, made journeys malodorous and suffocating.

Exhaust fans were first built into the underground system in 1902 at Bond Street. London County Council chemists had been called in to investigate pollution underground; they found that, though carbon dioxide was not a danger, sulphur and nitrous oxide were. The evil-smelling atmosphere seems to have been caused by excessive dryness: the tubes had an average humidity of 44.5 per cent, against average street humidity of 75.7 per cent. One gentleman of the Sudan Political Service, on furlough from Africa, complained that the smell of the Underground reminded him of a crocodile's breath.

Other fans were installed on the Central Line at British Museum station, but complaints continued. It was not until filtered, ozonised air was injected into the Underground in the 1920s and 1930s that passengers accepted underground travel as a comparatively painless pleasure. Ozonising plants were eventually built at Edgware Road, Goodge Street and Charing Cross. They are still visible – reminders of that period of London's history when passengers thought they could smell the sea in the Underground. At least the London Underground did not emulate the Paris Métro, whose trains at one time sprayed scent as they ran into a station.

Today the air is extracted from the tunnels by 130 powerful fans discharging 2400 cubic metres of air per second into purpose-built ducts, keeping the temperature at an average of 73°F (21°C), making the Underground warm in the winter and cool in the summer. Fresh air enters through natural openings like station entrances and staircase shafts, but supplementary fresh air is pumped into the system through shafts.

The trains are themselves a means of air circulation – like pistons, they push the air along in front and suck it along behind. Without this constant circulation, temperatures would rise to intolerable levels.

Experienced travellers know well in advance when a train is approaching. Long before the noise can be heard, either as a distant rumble or as a hum of vibration along the lines, there is the faintest air disturbance and a slight drop in temperature, which increases as the train emerges from the tunnel and the distant rumble turns into a deafening roar.

While ventilation continued to pose major problems, competition between the District and Metropolitan lines had not ceased, despite the merger of the two companies. But it was to become increasingly irrelevant. New underground railway companies were to be formed, charged with the task of tunnelling rather than cutting-and-covering their way through London's sub-strata.

The first of the new deep-level railways was the City and South London Line, running from King William Street to Stockwell, later to become the City Branch of the Northern Line. Greathead was the

*Above:*
*The City and South London was the first line not built by cut-and-cover.*

*Right:*
*The deep-level King William Street tunnel found a wartime role as an air-raid shelter, but now, dripping with stalactites, houses gas and water mains.*

engineer. The original City and South London Railway had a pair of tunnels crossing the Thames at an oblique angle. The line was later straightened from London Bridge to Monument, the original tunnel which leads to King William Street Station being given over to gas and water mains, and used, as we have seen, as an air-raid shelter during the Second World War.

The straightened line almost caused the demolition of Nicholas Hawksmoor's St Mary Woolnoth. Indeed, the Company obtained parliamentary sanction to knock down the church. So great was the public outcry that the City and South London Railway was obliged to underpin the church's foundations, while it constructed Bank station, directly underneath the church. The entrance to the station at King William Street is marked, appropriately, by the head of an angel.

By this time, the United States was well in advance of Britain in its use of electric traction. It had over 3500 miles of electrically-operated track carrying 250,000,000 passengers annually. These figures, together with the success of the Bessbrook and Newry Tramway in Ireland, and of Volk's electric railway along the sea front at Brighton, were enough to give the promoters second thoughts about running the lines by cable-hauling. They switched to electricity.

The trains consisted of three cars pulled by an electric locomotive. They ran at five-minute intervals and at eleven and a half miles per hour. The staff rode on small platforms between cars, calling out station names and opening and shutting doors. Admittedly, even if the station names had been visible, passengers would have been unable to see them: the cars were windowless. The theory was that since there was nothing to see, windows were pointless, and the lavish upholstery was swept right up to the small ventilation slits. (These cars became known as 'padded cells'.) Futher refinements were electric lamps and all-male smokers' cars. All you needed for a trip in a padded cell was twopence for the fare and a strong constitution.

The line was formally opened by the Prince of Wales (later Edward VII) on 4 November 1890. Six weeks later, when the staff had mastered the new technique, it was opened to the public: the first electrically-operated, deep-level railway in the world.

Next to be built was Dalrymple-Hay's Waterloo and City Line, nicknamed 'The Drain' – London's second-oldest deep-level tube – giving commuters access to the City from Waterloo. 'The Drain', like the 'Sewer Railway', was a name given to all tubes by those who automatically connected all underground structures with pipes, drains and sewers. And yet . . . there is a germ of truth in the nickname. 'The Drain' has an atmosphere and smell all of its own.

Unlike other Underground lines, the Waterloo and City Line today belongs not to London Transport, but to British Rail; its trains, once American, differ considerably from the rest of the rolling stock. They are made up of two motor-cars and three trailers, and instead of

*The interior of a 'padded cell' on the City and South London Railway – windowless but lavishly unholstered. Railway staff called out the names of the stations as the trains drew in.*

using London Transport's four-rail system of transmitting current, the Drain's is transmitted by a third, outer rail. The trains can operate on normal, above-surface British Rail lines, and frequently do, when being tested or sent for repair to the depot at Lancing.

The tunnels are cut obliquely under the Thames, about twenty-three feet beneath its river bed. At the Waterloo end, there used to be a hydraulic lift, for raising and lowering the carriages. Capable of carrying loads of up to thirty tons, the lift was also used to heave the coal when the independent generating station, which supplied the line, was steam-operated.

The success of the new underground railways stimulated a second burst of new railway projects under London in the 1890s and 1900s. There were proposals for central lines running east-west, for a railway under Kensington Gardens, for one running diagonally across London from Waterloo to Baker Street, for another running under the Great Northern tracks from Moorgate to Finsbury Park, for a line linking Piccadilly and Brompton, and even a suggestion for a vast central interchange station at Mansion House to bring all the lines together. On 9 May 1891, all the schemes were considered by a joint committee of the two Houses of Parliament. There was, they decided, to be uniformity of gauge and tunnel (with a minimum diameter of eleven and a half feet); the companies were to be given the right to tunnel beneath properties without paying compensation, and in return they were to be required to provide cheap and frequent public services.

The next two decades saw the building of the Central Line (1900) – the first line dug by tunnelling machine – the West End branch of the Northern Line (1904), and the Bakerloo, Piccadilly-to-Brompton and Hampstead Line, now part of the Northern Line (1907).

The railway bonanza did not only bring railways to London. It also brought railway tycoons: none more extraordinary, ruthless and megalomaniacal than the American monopoly capitalist, Charles

*Railway lines and railway junctions multiplied in the last decade of the nineteenth century. Gauge and tunnels were standardised by Parliament.*

*Right:*
*The junction of the Metropolitan Line and the Great Northern Railway at King's Cross. The Great Northern Line rises up to a platform on York Way.*

*Opposite:*
*A cross-section of the works at the junction of Hampstead Road, Euston Road and Tottenham Court Road.*

150

GULLY       VENTILATOR       GAS & WATER PIPES

PNEUMATIC DISPATCH COYS TUBE

SEWER

METROPOLITAN      RAILWAY

DRAIN

PROPOSED     HAMPSTEAD     MIDLAND    NORTH WESTERN &

CHARING CROSS    JUNCTION       RAILWAY

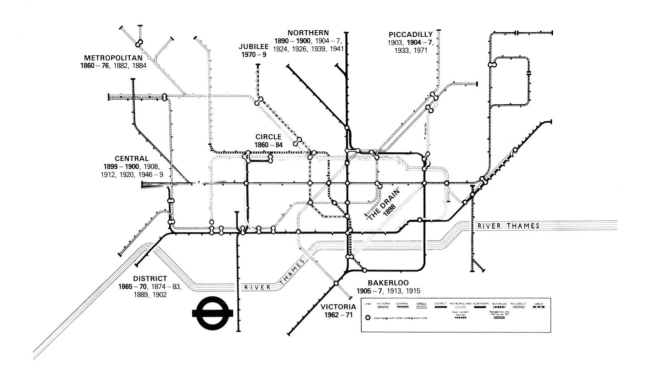

*London's Underground network. The principal dates of construction of each line are shown in bold.*

Tyson Yerkes. Born in 1837, son of a Quaker bank president, Yerkes started his own stockbroking company at the age of twenty-three, and was jailed for embezzlement at the age of twenty-four. After a year in prison, he moved into the streetcar business in Chicago. 'The secret of success in my business', he said, 'is to buy old junk, fix it up a little, and unload it upon other fellows.' He soon controlled all Chicago's streetcars, and within fifteen years was to draw forty million dollars' profit from the people of that city. He became one of its most powerful citizens, with the state government in his pocket. But when he overstepped himself, demanding perpetual monopolistic rights for his streetcar business, Chicago turned against him and he was forced to fly the city – to New York.

There he built a fantastic Italianate palace, furnished at a cost of one and a half million dollars. His picture collection was priceless, and he paid $80,000 for his bed, which had once belonged to the King of the Belgians. For the great Yerkes Observatory on Lake Geneva, Wisconsin, he ordered a telescope: 'Build the largest and the finest in the world. I'll pay the bill.'

In 1900 he arrived in London. The press kept abreast of his activities:

> The *Daily Express* is informed that the controlling interest in the Metropolitan and District Underground Railways has passed into the hands of Mr Charles T Yerkes, of Chicago. For a long time past, the *Express* has known that Mr Yerkes' agents were buying all the stock of the Underground that could be obtained; no block was too small, and none too

152

big for them to buy . . . Mr Yerkes will not discuss the matter. He will return to New York within two weeks, having already booked his passage.

The *Express* was wrong about the Metropolitan and District Railways – it was only the District that Yerkes had bought – but it was right about the scale of his ambition. Having built his own power station at Lots Road in Chelsea and electrified the District Line, his company later took over London's other lines: the Brompton and Piccadilly Line, and the Great Northern and Strand Lines (which he joined to form the Piccadilly Line), the Charing Cross-Euston-Hampstead Line and the City and South London Line (which he joined to form the Northern Line), the Central Line and the Bakerloo Line. Only the original Metropolitan Line remained independent of Yerkes. O S Nock wrote:

> His interest in railways, *as railways*, was absolutely nil. He neither knew nor cared about the day-to-day methods of operation, safety considerations, and such like, his sole and only concern was with the accounts.
>
> (*Underground Railways of the World*)

*Two of London's railway tycoons – Charles Tyson Yerkes (top), and Henry Stanley, later Lord Ashfield (above) – had strong American links. Both found their way to London – Yerkes to retrieve his reputation, Stanley to make his.*

Yerkes returned to America in 1905, dying at the Waldorf-Astoria Hotel that December. His empire passed to Albert Henry Stanley, the son of a Derbyshire coach painter. Stanley had emigrated to America; starting as a messenger boy, he ended up running the Detroit Street Railway Company at the age of twenty-eight. He fought in the US Navy in the Spanish-American War and returned to become general manager of the Street Railway Department of New Jersey. Coming to England, he became general manager of Yerkes' Underground Electric Railway Company and President of the Board of Trade in the 1914-18 War. In 1920, he was created Lord Ashfield. When a baby girl was born on a Bakerloo train, Ashfield was asked to be her godfather, and gave her a silver christening mug. She was named Thelma Ursula Beatrice Eleanor, so that her initials would remind her of her birthplace.

Although there were large-scale extensions to London's railways under Stanley's stewardship between the wars, most of them were overground, taking the network ever further into the suburbs. The three extensions underground were the Northern Line into north and south London, and the Central Line to Hainault in east London. The Central Line extension became a five-mile-long, underground, aircraft components factory during the war; but it was the Northern Line extension under Hampstead Heath that was the most interesting – and provoked the most opposition. One letter to *The Times* went so far as to claim that an Underground under the Heath would act as a drain: grass, gorse and trees would suffer from lack of moisture, while constant jarring of the environment as trains went by would loosen tree roots, presumably causing landslides down Hampstead High Street.

The tunnel for the extension, 200 feet below Hampstead Heath, was

*Above:*
*A perspective view of Piccadilly Circus station, which underwent a major, complicated and expensive reconstruction in 1923.*

*Opposite:*
*Escalators were installed at Earl's Court for Coronation Year, 1911.*

excavated and a new station – the Bull and Bush – built, with its entrance at North End, between Jack Straw's Castle and Manor House Hospital. But the strength of local opinion, somewhat more articulate in Hampstead than in the Rev William Denton's Cripplegate when the Metropolitan Line was being built, forced a compromise. The line was built to Golders Green, but the station under the Heath was abandoned. Thus the Northern Line, stretching north and south of London, became the longest continuous railway tunnel in the world, seventeen miles long, while the Bull and Bush – although it was later to have other uses – joined the long list of stations-that-might-have-been.

Henry Stanley, Lord Ashfield, continued to dominate London's Underground in the 1930s as he had in the 1920s, and when London Transport was brought under public control in 1933, Ashfield became chairman of the London Passenger Transport Board.

One major improvement between the wars was the reconstruction of Piccadilly Circus station. The first Piccadilly station had opened in 1906 to serve the combined Bakerloo and Piccadilly Lines. By the 1920s, it had become hopelessly out of date and overcrowded. Its reconstruction was authorised in 1923. One consideration overshadowed all others: there was no room for a new station of any size except beneath the Circus itself. The buildings surrounding it had deep and massive basements. Locating the underground services was the first task. There were neither maps nor records of what was there. Trenches were dug across six of the roads coming into the Circus, and the results revealed a maze of telegraph cables, telephone lines, Post Office pneumatic tubes, water pipes, hydraulic mains and sewers. Cables belonging to three different electricity companies were unearthed. The services were diverted into a twelve-foot tunnel. Eros was moved for the duration, and a full-scale mock-up of the booking hall was constructed in the Earl's Court Exhibition Hall.

At that time, escalators were comparatively new in the Underground system. Lifts to the platforms were considered first, but during building the decision was made to switch to escalators. The oval booking hall was eventually excavated to its full size under the Circus, its roof supported by steel uprights and joists, so that traffic could continue to run above it. Opened in 1928, it was regarded as a triumph of cooperation between engineer, designer, and bureaucrats.

Piccadilly was not the only station to acquire escalators during the inter-war years. The original Metropolitan and District Lines were still served by stairs, but the deeper the tube, the more impracticable this became.

At first, steam lifts were used, but they were banned by the government after a series of disasters. Hydraulic ones worked by water pressure took their place. Then, in the 1890s, electric lifts were developed, supported by four ropes, which would automatically stop if

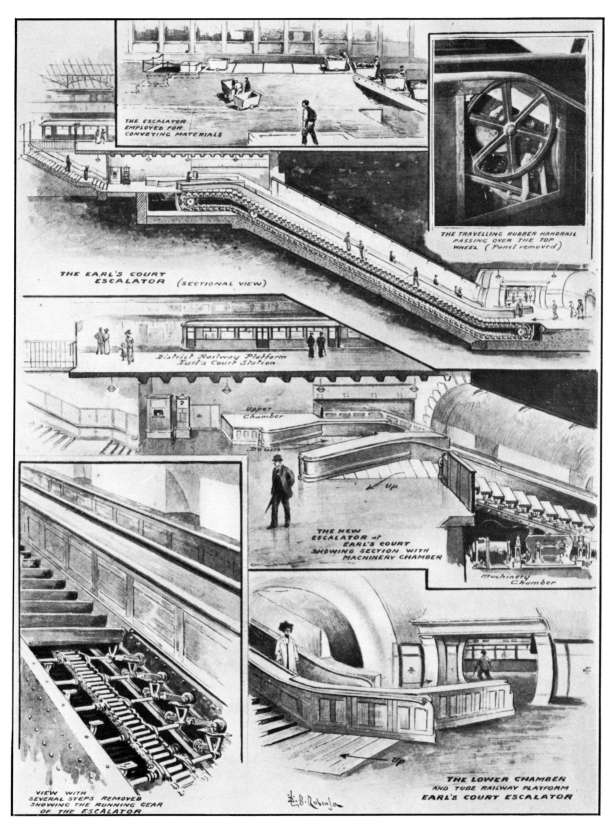

THE ESCALATOR EMPLOYED FOR CONVEYING MATERIALS

THE TRAVELLING RUBBER HANDRAIL PASSING OVER THE TOP WHEEL ( Panel removed )

THE EARL'S COURT ESCALATOR (SECTIONAL VIEW)

District Railway Platform Earl's Court Station

Upper Chamber

Down

Up

THE NEW ESCALATOR at EARL'S COURT SHOWING SECTION WITH MACHINERY CHAMBER

Machinery Chamber

VIEW WITH SEVERAL STEPS REMOVED SHOWING THE RUNNING GEAR OF THE ESCALATOR

Up

THE LOWER CHAMBER AND TUBE RAILWAY PLATFORM EARL'S COURT ESCALATOR

E. B. Rubinja

one broke. Doors were concealed inside each lift, and behind advertising posters, and the lifts were always built in pairs, so that if one broke down, the other could stop at the same level and take passengers off. The same system operates today.

Escalators offer continuous service, and carry more passengers per hour than lifts. They can even vary their speed, increasing it in response to the number of passengers using the escalator. The first one was a novelty for Coronation Year, installed at Earl's Court in 1911 to link the District and Piccadilly Lines. To allay passengers' fears, 'Bumper' Harris, a one-legged gentleman, was hired to travel up and down the escalator throughout the opening day.

The 1920s and 1930s saw a renaissance in Underground railway poster art. The first posters had been stuck on the wooden hoardings of the Metropolitan when it was being built in 1861. W Gunn Gwennet, a railway advertising illustrator, making a plea for artistic standards to be maintained, wrote:

> So thickly placarded are the stations on the Underground railway that it is not uncommon to hear two countrymen arguing whether they have arrived at Vinolia or Willing. It is thought that the guards on the Central London Railway shouted out: 'Next station Pears Soap, Beecham's Pills, Marblarch, Bovril . . .' Let some railway company more enterprising than its contemporaries resolve that its advertisements shall be more or less artistic, and other companies will eventually follow, though it is to be feared very slowly. The pioneer company will reap the greatest reward.

The man who put Gunn Gwennet's ideas into practice was Frank Pick, who rose from publicity director to become vice-chairman of the London Passenger Transport Board. A shy man, but not frightened of controversy, he became one of London's most influential patrons of contemporary artists in the inter-war years. He commissioned Epstein's 'Night' outside St James' Park Station (it was tarred and feathered), and was responsible for a whole range of posters: McKnight Kauffer's 'Winter Sales', Clive Gardiner's 'Windsor Castle', Laura Knight's 'Richmond Park' and Fred Taylor's 'Hampstead Fair'.

In 1916, Pick commissioned Edward Johnston to design an alphabet for all London Transport's stations. Still in use today, it is a model of typographical clarity and simplicity. Johnston's alphabet, which heralded the return of *sans serif* lettering, prompted Eric Gill to write:

> It is interesting to reflect that a development of such importance in the field of printing should owe its origin to an undertaking concerned primarily with transport; a convincing demonstration that design is indivisible.

Pick was also responsible for London Transport's information posters, including John Hassall's famous 'No need to ask a p'liceman'. When the London Underground came under public ownership, he commissioned four special posters, to be displayed in underground stations at fortnightly intervals. The first explained the

reasons for the take-over and the aims of the new board, the second showed London's Transport's territory under the new board, the third gave information about London Transport's services, and the fourth about the staff.

The last words on Underground poster art, however, should be Pick's own: 'A high standard of design in all things is essential to lasting prestige and therefore to the smooth running of a great public service.'

*Opposite:*
*Underground art flourished during the inter-war period, thanks largely to Frank Pick, who not only commissioned posters from well-known artists, and an alphabet from Edward Johnston, but also designed some of the moquettes used for the upholstery.*

The end of the Second World War gave the first chance for an overall plan of underground London. Sir Patrick Abercrombie's Greater London Plan of 1944 advocated the burial of mainline trains under London, as well as an extension of the Underground system. One plan was to link the deep-level bomb shelters under the Northern Line into a high-speed, deep-level tube. Another was to build large tunnels, seventeen feet in diameter, running diagonally under London for British Rail trains: one crossing north-east to south-west, roughly along the alignment of the future Victoria Line, the other north-west to south-east, roughly along the alignment of the partially-completed Jubilee Line.

In 1946, the Railway Committee proposed a new Underground line, 'Route 8', with tunnels large enough for British Rail rolling stock, from Finsbury Park, via King's Cross, Euston, Victoria and Brixton, to Croydon. Two years later the proposed route was slightly amended and rechristened 'Route C'. The new line was to link three major British Rail stations in London, benefiting not only passengers who used it, but also those who didn't, since 'Route C' would take the strain off the other lines. The capital itself was suffering from the growth in motor-car ownership and use. 'It is in no one's interest to allow personal transport to paralyse our urban amenities,' said Sir John Elliot, London Transport's chairman, in 1955. 'This will surely happen unless adequate steps are taken in the greatest interest of all.'

Powers for the new line were granted in 1955, and in December 1956 *Political and Economic Planning* claimed in a pamphlet that underground railways were better value than overground motorways: urban motorways cost £11m per mile, while underground railways cost only £4m per mile. Elliot continued to campaign for the new line. 'It became clearer that freedom of movement in the streets was (and is) in jeopardy,' he wrote in 1958. 'It also became clearer that more

157

people are travelling on the Underground, and this is further reason for starting to build the Victoria Line without delay.'

The project was given, once again, to Sir William Halcrow and Partners. It was to be one of the biggest engineering projects ever undertaken under London, with twelve stations and a line ten and a half miles long. It would start at Victoria, seventy feet down in clay, break through the upper clay and cross the Tyburn under Buckingham Palace, pass below six other major government buildings, return to the clay stratum between Oxford Circus and Warren Street, then dive below it at Euston and King's Cross. This last section, much of it in gravel, would be one of the most difficult. The line had to cross under the Fleet sewer and make its way through the spaghetti of Metropolitan, Northern and Piccadilly Lines as well as the Post Office's own underground railway. Even beyond King's Cross it would not be easy. The line would then encounter the high-level sewer between Highbury and Finsbury Park.

After digging an experimental tunnel between Finsbury Park and Tottenham Hale, 'a suitable area where there was little valuable property above', work began in 1963, simultaneously, at two-mile intervals. Accuracy was vital: in over 23,000 feet there could be no more than one inch of deviation in any direction.

*Before Oxford Circus station could be dug as part of the new Victoria Line in the 1950s, a steel umbrella had to be built over the concourse to maintain the free flow of traffic.*

The spectacle that attracted the most attention, however, was the steel umbrella covering the whole of Oxford Circus, over which cars and buses could drive via the steel ramps. Under the umbrella, a vast new concourse was built for London's biggest underground interchange system.

Before serious construction could begin, the engineers faced the usual problem of finding the underground mains of the public service. As with Piccadilly Circus, the mains were disclosed by trenches dug at night across the approach roads, when there was little traffic. All the familiar brands were discovered — a veritable 'snarl of services' — which now included television cables. A sewer was diverted and the other services were re-routed around the concourse.

The construction was an immense and complex task, involving the temporary destruction of the garden of Cavendish Square, the nearest practical location for the working site. To add to the engineers' difficulties at Oxford Circus, the new tunnels had to pass under the deep foundations of Peter Robinson. There was little room between them and the tunnel roof. The load had to be spread and to do this the store was underpinned with concrete blocks. The operation was carried out from a pilot tunnel 250 yards long, which passed under the Bakerloo Line.

There were some phenomenal engineering achievements. Water-bearing gravel was frozen by driving tubes into the ground and circulating liquid nitrogen at a temperature of -196°C, or 352°F below freezing. At King's Cross, the various lines had to be propped up on concrete stilts. There were some surprises, too. Six fossil nautiloids, fifty million years old, were discovered near Victoria, and a plague pit was uncovered near Green Park when a drum-digger began to churn up ground bones.

As every foot of tunnel was bored by the great rotating teeth of the hydraulically operated drum-diggers, the segments – made either of pre-cast concrete or cast-iron – were fixed, lining and supporting the tunnel. Behind the drum-diggers, the excavated refuse from the two rotating drums was disgorged by scoops and paddles onto a conveyor belt, which carried it back to spoil trucks on tracks; from there it was taken to shafts, where the trucks were hauled up by crane and their refuse unloaded into skips and trucks to fill in the disused gravel pits west of London. As the six tunnels under the city joined together, the two-foot-gauge tracks for spoil were taken out and the permanent track-layers moved in. Accuracy had to be as precise in the track-laying as in the tunnel-aligning – deviation of one-sixteenth of an inch only was allowed.

The Victoria Line was opened by the Queen on 7 March 1969. In six years, 2500 miners had excavated one million tons of earth, building London's most efficient and up-to-date Underground at a cost of £70m. The ten and a half miles of line are fitted with a closed-

*'A plague pit was uncovered near Green Park when a drum digger began to churn up ground bones.'*

circuit television network with seventy-four cameras and forty-two monitor sets. The trains, although they contain drivers, run automatically from signals transmitted along the pick-up rails. The issue of tickets is electronic.

Before work was finished on the Victoria Line, plans for its extension to Brixton were already under consideration. At last south London, virtually ignored by the Underground, was to get a decent line. By that time, the specialist equipment, contractors and – above all – the tunnellers, had been welded into an élite corps. If the government delayed its authorisation, Halcrow's team, who had first come together to excavate the raw water main, and had matured and expanded with the Victoria Line, would be dispersed; it would take years to build up such a workforce again. In the event it was a fairly close-run thing. Finally, in August 1967, Britain's first woman Minister of Transport, Barbara Castle, gave her consent. The extension was due to be completed by 1972. In fact, the three and a half miles were opened by Princess Alexandra in July 1971.

There was nothing as spectacular in building the Brixton extension as the creation of the Oxford Circus umbrella, or the massive new underground stations at King's Cross and Euston. But the ground through which the tunnels were driven was less firm than in the northern section, varying from gravel to blue clay. New stations were built at Pimlico, Vauxhall and Brixton, and a twin tunnel was bored twenty-five feet under the bed of the Thames, just above Vauxhall Bridge.

One of the underground railways suggested after the war had been a diagonal line running north-west to south-east, to be named the

Fleet. It would take over the Bakerloo tracks from Stanmore to Baker Street, then run in new twin tunnels via Bond Street, Green Park and Charing Cross, relieving the overcrowded central London section, then continue under Fleet Street and the City, and cross under the Thames to Lewisham. With the Piccadilly extension to Heathrow (which lies outside the frontier of this book), and the impoverishment of the inner cities, the cost was deemed prohibitive. A compromise was made. The Stanmore branch of the Bakerloo Line was taken over, three miles of new twin tunnels were built to Charing Cross, and the line was renamed 'Jubilee'. It was opened by the Prince of Wales in 1979.*

Work began in 1970: twelve-and-a-half-feet twin tunnels, which yielded 390,000 cubic metres of earth and were supported by 23,000 cast-iron and concrete rings. Trafalgar Square and the Strand were replaced by a new underground complex at Charing Cross, linking British Rail and the Underground, with subways to Covent Garden and Trafalgar Square. The old Bakerloo platform, which had cable links with the Whitehall tunnel system, was modernised, and the new line was aligned so as to have a crossover tunnel, thirty-one feet in diameter, directly under Admiralty Arch and the Duke of York Steps, with emergency access and cable ducts to Whitehall.

*The tunnels of the Jubilee actually extend from Charing Cross to Aldwych, but the last section is unused. In 1993 the go-ahead was given to extend the line to Stratford via Canary Wharf (see p. 223.)

*The Victoria Line was extended to Brixton. Vauxhall was one of the new stations along the route.*

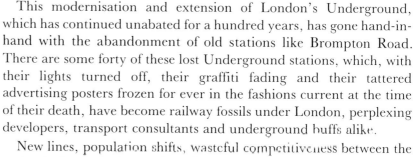

This modernisation and extension of London's Underground, which has continued unabated for a hundred years, has gone hand-in-hand with the abandonment of old stations like Brompton Road. There are some forty of these lost Underground stations, which, with their lights turned off, their graffiti fading and their tattered advertising posters frozen for ever in the fashions current at the time of their death, have become railway fossils under London, perplexing developers, transport consultants and underground buffs alike.

New lines, population shifts, wasteful competitiveness between the early rival companies, and straightforward bad planning, have left these subterranean monuments beneath us. Some of these will-o'-the-wisp stations had but a few years of active service. The Tower of London station on the Metropolitan Line was open for less than two years, from 1882 to 1884, when it was replaced by the rival District station. Hounslow Town station on the District Line lasted only from 1883 to 1886. It was revived again in 1903, only to be shut down six years later because of lack of use. Nine stations have been replaced by others close by – some losing their names, others retaining them: Hounslow Town, White City, Park Royal, Osterley and Spring Grove, Aldgate East, Chancery Lane, British Museum, Uxbridge Road and Wood Lane. Other stations have completely disappeared: St Mary's, City Road, South Kentish Town, York Road and King William Street with only facades remaining.

The Metropolitan Line northwards from Baker Street contains some fascinating old memories. There were stations at Lord's, Marlborough Road and Swiss Cottage. The Marlborough Road station was closed in 1939, after serving Londoners for seventy years, and has been converted into a Chinese restaurant. The old Swiss Cottage station disappeared to make way for the present station in 1940. The entrance used to be through an arcade, later converted into a shopping centre. Beyond Swiss Cottage are the abandoned stations of the Metropolitan's 'Brill' branch (once a private tramway, opened in 1871 and closed in 1935): Waddesdon Road, Woodsiding, Westcott and Wotton.

Meanwhile London Transport continues to carry its 541 million passengers each year, about one and three quarter million a day, over some 770 miles of track, served by an underground staff of 23,876, of which nearly 5000 guard and drive the trains. London's Underground network has a more extensive mileage than any other in the world. But the numbers using it are relatively small. The New York Subway carries 1296 million people a year, over double London's figure. The Paris Métro, which is smaller than London's, carries 1600 million, thrice London's figure. Moscow, with only 87 miles of track, handles few less than Paris – 1501 million; while Tokyo, whose 58 miles carry 190 million, employs a special staff to collect baskets of abandoned shoes and torn jacket sleeves at the end of each day.

*British Museum platform, one of the ghost stations created by 'new lines, population shifts, wasteful competitiveness . . . and straightforward bad planning'.*

The introduction of cheaper fares, travel concessions and modernisation, have increased numbers. Because the Paris Metro received three times as much investment as London's Underground in the 1970s, it is now the healthiest urban underground train service in the world. London's Underground need not die, and the long list of abandoned underground stations need not be extended. It was the first of its kind: an unlikely monument to Charles Pearson, yet somehow fitting for the man who first thought up the 'train in the drain'.

*The echoing tunnel of London's newest underground railway line – the Jubilee – at the Strand.*

# 7 The Nerves of the City

If the nineteenth century was the Age of Engineering, epitomised by Greathead's tunnels and Bazalgette's sewers, then the twentieth century is the Age of Technology, epitomised by the cable tunnels of the London Electricity Board and British Telecom.

This, the nervous system of London, started life in the mid-nineteenth century, above ground. But overhead clutter, storm damage and a train of accidents drove it underground about the turn of the century. It has been going deeper ever since.

At first, the wires and cables were carried in ducts about three or four feet below pavement level. The ducts were made of earthenware and were rectangular, linked with spigots and sockets to concrete manholes, or 'jointing chambers', every hundred yards or so.

But with so many manholes so easily accessible, governments considered cables in ducts 'insecure'. Continuous traffic overhead caused ripples in the ground below, stretching and breaking the cables. The ducts also interfered with construction schemes. The cost of diverting cables for, say, a new road interchange could be as high as sixty per cent of the cost of the total scheme. So, the cables went deeper underground.

Some were moved into the London Electricity Board's own small tunnels, others into British Telecom's deep-level tunnels. Some shared space in the Underground with London Transport cables. No matter how deep they went, they always had to come up again at the end of their run: up through the shafts and via shallow cable ducts to the distribution box and into the home.

## ELECTRICITY

Virtually every room in every building in London is girt about with wires and cables, hidden above ceilings, in walls, under floors, behind skirtings; marked only by protruding sockets and fixtures. For twentieth-century man electricity has become essential. Without it there would be no television, no record player, no fan, no electric light, no electric fire, no reading lamp. The tens of thousands of miles of cable coursing their way through London link us, like an umbilical cord, to our technology. Cut the cord, cut off the energy that runs through that cord, and something of our civilisation dies.

The miles of cable are fed ultimately by the National Grid, which comes into London at a dozen different points. Its cables run either in existing tunnels, or in ducts, or in conduits, or in their own, very small tunnels, which are excavated and then filled in afterwards. Electricity in Britain is conducted as alternating current (ac) and not direct current (dc). High voltages generate immense heat, known as super-conductivity and caused by the resistance set up within the cable by the

*Opposite:*
*A circuit-breaker at New Cross sub-station.*

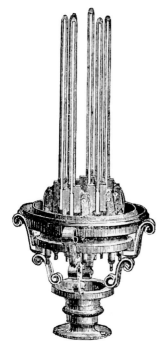

*Top:*
*Volta's battery – 'La Couronne de Tasses' – of about 1800 was the first device for creating an electric current. Cups were linked in a circle by alternate zinc and copper plates. The last copper and first zinc plate were then connected by an exterior wire.*

*Above:*
*The Jablochkoff candle of 1876 – the electric current passed through parallel carbon rods embedded in a coat of china clay. Jablochkoff himself, a Russian émigré, never made capital out of his invention: he disappeared without a trace a few years later.*

alternation of the current – particularly if the cables are laid underground. The cables have to be insulated heavily, some with gas-filled insulation, others through direct contact with earth or gravel. One of London's most ingenious runs of cable is along the Grand Union Canal, where the National Grid cables run under the tow-path and are cooled by the waters of the Canal.

Cables feed the electricity from the National Grid to sub-stations, where it is transformed to a lower voltage and transmitted by the London Electricity Board through 17,000 miles of low-voltage cable into the home. They are laid with the same variety of methods as their grander counterparts, the National Grid cables: in trenches, ducts, tunnels and conduits (depending on subterranean ecology, modern technology and the surface above).

The first recorded use of electricity was in April 1746, when the Abbé Nollet wired up a number of Carthusian monks in a 5400-foot circle. The contortions on the faces of the monks, all of whom had taken their Vow of Obedience, were judged sufficient proof that power could be transmitted.

The problem over the next hundred years was not how to transmit electricity down a wire, but how much electricity could be transmitted down a wire, and what to do with it once it had been transmitted. Progress was slow, but certain. In 1800, Alexandre Volta invented the battery. In 1831 Michael Faraday discovered electro-magnetic induction, which made generation a practical possibility. By 1858, Watson had built an electric lighting apparatus to illuminate London Bridge. Twenty years later, the old Gaiety Theatre in the Strand was lit by an 'electric light arc lamp', the West India Docks by 'electric candles' – designed by Paul Jablochkoff of the Russian Engineering Service – and Bazalgette's Embankment by a twenty-light electric generator, commissioned from a French firm by the Metropolitan Board of Works, who were to supply the coal.

The Embankment generator was successful, and a steam generator that worked under Holborn Viaduct extended electric lighting to Mansion House, the British Museum, and Waterloo and Blackfriars Bridges. But the company who supplied the generator could not ensure a steady supply. By 1884 the Board of Works was back to gas.

This was the moment the complacent Gas Light and Coke Company had been anticipating. They had published a report as early as 1878, which had 'evaluated' electricity's 'comparative adaptability with gas for general illuminating purposes'. Not surprisingly, they had found it wanting:

> We are satisfied that the electric light can never be applied without the production of an offensive smell which undoubtedly causes headaches and in its naked state it can never be used in rooms of even large size without danger to sight.

The danger of electrocution and the likelihood of electrolysis

*Left:*
*Jablochkoff candles were used to illuminate the Victoria Embankment in 1878, but the Jablochkoff Electric Lighting and Power Company lost its contract with the Metropolitan Board of Works six years later, due to the cost of the arc light – four times as expensive as gas. The Gas Light and Coke Company had real, if short-lived, reason for its early complacency.*

*Below:*
*The Holborn generator, which powered the lighting of the Holborn Viaduct in 1878, was modest in scale, driven by traction engines. The experiment lasted less than a year – the cost was again deemed prohibitive.*

underground were freely broadcast in the company's campaign to vilify the new source of light, which threatened to outshine their own. But despite their denigratory utterances, the popularity of electricity grew. At the Savoy Theatre and Crystal Palace, exhibitions extolled the spirit of electricity. New companies sprang up to take advantage of its progress. A house-to-house electric supply company registered and soon began to make its mark. Before long, an electric light generator, powered by steam and built by Sir John Fowler, of 'Fowler's Ghost' fame, was throbbing away underneath the arches of Cannon Street Station.

From its earliest infancy, a measure of public control was imposed on the new industry. The very public nature of the innovation made that necessary, and the monopolistic arrogance and corporate strength of the gas companies had taught the government a lesson. As George Orwell remarked, a millionaire cannot light up the street for himself and keep everyone else in darkness.

In 1882, Parliament enacted the Electric Lighting Bill, which curbed the power of the undertakings by giving vestries and local authorities power to purchase any private electricity supply undertaking in their district after twenty-one years. The problem was that checking their power by threat of sale weakened their ability to raise long-term capital, so the law was subsequently amended to give the companies forty-two years' grace before they could be taken over.

A year later, Sir Coutts Lindsay, at the prompting of a twenty-one-year-old prodigy called Sebastian Ziani de Ferranti, installed an electric generator in the basement of his Grosvenor Art Gallery in New Bond Street (now the BBC's Aeolian Hall), the basement of which still bears the marks of the generator. Encouraged by its efficacy,

*Above:*
*Sebastian Ziani de Ferranti (1864 – 1930). At 17 he was working in Woolwich for Sir William Siemens, experimenting with an electric furnace for making steel. 'There I really got what I wanted. I was surrounded by dynamos and everything electrical. I felt entirely happy.'*

*Right:*
*The generator installed by Ferranti in the basement of the Grosvenor Gallery for Sir Coutts Lindsay, founder of the London Electricity Supply Corporation.*

Lindsay extended his plant, wired up his neighbours, and in 1887 formed the London Electricity Supply Corporation.

Ferranti, Lindsay's amanuensis in all things, was Liverpudlian by birth, English, American, Dutch and Venetian by descent. He had sold his first generator for £5 while still at evening classes at University College, London. Lindsay's protégé was a prophet of electricity. He was to design the first paper-insulated electricity mains and to originate the idea of a National Grid.

'Whenever coal, gas or power are now used,' he said, 'everything for which they are used will be better done when electricity is the medium of application.'

Ferranti understood electricity and he understood the economics of electricity. Ten small generators powering ten buildings are no substitute for one large generator powering a hundred buildings. Big has never been beautiful in the electricity business, but it has always been bountiful.

Ferranti proposed a giant power station at Deptford, where Peter the Great had been a carpenter in the Royal Dockyard, and where John Evelyn had lived. It was to be the largest in the world, with enough power to light two million lamps. Like the gas men before him, he sited his power station alongside the River, so that the Thames could feed it with raw water and coal barges. Ferranti's idea was for ten-thousand-horsepower generators producing ten kilowatts. The engineering Establishment, Edison included, was aghast. Then a fire at the Grosvenor generator cast doubt on his abilities. Ten-thousand-horsepower generators were never installed; instead, Lindsay played safe with three-thousand-horsepower generators. Ferranti, who felt his competence was now in question, resigned in 1891 at the age of

*Top:*
*The exterior.*

*Above:*
*Ferranti's alternators.*

*Left:*
*The interior –*
*3000-horsepower generators*
*were to replace Ferranti's*
*10,000-horsepower after a fire*
*at the Grosvenor Gallery.*

twenty-six. Later his prophecies were to come true. The giant generators he envisaged were built, and Deptford became the precursor.

At first, Lindsay's London Electricity Supply Company – which by 1890 was to extend from Regent's Park to the River, and from Knightsbridge to the Law Courts – distributed supplies overhead. Gradually, distribution moved underground, as the clutter above ground proved unacceptable.

> Eventually the success of larger-scale electrification came to depend on the development of insulation techniques for high-voltage cables and cheaper ways of laying such cables in the streets, for in the densely-populated urban areas of Britain aesthetic and social considerations generally militate against the use of unsightly overhead wires. Fortunately the British cable manufacturers, who had already built up an unrivalled reputation in the telegraphic field, were able to respond, and wider distribution schemes became possible with rapid improvement in design and reductions in cost. (Leslie Hannah: *Electricity before Nationalisation*)

But as electricity moved underground, tensions surfaced, and feuds began between the undertakings, who regarded subterranean London as their fiefdom. The Post Office, the telegraph companies, the gas companies and the Metropolitan Board of Works all vied with each other. Private electricity companies sprang up in the richer residential districts of west London, while local councils established their generating plant in the poorer districts of east London.

London was rapidly turning into a patchwork of public and private, municipal and miscellaneous. The London County Council and radicals favoured public ownership. Government and traditionalists were loath to intervene. A Cabinet Committee investigating the electricity industry in 1917 bravely argued for public ownership, more out of logic than political conviction. 'To have as a permanent arrangement a large number of undertakings each operating its own system in a small area is as impractical as to have the railways of this country divided as between local authorities.'

Politically, Britain was not yet ready for nationalisation. The Labour government compromised in 1919 with a bill creating 'Joint Electricity Authorities'. According to Herbert Morrison, a member, they were 'all joint' and 'no authority'. The political climate meant that the bill changed little and London remained divided. In the decades that followed, the private companies, on the defensive against the advocates of public ownership, came together to build Battersea Power Station in west London in 1931. It was, quite literally, a cathedral of power, with aisles, chancels and naves, pristine halls faced in marble, wrought-iron stair rails, art deco control rooms and parquet flooring so perfect that the staff were obliged to wear carpet slippers. The municipalities reacted by joining together and building their own giant rival at Barking. By 1925 Philip Cunliffe-Lister was

*Giles Gilbert Scott's self-confident 'cathedral of power' at Battersea was built in 1931 by the private electricity companies in an attempt to ward off nationalisation.*

able to record that 'electricity is so inefficient today in this country that it has always been amazing to me that the Labour Government did not attempt to nationalise it.'

A year later Baldwin, in the hope of averting nationalisation, promoted the Electricity Supply Bill. Enacted, it set up a National Grid controlled by the government-appointed Central Electricity Board, which was to be able to transmit electricity from one area to

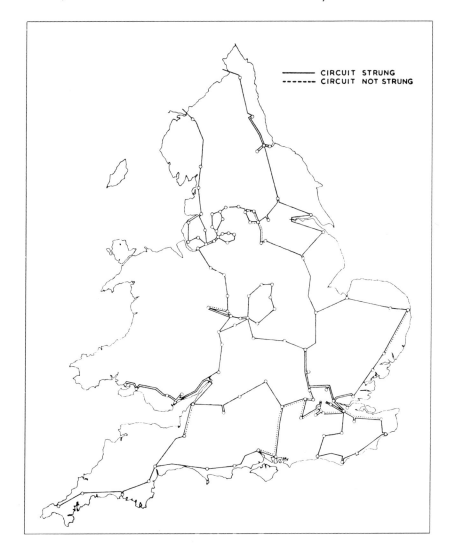

*With the building of the National Grid (1926-1933), the industry was nationalised in all but name. This map shows the state of electrification three years before completion.*

another, wherever it was most needed. Ineffective power stations would be closed down and larger and more economic ones would generate for the whole grid. Private companies and local municipalities would then buy electricity from the grid at a fixed rate.

The building of the National Grid started in 1926 and was effectively completed by 1934. Most of the cable went overhead on pylons ('monumental gateways of an Egyptian temple', according to

171

the Oxford English Dictionary), but in the Lake District, New Forest, parts of Sussex and London, it dropped underground. Apart from the Lea Valley, London has been spared 'those pillars/Bare like nude girls, giant girls that have no secrets', as Stephen Spender saw them.

Things would have been different if Herbert Morrison, the Minister of Transport, had had his way. 'They have a sense of majesty of their own and the cables stretching between them over the countryside gives one a sense of power, in the service of the people, marching over many miles of country.'

Between the wars, increasing demand for electricity made the National Grid, with its regional boards, effectively the controlling body. More and more houses were being given electricity at a rapidly declining cost – the cost of connection fell from £15 in 1919 to £5 in 1929. Hackney, where Morrison was the local electricity committee chairman, could boast of every house having been wired by 1926.

*Ploughshares into pylons – 'power, in the service of the people, marching over many miles of country', or 'giant girls that have no secrets'? A drawing in the* General Electric Review *at the time the National Grid was built.*

During the 1930s, the electricity industry expanded further with the popularisation of electric fires and labour-saving gadgets. A publicity film made for the industry – *Edward and Edna* – saved a romance and made a marriage, even though the couple could not afford a domestic servant, because Edna volunteered to do all the housework herself electrically.

The war consolidated the Central Electricity Board's control over the industry. A National Grid Control Centre was set up at Newgate Street off St Paul's, and an underground control centre built in the disused lift shaft of the old Post Office Underground Station. Though the control centre was bombed and the shaft flooded in 1940, the subterranean headquarters were completed two months later, linked to the grid by a three-quarter-mile cable run through the Central Line tunnel and a disused section of the Post Office Station. (Since the mid-1930s, London Transport has let space in its tunnels for both

*The National Grid Control Centre was set up during the war near St Paul's.*

Central Electricity Board and London Electricity Board cables. The first agreement London Transport made was with Bermondsey Council in 1933.)

After the war, the act of nationalisation hardly changed the industry. To all intents and purposes, it had been operating as a national industry for twenty years, ever since the building of the National Grid.

The London Electricity Board inherited three tunnels across the Thames from its power stations at Battersea, Deptford and Barking. an extension of the Deptford Tunnel under Westferry Road and Millwall Docks, a couple of tunnels under the Surrey Canal and another under the Old Kent Road.

By the standards of other utilities, they are small tunnels, built to overcome a particular obstacle. The London Electricity Board has no extensive system of tunnels under London, nor is it likely to have one in the future.

The power stations of London – those vast 'cathedrals of power' that once dominated the River – have now all been closed down. Ferranti's fantasy at Deptford, Giles Gilbert Scott's strikingly self-confident and assertive monument at Battersea and its municipal twin at Barking lie 'thrown dead' by the side of the Thames.

Visit them today, and you have to view them as industrial archaeology – technological dinosaurs seemingly beached up in an alluvial basin. Most of Barking Power Station has already been demolished – all that remains is one giant building with two tall chimneys and a litter of smaller buildings, decaying amid the wasteland. Yet when Barking was opened in June 1925, it was the biggest power station in Europe. Close by the River, in one of the few buildings left standing, is the shaft-house leading to the half-mile cable tunnel under the River to Woolwich Arsenal.

You can still see the lines of the old cables dropping down into the shaft, over eighty feet deep. The steps down the shaft are old and rusty, and inside the tunnel itself, seven feet in diameter, are white stalactites hanging down between the rust-covered, cast-iron segments of tunnel lining. Even the cables are rusty.

'I've been looking after this tunnel for twenty-six years,' says Bill, the Barking tunnel's 'corker'. (Corkers are so named from their original job of inserting cork between leaking tunnel-lining segments.) Each London Electricity Board tunnel has its own corker, who over the years has learnt the characteristics of his tunnel. Since the Barking tunnel was completed in 1926, it has had only five corkers.

'Over there at the other end of the tunnel,' says Bill, 'you used to have Woolwich Arsenal, with a dirty great moat. The tunnel shaft came up in their grounds, so they put barbed wire all around the shaft house. If you wanted to get out, some copper had to come with a key and open it up for you. Then you had the Beckton Gas Works on the other side of the Barking Creek, and all the Docks. It was a great place once upon a time.

'Oh, there was a lot going on once. You used to be working down here, and you could hear the ships' propellers churning round above you. And there'd be a dredger coming over twice a week. If you hadn't heard that before, you'd find it real scary. A few fellers did.'

The brackets on the tunnel walls are almost empty. A few tattered cables serving Thamesmead are all that remain — perhaps a dozen in all. Yet in its heyday the tunnel carried thirty-nine cables, and had its own two-foot-gauge railway to haul them; you can still see traces of it in the concrete floor. There are other marks on the tunnel: the scars of a night of vandalism by kids in 1979. Like Brunel's, Barking tunnel has seen better days.

Bill the Corker guards his tunnel, a latter-day Charon. Above him the derelict wasteland stretches along both banks of the Thames.

## THE POST OFFICE AND BRITISH TELECOM

Each time you lift your receiver and make a call, your voice makes a complex subterranean journey. It travels first into a cable duct about three feet beneath the pavement. From there, it journeys through oblong inspection chambers, visible as manholes, which occur every few hundred yards, to a sub-exchange – the little green boxes on the corner of many streets. Your telephone conversation will take place on two wires (one for each participant), contained in lead-covered cable, which may house as few as seven pairs of wires or as many as 2000. A cable only 2.7 inches in diameter can contain 542 pairs. If your call is local, very local, it may continue through pairs of wires in cable ducts just underneath the pavement and never drop any further underground. If you are calling a longer distance, it may be transferred to a 'quad' – four wires which transmit your conversation on 'carrier' frequency radio, each 'quad' carrying some twenty conversations at once. Or it may be transferred to coaxial cables – half-inch tubes, with copper wires down the centre, which carry up to 1000 calls through high-frequency radio waves. Some cables under London carry combinations of all three. Trunk calls can even be carried through optical fibres, with the conversation transmuted into waves of light. Water in the cables is one of British Telecom's biggest headaches, and lead cables are now being replaced by plastic ones, with pressurised areas inside them to keep out the water.

The cables run through ducts and then, once they get beyond the local exchange, drop down shafts, often a hundred feet deep, into one of the many networks of tunnels beneath London. For a call from Paddington to the City, for example, it might drop into British Telecom's own cable tunnels, or along the Post Office's old pneumatic tube system. Or it might run along the sides of London Transport's underground tunnels, changing from Circle to Central Line on the way. Sometimes a telephone call will pass through all of them, running through a labyrinth of cables beneath us, avoiding overloaded cable routes. Then, from the depths of London, the cable will emerge through a shaft to duct level, passing through sub-exchanges, manholes, telephone poles and overhead wires until it reaches the person called.

The Post Office and its coaxial child, British Telecom, are, after the Government, the most powerful organisations under London. Between them they have the most capital-intensive 'real estate' under the city and have probably spent more money under our streets than all the other subterranean organisations put together. Their underground domain includes a vast subterranean telephone exchange under Holborn, a six-and-a-half-mile underground railway, more than twelve miles of cable tunnels a hundred feet underground and thousands of miles of cable duct beneath the pavements.

The origins of this telecommunications network goes back to before 1868 – when the Post Office first obtained its monopoly in this country to supply telecommunications equipment – to 1763 (seven years after Abbé Nollet's experiments with his unfortunate Carthusian monks), when Charles Marshall, 'a clever man who could make lightning speak and write upon a wall', despatched the world's first telecommunication using twenty-six separate wires, one for each letter of the alphabet.

In the summer of 1816, half a century later, Francis Ronalds, a twenty-eight-year-old inventor, built the first underground electric telecommunications cable in his garden at Upper Mall by the Thames at Hammersmith. He threaded a wire 525 feet long through glass tubes and laid it in a four-foot trench, lined with tar – a method of insulation little different in principle from the one used today – and succeeded in transmitting electricity along the wire. When the Admiralty rejected his invention two months later, he turned to meteorology, all but abandoning electricity until 1870, a year before his death, when he was given a belated knighthood.

Ronalds' co-worker, William Fothergill Cooke, stayed with electricity, going to Prussia (where in 1832 electricity was already being used to explode mines) to study the new phenomenon. Returning to England in 1836, he approached the London Liverpool and Manchester Railway with a proposal for a telegraphic signalling system for their tunnel under Lime Street in Manchester. His idea was rejected, but as a result he made contact with Charles Wheatstone, Professor of Experimental Philosophy at King's College London, and a Fellow of the Royal Society. Wheatstone had experimented with electricity through long-distance cables, discovering that it travelled faster than the speed of light, and had built his own telegraph system based on the mechanisms of a music box. The two men went into partnership and took out a joint patent in May 1837.

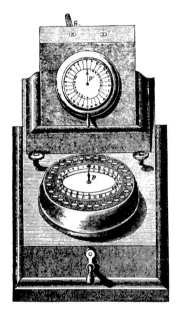

*Top:*
*Cooke and Wheatstone's five-needle telegraph instrument. Two of the five needles were deflected simultaneously by electric current, so that their direction converged onto a particular letter of the alphabet painted on the dial.*

*Above:*
*Wheatstone's ABC telegraph. The operator turned the handle at the front and pressed a key on the dial to generate the alternating electric currents which activated the same key on the receiver at the other end.*

That year saw a sudden leap in man's ability to exploit electrical impulses. In America, Samuel Morse gave his first public exhibition. In France, Steinheil contracted seven miles of telegraph, while in Britain Edward Davy coiled a mile of copper wire around the Inner Circle at Regent's Park, sending a signal round the Park, and developed a 'relay' for strengthening the signal as it passed down the line.

That same year saw the first electrical signals system installed on the North-Western Railway from Euston to Camden Town. It was a development of Cooke's original idea for the Lime Street tunnel in Manchester. In the event, it was found to be impractical and replaced by a pneumatic signal system based on compressed air, tubes and tin whistles. An obituary of this earliest of electrical signals systems appeared in Osborne's *Guide to the London-Birmingham Railway* of 1840:

> Electricity was thought to be a quicker signal agent, and some successful experiments were tried with it, but experience has proved that the whistles were more advantageous and suitable in every respect.

Although the Euston-Camden Town experiment had been a failure, it was seized upon by Isambard Kingdom Brunel, who had finally emerged from his tunnel and was now chief engineer of the Great Western Railway, due to open in June 1838. Brunel laid a line of six wires in a hollow tube insulated with cotton about a foot beneath the Great Western Line, from Paddington to West Drayton – a distance of thirteen and a half miles. 'The telegraph on the Great Western Railway has given great confidence and satisfaction,' wrote Cooke. A month later the *Railway Times* lyrically described how the system was so simple that even a deaf and dumb boy was able to work it.

The telegraph system spread rapidly across London. By May 1849, the Central Post Office had its own telegraph line. By 1861, a map of the London telegraph system shows the Post Office as the centre of the spider's web. From the Post Office's headquarters at St Martin's-le-Grand, next to St Paul's, the lines extended east to Limehouse and Whitechapel, north to King's Cross and Camden Town, west to Paddington and Shepherd's Bush, south-west to Westminster and Victoria, and south to Elephant and Castle and beyond.

Brunel's original idea of telegraph wires in hollow tubes beneath the tracks of the Great Western was taken a stage further by the London-Manchester Railway, who laid their gutta-percha-covered wires in a creosoted, wooden duct within a trench. But at £200 a mile it was very expensive. A cheaper method, using glazed earthenware pipes at £60 a mile, was tried, but the pipes kept breaking. So the telegraph wires were sent overhead – not without hazard. A violent storm in January 1866 brought miles of cables down.

By 1868 there were 3381 telegraph stations and 91,000 miles of wire in Britain, transmitting six million inland messages each year, with the railway companies operating about a third of the system. London was dominated by two companies, the London District Telegraph Company, which operated within a four-mile radius of King's Cross, and the Universal Private Telegraph Company, which provided direct links between London business premises. They offered betting services, financial news, commercial information, fire alarms, administrative control and weather forecasting services. The telegraph's supporters spoke enthusiastically not only of its successes, but also of its potential.

The greater the claims of the telegraph buffs, the greater the clamour for them to be taken under public control. One of the most articulate champions of public control was John Lewis Ricardo, previously a prominent free-trader and one-time chairman of the largest telegraph company in Britain, the Electric Telegraph Company. The telegraph, he wrote in a memorandum to Gladstone (then Chancellor of the Exchequer), was 'so powerful an engine of diplomacy, so important an aid to civil and military administration, so effective a service to trade and commerce', that society would not be safe until it was in government hands. The takeover, he estimated, would cost a mere £2m. Nationalisation of the telegraph system became a liberal *cause célèbre*, finding supporters in Edwin Chadwick and the *Quarterly Review*.

*A map of the Post Office telegraph system in 1890.*

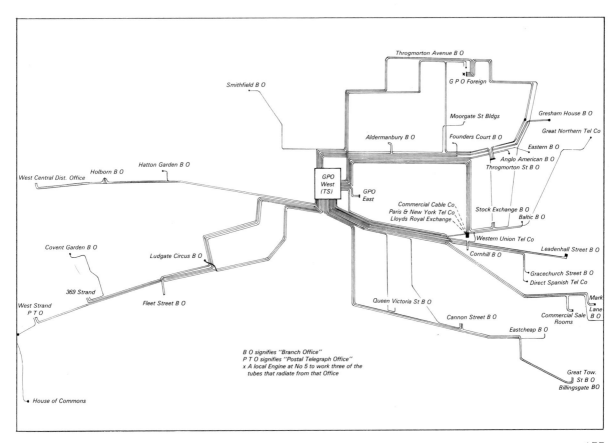

It was not cheap, however. Nationalisation cost £8m, and the bought-out telegraph companies made fortunes. To compound it all, in 1873 the Post Office was discovered to have misappropriated £812,000 secretly from the Post Office Savings Bank to finance the takeover. The Post Office official in charge, Charles Scudmore, was hastily pensioned off with a £20,000 golden handshake, and retired to Turkey for the rest of his life.

Within eight years of the takeover, Alexander Graham Bell patented the telephone, destined – as anyone with foresight would have realised – to make the telegraph obsolete. The Postmaster General, Lord John Manners, swallowed hard and said that the telephone was no threat to the telegraph; the Post Office gulped at the £8m just spent on what had turned out to be a technological dead-end.

Predictably, the Post Office tried to take over and suppress the new private telephone companies. When its bid proved unsuccessful, it did

*An early telephone exchange.*

all it could to obstruct them. The Post Office claimed that the new wires would interfere with its existing cables; it was joined by the gas companies, who resented anything electronic under the ground on principle. The new companies were not allowed to run telephone wires either over or under private houses without householders' permission; they were to pay ten per cent of their gross income to the Post Office; their working area was to be limited to a five-mile radius. Faced by these restrictions, the smaller companies vanished, leaving one monolith, the National Telephone Company.

In a new clause, the Post Office attempted to defeat its competitors by defining telephones as telegrams within the meaning of the Act being promulgated in 1878. It was struck out by the Commons. But in 1880, a Court Judgement by Mr Justice Stephens and Mr Justice Prolock ruled that a telephone was a telegraph within the meaning of the Act, and that telephones were thus a monopoly of the Post Office.

Instead of taking over the National Telephone Company, the Post Office went into competition. It could hardly do otherwise. The Post Office was in no position to ask for funds after 'the improvidence of the bargain by which the telegraph was taken over', as *The Times* thundered, 'at terms scarcely bearing impartial examination.'

The result was chaos: the Post Office gained the main lines, the National Telephone Company retained the local lines. It became even more confused in 1890, when the London County Council, fearing the monopoly of the National Telephone Company, refused to cooperate with it, and even considered starting its own telephone company.

Overhead, clutter was becoming intolerable. Telegraph, telephone and electricity competed for skyspace. Underground offered the only neutral territory. Or did it? In July 1900, the Post Office issued an injunction to prevent the National Telephone Company from opening up any street without the consent of the Postmaster-General and of the London County Council. By November of the following year, the Post Office and the National Telephone Company finally reached agreement: the Post Office would rent out underground space to the National Telephone Company; in return, the Post Office would acquire the plant of the Company. When the Company's charter ran out in 1911, the Post Office stepped in and took over the entire system.

By then, in any case, almost half of London's telecommunication cables had moved below ground. Other Post Office services were already there. In February 1863, the Post Office had opened an underground, pneumatic railway, running from the District Post

*The popularity of electricity and the invention of the telephone increased the clutter of overhead wires and cables. A cross-section of Holborn Viaduct shows the logical solution – to put all the cables underground.*

*The first despatch of the Post Office's underground pneumatic railway from Euston to Eversholt in February 1863. The 500-yard journey took three minutes. Extended to St Martin's-le-Grand in 1865, the railway was nonetheless a failure, and by 1880 was abandoned and all but forgotten.*

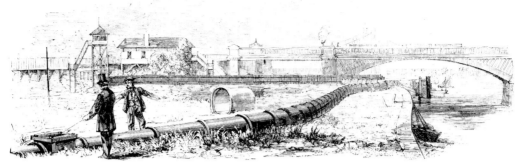

THE PNEUMATIC LETTER AND PARCEL CONVEYANCE : THE DESPATCH-TUBE AT BATTERSEA.

SECTION OF DISC IN THE ENGINE-HOUSE.

THE MOUTH OF THE TUBE, AND CARRIAGE.—SEE PAGE 187.

Office in Eversholt Street to Euston Station. Compressed air pushed the train from behind, air vacuum pulled it from the front. On its first outing, the driverless train-in-a-drain, carrying thirty-five mail bags, left Euston at 9.45 and arrived at Eversholt Station three minutes later – a journey of about 500 yards on two-and-a-half-foot rails in a tunnel seven feet in diameter.

The system was extended to the General Post Office at St Martin's-Le-Grand in 1865. It was opened by the Duke of Buckingham, who rode in one of the cars through the arched tunnel. Made of brick and with a cast-iron lining, it was about four feet high and four and a half feet wide. 'The sensation of starting, and still more of arriving', those who accompanied the Duke of Buckingham informed the *Illustrated London News*, 'was not agreeable . . . But once fairly within the tube, these sensations were got rid of, or left behind.'

Mechanical faults began to develop: there were constant air leakages, and gradually plans for extending the pneumatic railway system were dropped. The tube was then converted into an electric railway by George Threlfall, but to no avail. In 1880 it was abandoned, forgotten by all save Threlfall himself, who sold it for a profit. It remained buried for fifty years, until a large gas explosion on 20 December 1928 revealed several of the original mail-cars still in the tunnel. One of them is now in the Science Museum. The Post Office, reminded of the tunnel's existence, decided to use it to carry telecommunications cables.

If the pneumatic railway was dead, the pneumatic principle was not. Under London a spider's web of pneumatic tubes, two and a half inches in diameter, was built by the Post Office to link seventy of its post offices. The system – like one still in use in Harrods – utilised compressed air to propel a cylinder down a tube at about twenty miles an hour, for a distance of three miles. The pneumatic tubes are still there, a few used as cable conduits, but most of them are forgotten. In the 1970s, batteries of them were to be seen lining Post Office excavations at St Paul's, amputated by the diggers of the contractors.

If pneumatic dispatch tubes had speeded telegraph traffic (the original message could pass through tubes and obviate mistakes), letter and parcel post travelling above spent as long in traffic jams in the metropolis as on inter-city trains to their destinations. Pneumatic systems had been tried and had failed. Something else was needed.

The Post Office's answer was yet again to tunnel underground. It was decided to build an electric railway with an engine, using exactly the same principle as a child's Dublo Hornby. It was to be the Post Office's own underground railway, and work on the line, under the direction of London Transport's ageing tunnelling consultant, Dalrymple-Hay, began in 1913. From the Eastern District Post Office on Whitechapel Road, it was to pass under Liverpool Street Station, where chutes and lifts were to connect it with the mainline station.

*Opposite:*
*A tube powered by compressed air was constructed at Battersea in 1861 by the Pneumatic Despatch Company to carry letters and parcels (top). The engine house supplied the air suction (centre). The cars (below) were drawn through the tube at 25mph. The system became obsolete when the Post Office built its own railway two years later.*

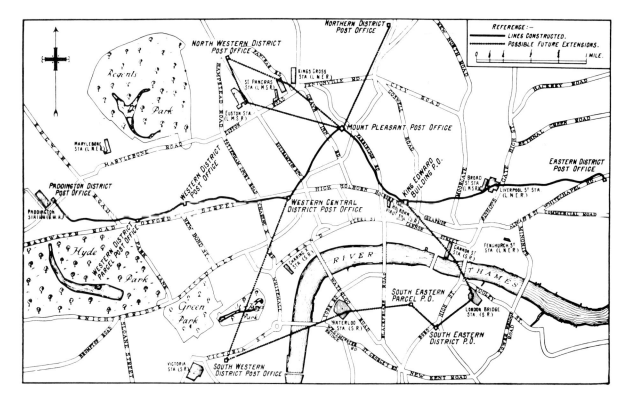

*The Post Office electric railway in 1927.*

Then it was to run beneath the old Roman Wall, London Wall, to the General Post Office headquarters at King Edward Buildings, just north of St Paul's Cathedral. From there, the line was to swing north-west to Farringdon Road and to run under the Fleet Valley to the Mount Pleasant Sorting Office. From Mount Pleasant it was to take a turn south-west under Russell Square to the Western Central District Post Office off High Holborn. Next it was to branch under where Centre Point today stands along to Oxford Street and beyond, to the Western District Post Office in Wimpole Street, and on to the Western District Parcels Office behind Selfridges. From there it was to move across Edgware Road and to end up at the Paddington District Post Office. Six and a half miles in all, it was to serve central London quietly, smoothly, and underground.

Construction work was suspended at the outset of the First World War and the single nine-foot-diameter tunnel was used to store the Elgin Marbles. In 1923, work resumed, and, General Strike apart, continued for four years. The line opened in time for the Christmas mail rush of 1927; within a year, one quarter of London's mail vans disappeared from the streets.

The railway is fully automatic, the electric engines driverless and the train's speed governed by the amount of electricity running through the central rail. Designed to avoid crashes, the section behind goes 'dead' as the train passes each section of track. The stations themselves, like their Underground counterparts, are slightly raised so

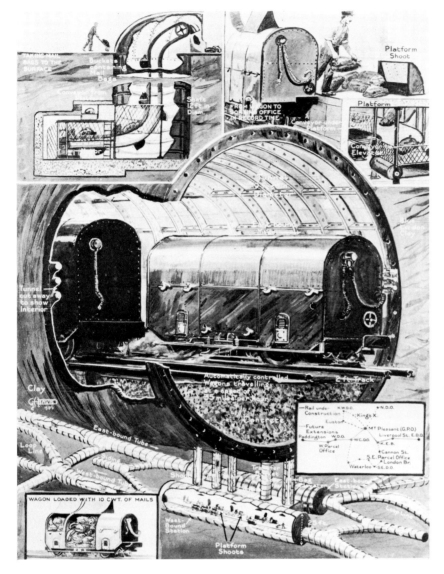

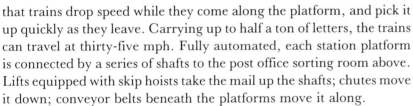

*Top:*
*A repair workshop at Mount Pleasant.*

*Above:*
*The letters are loaded into driverless containers, half a ton at a time.*

*Left:*
*A series of explanatory drawings of the railway, which runs from the Eastern District Post Office at Whitechapel to the Paddington District Post Office.*

that trains drop speed while they come along the platform, and pick it up quickly as they leave. Carrying up to half a ton of letters, the trains can travel at thirty-five mph. Fully automated, each station platform is connected by a series of shafts to the post office sorting room above. Lifts equipped with skip hoists take the mail up the shafts; chutes move it down; conveyor belts beneath the platforms move it along.

Of the eight on the line the three key stations are Paddington, Mount Pleasant and the GPO headquarters. At Paddington, the line originally extended from the District Post Office, directly underneath Platforms 11 and 12 of the mainline station, where there were eight chutes. Another chute came down from 'the Lawn' in the middle of the station. The system was changed with the modernisation of Paddington in the 1930s, but the changes were a matter of detail, not of principle. The station at Mount Pleasant contains stabling tunnels, underground depots, repair workshops, cross-over points and turn-around tunnels, all arranged in tight curves to conserve space. The GPO headquarters under King Edward Building is a similar maze of tunnels, all arranged in a figure-of-eight.

At both Mount Pleasant and King Edward Building, there are twin 'blind' tunnels, leading nowhere. At King Edward Building, they run under Angel Street (where there are shaft connections with the Post Office's deep-level tunnels) and stop abruptly. At Mount Pleasant they run briefly under Cubitt Street, along the Fleet Valley; then they, too, stop.

These 'blind' tunnels were to be the extensions of the railway: north-west from Mount Pleasant to King's Cross, Euston and the North-Eastern District Post Office in Mornington Crescent; and south-east from King Edward Building under the River to London Bridge, Elephant and Castle and Waterloo; then to run north via Victoria to link up with Paddington. Had the tunnels been completed in the 1930s, they would have changed the entire Post Office Railway. It would have had its very own 'circle line'. It never happened. But the elephantine Post Office never forgot. The idea was to reappear twenty years later in a slightly different form.

The railway whetted the Post Office's appetite for underground empire-building. Before the railway had even been opened, their tunnelling equipment was being used to build a tunnel under Wood Street, to link the Post Office railway and the GPO with the Faraday International Exchange at Electra House. It was to be the first tunnel built by William Halcrow.

The Munich Crisis in 1938 provided the Post Office with the occasion, if not the cause, to stake its claims to space underground. In 1939, it was to dig a second cable tunnel, running from the telephone exchange under High Holborn to its headquarters at St Martin's-le-Grand, where it was to form a 'T' with the Wood Street tunnel. It was to be more than just a tunnel. The Holborn Exchange at one end brought together the telephone lines of every government department and had a direct link with Whitehall's own 'Federal' Exchange (you used to dial FED or 333 and then the number), and passed them to the Faraday International Exchange at the other end of the tunnel. It was the bottleneck through which virtually all overseas telecommunications passed.

These tunnels were unspoken witnesses of the Second World War. How essential were they to the Post Office? Were they, like other wartime journeys, really necessary? Tunnelling under London is expensive, and use of London Transport's tunnel network had been available to the Post Office from 1939. But the Post Office was not prepared to rent space in London Transport's tunnels. Like all empire-builders, it wanted outright ownership. It had tried something similar before, with its proposal to extend its railway. But the Post Office's plans had been turned down by the government of the day.

The detonation of the first atomic bomb in 1945 changed government attitudes overnight. It suddenly wanted deep-level tunnels beneath London to protect its communications system. And it wanted the tunnels to be 'secure'. The Post Office, seeing the opportunities available, persuaded the government to finance the excavation of a series of tunnels under London. It was the biggest subterranean project since Bazalgette's sewers. These new Post Office tunnels under London were designed to ensure that government communications could continue below while all above was devastation. They were not conceived, as some thought, as bunkers for top people. They were designed in an era when it was thought that the effects of an atomic bomb were little different from those of a conventional bomb – although bigger.

In the urgency for these cable tunnels to be built, the Post Office sought help from the major electrical contractors, who agreed between themselves to act as a consortium. This somewhat unusual alliance between the Post Office and its suppliers had its origins after the First World War. Then the Post Office desperately needed to modernise its equipment and wanted a large number of new telephone exchanges in a hurry. The five largest manufacturers of telecommunications equipment came together and persuaded the Post Office to grant them the exclusive right to make telephone equipment. The five companies, like the water and gas companies before them, perfectly sensibly divided up the underground telecommunications empire between them. The firms were Plessey, Automatic Telephone and Electric Company, Associated Electrical Industries, Standard Telephone and Cables, and General Electric.

The most profitable single item sold by the consortium to the Post Office was the Strowger Automatic Telephone Exchange. It had been invented in 1889, by a Kansas City undertaker, who was convinced that switchboard girls were listening in on his conversations. To defeat them he had invented an automatic exchange by-passing pryers: it consisted of a cylinder with banks of numbers on it. As the caller dialled the number, a mechanical arm found each number on the side of the cylinder in turn, contact was made and – hopefully – the receiver's telephone rang. It was a laborious process, and by the end of the Second World War, when the machines were being made over here under licence and supplied at handsome profit margins by the consortium, they were about as modern as Kansas City itself.

The managing director of Pye, J R Brinkley (whose firm was not a member of the consortium), wrote to *The Times* on 24 June 1964:

> The present arrangements by which the Post Office purchases its telephone equipment are not in the public interest. These Post Office Bulk Supply Agreements are amongst the most restrictive documents I have

ever seen and it is impossible to reconcile them with a modern competitive industrial situation.

The whole episode had the stamp of historical inevitability about it: the Post Office was too busy trying to create the underground empire it had always yearned for; the government was too concerned with making its communications secure by creating an underground citadel capable of surviving an atomic bomb; and the entrepreneurs were only too happy securing maximum profits by selling a somewhat cumbrous piece of machinery to an undemanding customer. The Offical Secrets Act was enough to ensure that there would be no public discussion. So everybody was happy – everybody, that is, except the taxpayer, who knew nothing about it until Brinkley raised the issue in *The Times*.

The Post Office pressed on with building its empire underground. Excavations began in 1951 for a vast underground telephone exchange at Kingsway. The backbone of the exchange was a twin tunnel 100 feet down on the northern side of High Holborn, between Hatton Garden and Red Lion Square, with Gray's Inn Road running over it. Eating, sleeping and working facilities were provided on the Red Lion Square side. Telecommunications plant, generators and repeating stations occupy most of the Hatton Garden side, while four extension tunnels, running beneath Chancery Lane Underground station, house switching units and an artesian well. A short cable tunnel links the exchange to the Post Office's Holborn cable tunnel. The exchange, opened in October 1954, could handle two million calls a week and the equipment was again supplied by the consortium.

At the same time, the Post Office extended its Holborn and Wood Street tunnels. From the northern tip of Wood Street a new tunnel was driven east under London Wall (on the same alignment as the Post Office Railway) via the Moorgate Exchange (code-named 'Fortress') to the Houndsditch Exchange near Liverpool Street Station, then north-east to Bishopsgate and Bethnal Green. From the southern tip of Wood Street, at the Faraday Exchange (code-named 'Citadel'), a tunnel was dug under the Thames to the South Bank Exchange at Colombo House on Blackfriars Road. From the other end of the Post Office's Holborn tunnel, two extensions were made, one north-west under Gerrard Street Post Office, Newman Street Post Office (not far from the Post Office Tower), then west to Paddington District Post Office; the other, via the Covent Garden Exchange, to Trafalgar Square Post Office, where it linked up with the government's own tunnels under Whitehall.

These early tunnels, built by William Halcrow, total eight miles. They are relatively large – some sixteen and a half feet in diameter – and are lined with pre-cast concrete segments. Banks of cables flank the two-foot-gauge railway line which hauls the cables. In more recent Post Office cable tunnels, which are smaller in diameter, the railway has been replaced by battery-powered trucks. The tunnels are well ventilated and neon-lit; access to them is either through the post offices above or through a number of very ordinary manhole covers dotted about London. The manhole covers make the system easily penetrable: in December 1980 the *New Statesman* held its Christmas party in one of them.

Within a year of the system being completed in 1954, Russia exploded a hydrogen bomb, and the whole inverted Tower of Babel became obsolete. In spite of that the Post Office persuaded the government to finance three more extensions: one in the 1950s joining the Faraday to the Covent Garden Exchange, another in 1966 linking the Trafalgar Square Post Office with Colombo House via Waterloo; a third in 1976 extending the Paddington tunnel to Shepherd's Bush.

The final tunnel system looks remarkably like both the original telegraph lines in 1861 and the projected Post Office railway extensions of the 1930s: a sign that, in spite of the changing nature of telecommunications under London, the direction of these communications has not changed in 100 years.

The consortium did handsomely enough out of what they supplied for these deep-level cable tunnels. Excess profits from government contracts were not yet seen as the unacceptable face of capitalism. Faced with criticism, the consortium members might have been wise to plough back some of their profits into up-to-date capital telecommunications equipment. Their critics have complained that they did nothing of the kind. When finally mutterings began and they were criticised for poor export performance and high prices (twenty-five per cent above competitors outside the consortium), they announced defensively that they were going to leap-frog one stage in telecommunications and build an all-automatic computer exchange. It was a technological disaster. The first exchange opened at Highgate Wood in December 1962. It closed on the same day. For the consortium this might have been the end of the line. When the Post Office was turned into a public corporation in October 1969, it was, in theory, free to make contracts with whomsoever it wanted. In practice, caught with outdated equipment, insufficient capital for new equipment, and poorly qualified and underpaid technical staff to evaluate new technology, it still relied too heavily on too small a number of contractors; as late as 1982 eighty per cent of its equipment came from just three firms. Only now that the Post Office has been divided between British Telecom, the Post Office and Giro Bank does it look as if this over-dependence on the few but powerful will finally be broken, with British Telecom importing equipment from Sweden and America for the new computerised System X, and even threatening to manufacture its own equipment if its contractors are not competitive. The renewal of Britain's outworn telephone system is a billion pound programme. To date six computerised exchanges are in operation. 1230 will be installed in the next decade.

*Overleaf:*
*One of the first of the new computerised exchanges, System X, to be installed in British Telecom's 6700 automatic exchanges over the next few decades.*

## CABLE TELEVISION

Inevitably, it began in America. A Mrs L E Parsons of Astoria, Oregon, whose husband operated a local radio station, had a craving for watching television. But the nearest station was in Seattle, 125 miles away. So, in 1949, Mr Parsons put up a large antenna, fifty feet high, joined by cable to his home, and his wife got her television picture. Neighbours were quick to link up with Mr Parsons' antenna, and Mr Parsons was even quicker to charge them a hundred dollars a link, plus the cost of a television, which they also had to buy from the enterprising Mr Parsons.

Soon it was discovered that cable television was as effective in urban as in rural areas – skyscrapers and high-rise developments block signals and ruin reception. By the mid-1950s, substantial areas of New York City had been linked by cable. More were to follow.

The system, as Mr Parsons had shown, was simple. One large and sophisticated aerial can pick up any number of television stations, and it can be linked to subscribers by special cable well capable of transmitting any number of programmes simultaneously. By contrast, the number of stations that can be broadcast over the air is limited. The greater the number of stations, the greater the interference. The potential of cable transmission is that it can be used for more than just television programmes. A report on cable television in 1982 found:

> The vital attraction for home subscribers would be the extra television entertainment channels. However, the main role of cable systems eventually will be the delivery of many information, financial and other services to the home and the joining of business and home by high capacity data links.

Cable television can open new doors. It can also close some. The airwaves may be cluttered, but at least the receiver is free to tune in to any wavelength, authorised or unauthorised, and no one can stop him. Cable television can provide information, but it can also exclude information; the authorities can decide, simply by pulling a switch, who will watch what. Ominously, one of the countries most interested in cable television is South Africa.

And quantity is no guarantee of quality. 'Viewers wanting to find top notch programmes on Cable TV had better put on their swamp boots,' reported Richard Zachs from New York. 'They'll come in handy for wading through the muck of endless babbling hosts, soap operas of every flavour, low-rent movies, obscure sporting events and network reruns.'

Although cable television started in America, cable broadcasting is far older, and started in England. It began in Hythe, Hampshire, in 1924. Parts of Hythe were without electricity, so another enterprising owner of a local radio shop, a Mr Maxton, attached wires to his radio receiver and ran them to loudspeakers in the homes of friends and neighbours. Within ten years it had spread to most working-class areas without electricity. It sprang up almost spontaneously, but was frowned on by both the Post Office and the BBC: most of the cables laid in London were laid without official permission. Twice between the wars the system was nearly taken over: once by the BBC, who were stopped by the Post Office, and once by the Post Office, who were stopped by the BBC.

The new cable companies that grew up were continually held in check by the Post Office and the BBC. No relay company was allowed to send out original material and no information on the results of sweepstakes (ie no Irish programmes) could be broadcast. Gradually the smaller companies were swallowed up by three larger groups: Rediffusion (who now have holdings in Capital Radio and Thames Television), Radio Rentals (owned by Thorn EMI) and British Relay Wireless and Television Limited (owned by Philips). The companies moved into cable television in the 1950s, using a pair of wires, like the telephone line. Despite their blandishments of clearer pictures in areas well-served by transmitters, their cable services never really got off the ground. Of the 170,000 homes which Relay Wireless and Television pass with their 'Showcase', only 5800 have taken up the service.

Coaxial cable and other technical developments are likely to change all that. The coaxial cable made cable television in America a practical proposition. Developed as long-distance telephone cables in 1941, they already carry about twenty-five per cent of British telephone traffic. The cables carry radio waves along a thin copper wire protected by a copper sheath: the wire and the sheath, with a fine tube of insulating plastic between them, share the same axis. Previously, telephone conversations ran through 'pairs' or 'quads'. But because the coaxial cable carries radio waves over a large number of frequencies, it can carry hundreds of telephone conversations at once.

After coaxial cables came waveguides. Waveguides carry millimetre waves, so tiny that they can go through neither the air nor a coaxial cable without dispersing and disappearing. But by confining them in tiny tubes, protected by a carefully wound helix or wire, they can be utilised, and each tube can carry thousands of telephone calls. The problem with waveguides is cost of cabling. They cannot go round sharp corners and existing tunnels and cable ducts have too many right angles in them. Waveguides would have meant creating a whole new underground system. The cost of waveleaves, tunnels, shafts and ducts would have run into millions of pounds, even if there had been room under London to put the stuff.

Hardly had waveguides made their appearance in the 1960s than they were overtaken by optic fibres, using waves of light or lasers. Electrical signals are transformed into waves of light which travel down hair-like threads of pure glass and are converted back at the other end into electric signals. Each optic fibre can carry tens of thousands of separate signals, and unlike electrical transmission they do not dissipate their power and require constant boosting over long distances. British Telecom have transmitted a signal for over sixty miles without regeneration.

Optic fibres provide almost limitless possibilities for cable communications under London. They are small, easy to thread through existing ducts and cheap to produce. There are two problems: first, they cannot, like coaxial cables, be split to form branches running from the trunk; second – though the cost of cabling would be no different from any other cabling – the cost of transformers would be astronomic. It comes down to economics of scale. Thus British Telecom are using optic fibres for their trunk routes, and the older 'pairs', 'quads', and coaxial cables, for their local ones.

So far there are two different systems of cabling to choose from: the 'tree and branch' system, and the 'switched multi-star' system. The 'tree and branch' is made up of a trunk with branches splitting off to individual houses, each branch capable of carrying all the programmes and services supplied by the trunk. The 'switched multi-star' is based on the idea of a network of stars, linked by optic fibre trunks, and with local leads to individual houses made of coaxial cable. The star acts as an exchange and the viewer can choose what to watch, very much in the same way as he chooses whom to speak to when he dials a number on his telephone. This is the method most favoured by the Post Office.

It was these technological developments, rather than public demand, that spurred on the developing network of cables under London. 'All forms of telecommunication can now be made over one single system,' wrote the Greater London Council's Economic Policy Planning Group in its report on cable television. 'In principle every part of that system can be linked to every other part.'

Already we are seeing a repeat of the nineteenth-century battles over water, gas and electricity. The government favours private enterprise. The GLC wants public control.

Another consideration is the actual cost of cabling. There are no profits to be made from just digging up a street and laying a cable. Nor would cable television be a great generator of employment. The cabling of the Barbican by 'Visionhire' (part of British Relay Wireless and Television), which connected 2000 homes, took sixteen workers six months. At that rate, it would take a mere thousand workers seven years to connect all London by cable. It is, however, capital-intensive. At an average cost of £149 per home, is it worth it?

One key determinant of the cost will be how much of the present underground system can be utilised. An obvious solution would be to make use of the miles and miles of Post Office cable tunnels and ducts. But the security-conscious British Telecom shows little interest in sharing its tunnels with people and organisations it does not control. London Transport, on the other hand, is anxious to rent out space underground, in its tunnels, in its abandoned underground stations and in its old tramway ducts. Already London Transport tunnels carry Mercury, Rediffusion and Visionhire cables, and London Transport has linked up seven London teaching hospitals so that students can simultaneously watch operations without physically having to be present. The old London hydraulic power pipes, now owned by Rothschild's, are also available to carry cables. There have even been suggestions that sewers could carry cables direct into the home – brain drain in reverse.

One thing is certain. There will be no new tunnels under London for cable television. Subterranean development is the prerogative of the very rich, and London is no longer rich. But what has the underground London of coaxial cables, waveguides and optic fibres got in common with the underground London of John Stow, John Evelyn, or Joseph Bazalgette?

But then what have you in common with the child of five whose photograph your mother keeps on the mantelpiece? Nothing except that you happen to be the same person.

(George Orwell: *The Lion and the Unicorn*)

# 8 The Defence of the City

Subterranean London came into its own – as we have seen – during the Second World War, but it was not the first time that it had provided the government with a bolt-hole. In May 1915, a Zeppelin had dropped a ton of bombs on London, killing seven people and injuring thirty-five. King George V had promptly been put aboard the Royal Train and towed to a tunnel, completely disrupting rail traffic; the Elgin Marbles had been stored in the foundations of the Post Office Railway; and the Cabinet and War Office had trooped down below into the Piccadilly extension between Holborn and Aldwych. Part of the Underground had been commandeered for troop movements, and, with extreme reluctance, Underground stations had been sanctioned by the government for use as air-raid shelters.

## AIR RAID SHELTERS

Persons may shelter here at their own risk after the take cover notice has been given. Person sheltering here are not allowed to take Birds, Dogs, Cats, or other Animals, as well as Mailcarts, on the Company's premises.

Even before the First World War the government had made use of subterranean London. The importance of London's tunnels in another kind of war – the clandestine war of terrorism – had been recognised by the police as far back as 1875, when they were negotiating to purchase a site for their new headquarters. That year, a national opera house was being built just a hundred yards from Whitehall on the Thames Embankment. The creation of the operatic impresario Colonel J H Mapleson, it was intended to rival La Scala in Milan, and to be connected by tunnel to the Houses of Parliament and the District Line. Bazalgette's Embankment had already been excavated to provide the opera with its own Underground station. The opera house had cost £103,000 to date, but it was never to be completed. The site was finally bought by the Metropolitan Police in 1890, its buildings cleared and Norman Shaw commissioned to build the 'old' New Scotland Yard there. The great advantage of the site, the chief engineer of the Metropolitan Police argued, was its tunnels, which would allow police to be moved swiftly from one part of London to another using the Underground.

Their recent experience with the Fenians had been a salutary lesson.

In the nineties in England – as indeed in the United States, France, Germany, Spain and Italy, and subterraneously in Russia . . . there were Anarchists . . . Irish Fenians, and Russian nihilists. The outrages in London and the North of England were mostly committed by Fenians. The idea was to terrorize England into granting freedom to Ireland. They dynamited . . . underground railways, theatres, the Houses of Parliament and docks.                                   (Ford Madox Ford: *Memories and Impressions*)

Fenian terrorists had, on 30 October 1881, detonated two nitro-

*A Fenian bomb exploded in 1883 outside a local government office in Charles II street, Westminster.*

*Opposite:*
*Friend or foe? Two men stand outlined at the entrance to the twin tunnels of the Fleet Sewer. London's underbelly may appear vulnerable; but terrorists have, with reason, chosen to attack the city from above.*

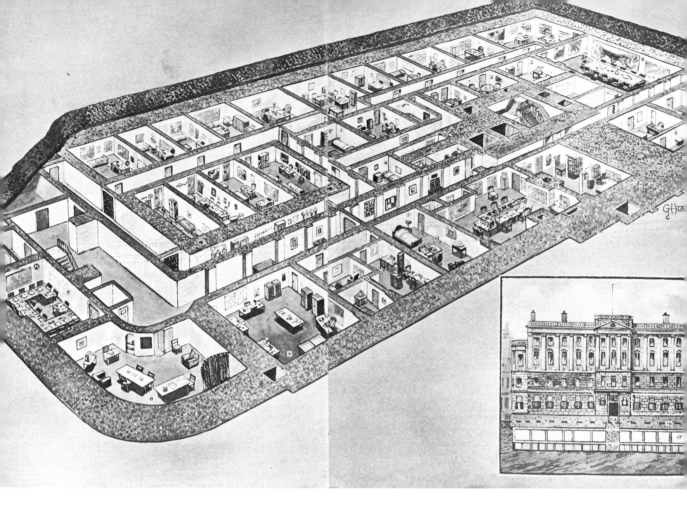

*Above:*
The 'Hole in the Ground' –
600 acres of office space
constructed under Storey's Gate
during the build-up to World
War II, protected by seventeen
feet of concrete.

*Right:*
'Paddock', an underground
shelter built to house Cabinet
Office.

glycerine bombs in the Underground, one at Praed Street and the other between Westminster and Charing Cross, almost on the site of the national opera house. On 27 February 1884, they had exploded a third in the cloakroom at Victoria Station, and on 2 January 1885 a fourth went off at Gower Street. The last Fenian bomb in the London Underground was set off on 30 April 1897.

Fenian bombs and Zeppelin raids finally pushed the government to take civil defence seriously and their own safety first. A government research report, estimating future casualties in an air raid over London, took as its starting-point the rate of deaths in the 1915-18 bombardment: eleven and a half dead per ton of explosive used. Air raids on London, the Air Staff predicted in 1924, would kill 1700 people in the first twenty-four hours, 1275 in the second twenty-four hours, and 850 every twenty-four hours following. Society would break down.

The government's answer was to dig itself in underground but keep the people battened down up above. The luckless population was offered gratuitous advice on self-preservation by the Home Office in a booklet published in 1938: *The Protection of your Home against Air Raid*. It contained excellent advice on the evacuation of pets, but omitted, among 'things to have', a shovel to dig yourself out with afterwards.

The London County Council disagreed with the government. They wanted trenches for people, not just bunkers for top people. Accordingly, they dug underground themselves. A trench network was dug, seven foot deep and 1430 feet long, under Lincoln's Inn Fields. The trenches were then covered with concrete and two foot of earth, and fitted with airlocks at the entrances to keep out poison gas. Similar trench systems were built in Queen, Bloomsbury, Russell and Woburn Squares. One of the most impressive local civil defence excavations was in the London borough of Finsbury, where an air raid shelter thirty-four foot deep was excavated to provide safety for 12,000 people. (It is now used as an underground car park, concealed by an ornamental garden on top.)

*Above:*
*Three of the subterranean war rooms at 'Paddock'.*

*Below:*
*'That vast monstrosity that weighs on Horse Guards Parade', the ivy-clad Admiralty building, whose bulk extended likewise below the surface.*

All the while, the government had been digging for all it was worth. In the suburbs, three subterranean citadels had been built in 1933: the Admiralty's at Cricklewood (which was to be used during the Falklands War), the Air Ministry's at Harrow, and the Cabinet Office's, code-named 'Paddock', under the Post Office Research Station at Dollis Hill. At the same time a subterranean office block had been excavated under the Treasury at Storey's Gate. Protected by seventeen feet of concrete, reinforced by iron rails, it contained 200 rooms in 600 acres of office space. The Cabinet Secretariat called it the 'Hole in the Ground'. Parts of it are now open to the public.

The government continued digging throughout the phoney war: extending the Whitehall troglodyte city with another citadel for the Admiralty ('that vast monstrosity that weighs on Horse Guards

Parade', as Winston Churchill called it) and a subterranean fortress for the Army at Montagu House (site of the present Ministry of Defence).

These were the months when the Ministry of Home Security was distributing cardboard, fold-up coffins to local authorities and debating – should the coffins prove insufficient – whether the dead should be buried in mass graves soaked with lime, or taken in hoppers and dropped into the North Sea, or dumped into the Thames like pre-Bazalgette sewage.

London Transport's main fear was of flooding in its tunnels. A single bomb fracturing a tunnel between Charing Cross and Waterloo could cause the entire Underground from Clapham Common to King's Cross to flood. Accordingly, six-ton flood gates, thirteen inches thick, were built at stations on either side of the Underground tunnels which crossed under the Thames. During raids, when no trains were allowed to run under the Thames, the passengers were turned off their trains at the Strand, and obliged to walk across the River, using the Hungerford footbridge, to join another train at Waterloo.

In the trains themselves, London Transport covered the carriage windows with heavy netting to provide protection for passengers from flying glass. The netting so darkened the carriages that passengers regularly tore it off. This produced the inevitable polite reproof from the awful Buzby of the Underground, Billy Brown of London Town:

> I trust you'll pardon my correction
> This stuff is here for your protection.

To which the graffiti writers replied:

*At the time of the Munich Crisis, London Transport equipped its tubes on either side of the River with six-ton manually operated floodgates. Their number has since been increased so that they girdle the centre of London.*

196

We thank you for your information
But we can't see the bloody station.

Further afield, the three-mile section for the Central Line from Leytonstone to Gants Hill, excavated but not yet opened, was turned into an aircraft components factory, operated by Plessey. The Post Office took additional cable space in London Transport's tubes, laying a cable from the government's Whitehall underground complex to the Post Office's at Holborn.

The Metropolitan Water Board was also making preparations for war. The Board's mains were likely to be inadequate in the face of heavy air raids. So, from 1937, water requirements were constantly reviewed. Rivers, streams and even swimming pools were systematically surveyed. In 1939, 5000-gallon storage tanks made of sheet steel were supplied to local authorities. Eventually, twenty supertanks, holding 200,000 gallons apiece, were built in London's squares and gardens. New mains were sunk, hydrants put on trunk mains, and miles of portable six-inch steel surface pipes manufactured for rapid installation in emergencies. Extra pumping stations were built on the River at Blackfriars and Hungerford Bridges, from where a short extension led to Trafalgar Square. Five eight-inch mains, built especially for fire-fighting, radiated from the Serpentine and the Round Pond in Kensington Gardens, and three twenty-four-inch raw water mains were constructed in and around central London. A City main connected the Thames near Cannon Street with the Grand Union Canal at City Road, with pumping stations at each end. A West End main ran from the Grand Union Canal at Regent's Park to Shaftesbury Avenue. A third connected St Katharine's Docks with the City mains.

*Top:*
*A diagram of the Plessey aircraft components factory which occupied part of the Central Line in East London.*

*Above: Plessey technicians at work in the underground factory.*

It became a moral offence to waste water. Inverted snobbery was used: not only was a daily bath unnecessary, it was actually bad for you. Moreover, as one MP pointed out, it was only a suburban snob cult. And if you really insist on keeping clean, then no more than five inches of water please . . . and don't pull the lavatory chain so much either.

All the preparations made by the various ministries and local authorities in the years leading up to the war had constantly to be reviewed and modified when the bombs began to fall on London. A single night of the Blitz, 29 December 1940, was enough to fracture twelve water mains and the City raw water main. All through the City, six-inch portable steel mains ran along the gutters. Even greater conservation of water was clearly required. The hundreds of bomb craters in London's basements were almost ready-made water tanks. The floors and sides of basements were 'made good' and waterproofed with bitumen. They were called 'static water tanks' – prompting the inevitable 'Gin and Static, please'.

*Drains and pipes (above) – even the northern outfall sewer (below) – were victims of the Blitz.*

Since the War, the Ministry of Defence has become the biggest carpet-bagger of real estate under London since Charles Tyson Yerkes. British Museum Station, on the Central Line, which closed in 1933 (replaced by a joint Central and Piccadilly Line station at Holborn), was taken over and later turned into an administrative office for the Brigade of Guards, able, in time of crisis, to double up as the emergency headquarters of the London District Military Command. The old Post Office Station on the Central Line was turned into a deep-level communications headquarters for the Central Electricity Board. And the never-used Bull and Bush under Hampstead Heath – at 200 feet down, London's deepest station – was used in the 1950s as London Transport's emergency headquarters in the event of a nuclear attack. Later still it became the control centre for the Underground's string of floodgates, built in the tunnels running under central London, which could be lowered through gaps in the tunnel roofs at the turn of a switch. Now abandoned, the Bull and Bush features on London Transport's list of disused Underground stations offered for rent.

The post-war fate of the deep-level underground shelters, built on Churchill's insistence, has varied. Goodge Street was turned into a processing centre for British troops passing through London until a fire in 1956, and was later offered to the British Library for book storage, but they turned it down. Chancery Lane was taken over by the Post Office and annexed to the Kingsway underground exchange. Clapham South became a youth hostel during the Festival of Britain. Camden Town was used as a set for a 'Doctor Who' series, and later, in 1976, was leased, together with Belsize Park, to Security Archives Limited. (There is a clause in the lease allowing government reoccupation should the need arise.) The rest are empty, awaiting a tenant.

With the end of the war, only government seemed reluctant to come up from underground. Old fears were replaced by new fears: of atomic war, flooding, terrorism. The government's response, like that of the ostrich, was to bury its head ever deeper.

The first threat was atomic. The government's reaction was mediaeval: 'Fortress London', with the Whitehall complex linked to 'Citadel' at St Paul's, 'Bastion' at Covent Garden, 'Rampart' at Waterloo, and 'Fortress' at Moorgate. This subterranean system tunnelled its way through the brain of some Whitehall Dr Strangelove until 1955, when Russia exploded her first nuclear bomb, and the tunnels under London became as useful to modern warfare as the Tower of London.

Now, the Post Office cable tunnels under London are no more than Post Office cable tunnels. 'Fortress London' has been buried and forgotten. Most of Churchill's Whitehall excavations have been turned into convenient office space for the Civil Service. The cable tunnel under Whitehall, which links up with the Whitehall telephone exchange on Northumberland Avenue, is still in use, but Churchill's extension to the Rotunda has been abandoned. It is dark and damp, dripping with stalactities, already a subterranean fossil. It had been built in difficult ground, in the estuary of the River Tyburn, and Halcrow had to harden the gravel with injected chemicals before he could excavate. It flooded in March 1983. For three weeks nothing was done: no government department accepted responsibility (so long as the waters did not penetrate beyond the flood-gates into the section under Whitehall itself). Finally, the Department of the Environment had to borrow a Post Office cable tunnel pump to dry it out.

By the 1960s, the government had given up hope of fighting a nuclear war from under London and surviving. A survey of all underground rivers, wells and springs was made, and the government issued Thames Water with emergency pumps – which came in useful during the 1976 drought. No more attempts were made to conscript subterranean London. The tunnels and underground workings were given their obituary notice as early as 28 December 1959 by Chapman Pincher in the *Daily Express*: 'These tunnels, which are below Whitehall, Leicester Square, Holborn and Victoria, are not deep enough to withstand a near miss with an H-Bomb.'

Hardly had the government jettisoned its nether city than another threat appeared: flooding. The reason was simple. Since Roman times London has sunk fifteen feet. Severe weather, combined with an abnormally high tide, threatened to engulf forty-five square miles of the centre, including most of Westminster, the City and London's valleys. John Stow's rivers would have surfaced once again. The Cabinet would have moved to Holborn, Parliament to Queensway, and the Ministry of Defence to Lacon House in Theobald's Road.

It never happened, and at a cost of £460m, a monster flood barrier, spanning 570 yards across Woolwich Reach on the Thames Estuary, with two service tunnels running beneath it, was built between 1975 and 1982 to protect the capital. With four 3700-ton gates, each as wide as the opening of Tower Bridge, it is the largest flood barrier in the world.

This is, perhaps, fortunate. The Greater London Council, in its municipal wisdom, has sited its flood control centre twenty feet *underground* in the disused Kingsway tram tunnel just under the junction of Southampton Row and Theobald's Road (you can see the entrance, guarded by iron railings, descending down the middle of Southampton Row by the Jeanette Cochrane Theatre), almost directly above one of London's main interceptory sewers. The British Army, in its military wisdom, has done four times better. It has sited its flood control centre *eighty* feet underground, in its alternative London Region headquarters in the old British Museum station, almost directly beneath the same interceptory sewer. Both control centres were supposed to have been sited above flood level, though this would not have prevented the sewers themselves from overflowing. The Thames Barrier will for a time at least deny Londoners a spectacle comparable with the fate of Richard the Raker, who, the reader will recall, 'drowned monstrously in his own excrement'.

*The Thames Flood Barrier is the largest in the world.*

Fear of flooding has given way to fear of terrorism. Guy Fawkes' memory lives on. Attack from below, which he pioneered, is an ever-present worry to government and police alike. Responsibility for security under London is centralised in one New Scotland Yard office, yet neither the Metropolitan Police nor the statutory undertakings have the manpower to patrol all of underground London; some subterranean routes, like Bazalgette's tunnel under the Embankment and the Tyburn sewer, are a security officer's nightmare.

The problem of protecting London from terrorists underground is its manholes. Underground tunnels and subways need access. Manholes provide it. Ingress for the aggressor is there for the making. Yet, although unofficial access theoretically is easy in most parts of underground London, security in those vital areas below public installations and in sensitive areas such as Parliament and Buckingham Palace is far more effective than meets the eye. Initially, shortage of police manpower may have turned out to be an advantage, since the underground authorities themselves (far more knowledgeable about their local demesnes than policemen could ever be) have perforce had to take on most of the legwork, like a subterranean militia. And closed-circuit television monitoring is beginning to do away with the legwork.

The underground is a far less friendly place than the makers of B-

*London's first underground terrorist was Guy Fawkes, whose plot to blow up the Houses of Parliament in 1605 was planned for the cellars under the Palace of Westminster. The pillars have been lopped off by the artist to reveal the full span of the cellar.*

movies would have us believe. A terrorist does not like a deserted sewer to hide in. He prefers to hide among people. He needs no secret tunnel to get from his safe house to his target. He is far safer simply purchasing a ticket and seeking anonymity on the Underground. Shallow tunnels, sewers and subways are regularly patrolled and used by maintenance parties and flusher gangs, while deep-level tunnels such as the Post Office's cable tunnels are so deep and strongly built (to resist atomic bombs) that 500 pounds of gelignite would cause scarcely a ripple on the surface. As for a 500-pound bomb in a London sewer, given the chemical instability of gelignite and the environmental instability of the sewer itself, the terrorist is more likely to damage himself than his target. Even the bomb which killed Airey Neave in the Houses of Parliament underground car park was incidental to the underground. It was fixed under his car outside his flat – at street level. Only by chance did it go off underground.

Besides, terrorists have no master intelligence system. To find your way around the intricate system of tunnels, sewers and subways beneath London requires a degree of intimate knowledge that only resides with the people who work in them. With London's underground divided and subdivided into separate empires, no one group of workers has a grasp of the entire system. Just as terrorists consciously protect themselves by dividing into cells, so subterranean London accidentally protects itself by dividing into systems and subsystems. You can walk down the Tyburn sewer from Hampstead, under the American Ambassador's residence in Regent's Park, under the MI5 headquarters and Buckingham Palace to Westminster – as long as you do it outside working hours. But you cannot change from the Tyburn sewer to the Victoria Line under Buckingham Palace, nor from the Victoria Line to the Post Office cable tunnels under New Cavendish Street. Nor is there any way of knowing whether you are under Buckingham Palace or New Cavendish Street. And you will be monitored by closed-circuit television cameras.

Of course the underground systems of other cities have been used by terrorists in the past. The Basque bomb that killed Admiral Carraras had been planted in a Madrid manhole. Egyptian terrorists crawled through water pipes to attack British bases in the Suez Canal Zone in the early 1950s. But they did so in order to avoid a clearly defined physical obstruction, a guarded perimeter. No such perimeters exist in London (yet), and a terrorist is more likely to take to the Underground than to the underground.

# 9 Orphanage for Oddities

If the empire-building passions of the metropolitan authorities and statutory undertakers have stolen the limelight of subterranean London, not to be forgotten are London's lesser-known tunnels, tramways, artesian wells, crypts, undercrofts, cellars, 'caves', bonded warehouses and covered canals, and its animal kingdom of rats, eels, mice and frogs.

The most inexplicable and oldest burrowings of man in London are to be found in Greenwich Park. West of the Observatory is a series of man-made burial mounds, with tunnels running underneath them. Dug in the Bronze Age, they are still visible. The Danes used them in the eleventh century as a base for an attack on London.

Not far from Greenwich Park, beneath the old Woolwich Arsenal, is another system of tunnels, more intricate and more modern, extending from Thamesmead to Shooters Hill. These tunnels date from 1716, the year the Royal Artillery was founded and the Royal Arsenal built, and it was they who gave the Arsenal its nickname — 'the Warren' — still remembered in its approach road, Warren Lane. The Arsenal was extended, first by Sir John Vanburgh, then again in the nineteenth century, by which time much of Woolwich had become army property. There were the Royal Artillery Barracks – a classical facade a quarter of a mile long; the Royal Military Academy, known as 'the Shop'; and even the remains of the Prince of Wales' pagoda, the Rotunda, blown up by a gas explosion in St James's Park, then removed and repaired by the Royal Artillery for use as a museum. As Woolwich expanded outwards, so it expanded downwards, with the original tunnels of 'the Warren' strengthened, widened and lengthened. By the 1914-18 War, Woolwich Arsenal was employing 90,000 people and had its own underground railway. Now, abandoned as an arsenal, it is used as a book store by the British Library.

Another little-known complex of tunnels and vaults lies in Camden Town near the Roundhouse: the Camden Catacombs, owned by British Rail, who use them for storage. Built in the nineteenth century as stables for horses and for the pit ponies used to shunt railway wagons, the tunnels run under the Euston mainline, under the goods depot at Primrose Hill, beneath Gilbey's bonded warehouse on the Regent's Canal, under the Canal itself and under Camden Lock Market and Dingwall's Discotheque. Their route can be traced from the distinctive cast-iron grilles set at regular intervals into the road surface – originally the only source of light for the horses below.

The Regent's Canal itself has a place amongst the oddities under London. A little to the east of Camden Lock, the canal goes underground – first under the St Pancras mainline, then again just

*Opposite:*
*The Kingsway tram tunnel of 1908 is the only outward and visible sign of a subterranean tramway system which was proposed by Royal Commission but never adopted.*

*Below: The Camden Catacombs today.*

beyond Caledonian Road, from where it flows in a tunnel beneath Islington, emerging again just east of Upper Street near City Road Basin. The tunnel, built by Nash between 1812 and 1820, is a thousand feet long, seventeen and a half feet deep and nineteen and a half feet wide. Barges were originally propelled through the tunnel by navvies, who lay on their backs and pushed against the arched ceiling of the tunnel with their feet. By 1826 navvy-power had given way to steam-power, the barges being towed by a miniature steamboat.

'The passage of this mode has a truly tartarean aspect,' wrote Thomas Cromwell in his *Walks in Islington* (1835). 'The smoke, the fire, and the noise of the engine, uniting with the black gloom of the arch, the blackness of the water, the crashing of the vessels against the sides of the tunnel and each other, and the lurid light that glimmers beyond each distant extremity, form an aggregate of *infernalia* that must be witnessed to be adequately conceived.'

*The double lock on Regent's Canal, drawn by T H Shepherd, just before it goes underground under Islington. Nash's 1000-foot tunnel is in the background.*

King's Cross, through which the Regent's Canal meanders – between its two subterranean passageways – is catacombed by a whole maze of tunnels: a Post Office tunnel, the Circle and Metropolitan Line tunnels, the Victoria, Piccadilly and Northern Line tunnels, and the Fleet sewer. Add to those a whole network of British Rail tunnels, and the King's Cross substratum begins to look like a colander. The King's Cross tunnels are linked to the main line, through an opening that gradually rises from a siding at the station on the York Way side. Others were part of the original connection of the Metropolitan and Northern Lines; another started as Metropolitan stabling for trains and carriages and now extends as far as Farringdon Street, weaving between the Post Office's own railway and several sewers on the way, where it joins with another tunnel under Snow Hill to Blackfriars, and is soon to be reopened by British Rail to provide a direct link between King's Cross and Moorgate to the north and

Holborn Viaduct and Blackfriars to the south.

The Kingsway underpass qualifies for inclusion among the oddities because of its original role as tram tunnel. As the new street, Kingsway, was built, so the tunnel was excavated beneath it: just over half a mile long, it began under Waterloo Bridge as cut-and-cover, became deep-level under the Strand, and reverted to cut-and-cover under Kingsway, with a stairwell at Holborn, before finally rising into Theobald's Road. Its role was to link the south London tramways that spread out from the Embankment to the north London tramways that stretched out from Theobald's Road; it opened in 1908, to a fanfare of publicity. (Unsung, it was to close half a century later).

In 1931 its arched roof under the cut-and-cover was replaced by a steel roof high enough to accommodate London's new double-deckers. It was the heart of the London tram system until 5 July 1952, when London's last tram left Kingsway tram tunnel and rode off in the

*Kingsway underpass was converted out of the old Kingsway tram tunnel (see page 204).*

sunset to the scrap yard. In the 1970s, the Waterloo-to-Holborn section of the tunnel was converted into a traffic underpass, with a new approach from Waterloo Bridge. The section from Holborn to Theobald's Road remains empty, and the former tram station at Theobald's Road, with its white glazed tiles and empty poster sites, lies undisturbed and unused. Undisturbed, that is, except by the Greater London Council, who equipped it as an emergency headquarters, with a white caravan and 'portaloo', in order to be able to save London in the event of fire, flood, or acts of God.

The tram system that Kingsway served has its place in the annals of underground history, not only for the miles of tramway ducts still underneath London's pavements, but also for the subterranean tramway system that never was. The ducts – four-inch clay pipes embedded in concrete a few feet beneath the pavement, and marked by manhole covers every hundred yards or so – originally carried the power cables for the trams; they extend for hundreds of miles under London's streets. Now, after lying fallow for thirty years, a new use may be found for them: carrying cable television.

The trams themselves were destined to go underground, if the Royal Commission on London Traffic (sitting in the 1900s at the same time as horse-drawn trams were giving way to electrically-operated trams) had had its way. The Commission proposed a subterranean tramway system based on the points of the compass, with an east-west line running from Bayswater, under Oxford Street and Liverpool Street, to Aldgate, and a north-south line running from Holloway Road under Caledonian Road, King's Cross, Grays Inn Road and Blackfriars Bridge to Elephant and Castle. There were to be extensions to Victoria, Knightsbridge and London Docks. Considering that the scheme would virtually have duplicated the existing Underground network, it must rank as one of the most unnecessary extravaganzas ever proposed under London. Now the idea of subterranean tramways may be resurrected. There are plans for the National Bus Company to take over Marylebone Station, and to tarmac ten miles of its main line, through three tunnels, to the outskirts of London.

From subterranean tramways it is but a short step to pedestrian subways: the nearest our subterranean authorities have got to putting Londoners into pipes and treating them like all the other services. In general, subways are not popular with the public, possibly because of their lingering association with public lavatories, more because of their harbouring of muggers, rapists and criminals. Not surprisingly, the public go to great lengths and risks to avoid subways. A recent, seemingly unnecessary study showed that ninety per cent of pedestrians will not use a subway if it is as quick to cross on the surface, but local authorities will almost certainly continue to build subways as part of road widening and underpass schemes. Inevitably in the nineteenth century there were those who wanted to take the subway to its logical conclusion. Subterranean relief roads, rather like storm relief sewers, were proposed, which would carry not only pipes for gas and water, but also carts, wagons and the lower orders; leaving the surface free for carriages, omnibuses and people of consequence. The scheme was scotched by the Metropolitan Police, who feared that they would become a haven for muggers, and by advocates of fresh air, who in their turn feared that they would become a breeding-ground for pestilence and poisonous fumes.

Another suggestion in 1872 was John Keith's; he proposed to up-date Brunel by tunnelling a 'sub-riverian arcade' along the River bed in place of the projected Tower Bridge. Since then, proposals for underground shopping arcades have been made again and again. Peter Palumbo's Mansion House Square proposal is merely the latest in a long line. There have been a few half-hearted efforts, such as the Elephant and Castle shopping precinct, but London in the 1980s –

*Opposite:*
*John Evelyn's plan for a subterranean city to service London was given a slightly different form in the nineteenth century. The gas-lit streets would carry pipes, cables and heavy goods traffic. Like Evelyn's proposal, it never saw the light of day.*

METROPOLITAN TRAFFIC RELIEF.

unlike Paris in the 1970s – cannot afford such prestigious projects. There are times when we can be grateful for poverty.

Private tunnels and subways are a common enough feature of nineteenth-century department stores and office blocks. Generally they were designed to link buildings on either side of a street. The most famous of these runs diagonally under Brompton Road, connecting Harrods with its warehouse in Trevor Place. From this tunnel runs a network of smaller tunnels and cellars: Frosty Way, which leads to the deep freeze rooms; Wine Cellar Close, lined by thousands of bottles; and the Lock-Up, where retired Sweeneyman Frank Nichols and his fifty uniformed guards and twenty plain-clothes detectives detain Harrods' unsuccessful shoplifters. Harrods even has its own underground transport system – a fleet of silent, or semi-silent, green trolleys, electrically operated, which purr under Brompton Road much as the old Harrods delivery vans once did on the surface.

Harrods also has its own bore-hole, an artesian well. In this Harrods is not alone. Hundreds of buildings in London, including Dolphin Square, Kingsway telecommunication exchange, the Ministry of Defence, the Bank of England (which, incidentally, has its own underground railway and tunnel system under the City, taking notes and coins to the London clearing banks), and several large hotels, have their own bore-holes. Indeed, so prevalent are these artesian wells sunk under London that the level of water beneath the metropolis has sunk, and their efficacy is progressively reduced as a result. The three bore-holes sunk at the back of the National Gallery in 1847, to supply the Houses of Parliament, Whitehall, Millbank Prison and the fountains of Trafalgar Square were all dry by 1911. By the year 2011, the Harrods well will be dry. So will most of the other wells under London.

If wells are drying up all over London, crypts, cellars and especially their modern equivalent – underground car parks – abound. Amongst the least known of the crypts is that of the Carmelite monastery (whose monks had complained in the Middle Ages about the smell of the Fleet) to be found under the *News of the World* on Bouverie Street, between Fleet Street and the River. It was excavated in 1867 and used as a coal cellar for thirty years. In 1910 a Committee of the British Archaeological Society reported: 'The vaulted crypt is a gem of its kind, and dates probably from the latter half of the fourteenth century.'

Also in the City – on the other side of Fleet Street – under the Cheshire Cheese, is another cellar, once the vault of a monastery's northern gatehouse. The original Cheshire Cheese (burnt down in the Second World War) was built after the Great Fire, just over one hundred years after the dissolution of the monasteries. You can still see the lines of the vault's narrow, pointed arches under the pub today.

But by far the most interesting of London's non-ecclesiastical cellars

lies under Montagu House, once the site of Cardinal Wolsey's Whitehall Palace and now the Ministry of Defence: the Cardinal's wine cellar. It lies nineteen feet beneath the MOD, is sixty-four feet long, thirty-two feet wide, and twenty feet high. In 1947, when the government deepened its underground citadel beneath the ministry, the wine cellar – girded by steel and cushioned on mahogany blocks – was moved bodily on rollers, a quarter of an inch at a time, for forty-three and a half feet. The excavations were made, and in 1949 the cellar was restored to its original position by the same meticulous method. It is now open to the public once a month.

*Cardinal Wolsey's wine cellar, over 400 years old, was moved 43½ feet during subterranean extensions to the Ministry of Defence in 1947, then moved 43½ feet back.*

There are also innumerable ecclesiastical crypts under the City's churches. Some of these, beneath churches bombed in the Blitz – Austin Friars, St Mildred's Bread Street and St Stephen's Coleman Street – have completely disappeared. Others are well worth a visit. The largest and best-known lies under St Paul's Cathedral. But one of the most interesting is St Stephen's Walbrook. In the mid-1960s the Rector, the Rev Chad Varah, founder of the Samaritans, rediscovered it after it had been hidden for centuries. It had been used as a burial vault. The Rector cleared out the coffins and converted the crypt into the Samaritans' telephone operations room.

The Adelphi Arches are another series of fascinating cellars under London. They run forty feet down, under Robert Adam Street, from Charing Cross mainline station to the Savoy car park. Originally

*Right:*
The vaults of Gray's Inn Wine
Establishment at High
Holborn.

*Below:* The largest and best-
known of London's crypts lies
under St Paul's Cathedral.

wine cellars, the vaults below the gay night club 'Heaven Underneath the Arches' now serve other purposes.

Though many of London's finest mediaeval cellars were destroyed during the Second World War, the Norman crypt of St Bartholomew the Great in Smithfield and the Decorated crypt of St Etheldreda in Ely Place, with their columns and vaults, serve as a reminder of the mediaeval passion for building underground. One of the finest eighteenth-century vaults, untouched from the date it was built (unlike its church above, which was gutted by fire and has now been rebuilt as a replica), is Archer's St John's, Smith Square.

Probably the best-known of all London's cellars is the Chancery Lane Safe Deposit, opened in 1882, and patrolled for the first decades of its existence by para-military guards with sawn-off shotguns. Buried deep under Chancery Lane, it has held the private papers of Lloyd George and the public papers of the Spanish Republican Government. We will never know all that its 5000 safes have contained. But during the War, when the Safe Depository was bombed and flooded, safes whose owners could not be traced were opened up. Amongst them was a safe containing a pair of Edwardian frilly lace knickers. Attached to the knickers was a luggage label, on which was written: 'My life's undoing'.

The largest area of private enterprise underground in the last fifty years has, of course, been the building of countless basement and sub-basement car parks. The result of a planning requirement, first by the LCC and then by the GLC, that every new office should 'house' at least a proportion of its workers' cars, led in the 1960s and 1970s to a rash of underground car parks. The City abounds with them, but even

*Left:*
*The 450-place Bloomsbury Square car park was built seven storeys deep and with twin helical ramps to minimise damage to the trees in the square.*

London's parks have had their share: beneath Bowater House, and the enormous cut-and-cover car park built under Hyde Park as part of the Park Lane improvement scheme. Some of London's squares, too, have been turned into subterranean car parks – Cadogan, Cavendish and Finsbury Squares amongst them. All these were built by the cut-and-cover method; the number of trees cut down as a result caused a public outcry.

The Cavendish Square car park was particularly controversial, since it was privately owned, and had one of the finest collections of mature plane trees in London. The original landscape plans, designed to hide the entrances, air vents and stairways, was cut on grounds of cost. An earthbank and a moat were abandoned as too heavy for the car park roof. 'Londoners now are 300 car-parking spaces and an anti-clockwise roundabout to the good and one square to the worse, but so many opportunities have been lost,' commented *The Architects' Journal*, on 18 August 1971.

Perhaps the most extraordinary car park in a square, and the deepest in London, is the one built in the 1960s in Bloomsbury Square. A conventional subterranean car park would have destroyed most of the square's trees, so instead Camden Council built seven storeys downwards, taking up less than half the square. Helical ramps descend like a corkscrew down a concrete drum sixty feet deep. When it was proposed, its designer claimed that the 450-space car park would cause little damage to the square, preserve all the trees and be the first of many. No similar car park has been built, and a very unpleasant place it is. With hindsight, the GLC decided in the 1980s to restrict rather than encourage parking within buildings, so private car parking underground is less likely to be a major feature of the offices of the future.

Regrettably, the oddest of oddities under London are things that never happened. Some of these we have already encountered: Charles Pearson, John Martin and the lady who proposed a sewage system based on the spokes of a wheel, so that London's waste could be sold to farmers in little shops. With the utilisation of compressed air, even these were outpaced by one H J Leaning, who shot under London in a pneumatic tube. Leaning, whose lack of practicality was on a scale that deserves to be remembered by posterity with more than just a brace of initials, could be called the prophet of the pneumatic. Writing just after the First World War, he called for the spirit of ingenuity and imagination displayed in war to be mobilised in peace, and then went on to propound a vision so defiant of the laws of proportion and common sense as to be almost heroic. The Post Office has already led the way with pneumatic tubes, he enthused, let others follow. Beneath London there could be a great grid of pneumatic tubes, linking railway stations, shops, office blocks, hotels and residential districts. Why should pneumatic tubes be limited to four inches carrying letters in brass cylinders? Why not larger tubes, carrying consignments by the hundredweight? This, Leaning pointed out, would relieve London's traffic by reducing the number of taxis and delivery vehicles in the capital. Fortunately for London, and thanks to the opposition of a large number of sensible people, including taxicab drivers, Leaning was never able to put his ideas into practice, nor to take them to his logical conclusion – the transmission of people by pneumatic tubes. This was fortunate for Mr Leaning, and even more fortunate for Londoners, since a high proportion of his passengers would have died of the bends.

Hard evidence of what lies underneath London are the hundreds of thousands of manhole covers, grates, stop-cock covers, 'keyholes' and inspection chambers set in the pavements and roads. Already these covers and grates have been promoted from municipal scrap into industrial archaeology, and have even become subjects for brass rubbing. Over the years the raised pattern incorporated in the design to prevent people slipping on them has been worn silver-smooth by countless feet. Thus the familiar Tolkienesque 'ELF KING' on manhole covers is all that is left of the original letters and logo of 'SELF LOCKING PLATE'. These covers have a collective language of their own. Many are easy to recognise: Metropolitan Water Board, North Thames Gas, GPO, LEB. Others are less well known. AV signifies Air Valve, HV is Hydrant Valve, EV an Emptying Valve, SV a Sluice Valve and OSV an Outside Valve – the pear-shaped one outside your house.

Some of the manhole covers in our pavements are the last signposts left to London's imperial subterranean past. In North London there are covers stamped NR. Northern Railway? Non-returnable? No. The New River Company. And what about GLCC? No, it is nothing

to do with the Greater London Council. It stands for the old Gas Light and Coke Company. There are still Chelsea Water Company manhole covers to be found in west London and Lambeth Water Company ones in south London. Numerous manholes are marked with the logos of the old borough council electricity supply companies, and throughout central London there are the manhole covers marked METESCO (Metropolitan Electric Supply Company), CLESCO (Central London Electric Supply Company), CCESCO (Charing Cross Electric Supply Company), and LHP (London Hydraulic Power Company).

Down those manholes and through those grilles, whatever tunnels or tubes, pipes or sewers they lead to, run, crawl, slip the animals of London's underworld. Animal life has not declined under London; it flourishes. The debris of the city above finds its way through drains, gutters, pipes and shafts into the nether regions below, where a strange world of rats, fungi, algae, eels, mice and a hundred other forms of animal and vegetable life pursue their subterranean existence, leaving their imprint on life above in the form of plagues, pestilences and paranoia.

The most populous animal under London is the brown rat (*rattus norvegicus*). An immigrant from Russia in the eighteenth century, more fertile and ferocious than the native black rat, it soon dominated the underworld. In one winter alone, 1963-64, 650,000 brown rats were killed in London's sewers.

Londoners will be pleased to know that the largest population of rats lies under Westminster. They are believed to have arrived from Kensington, attracted by the wastes of West End restaurants, thus reversing the traditional east-to-west flow of empires. An extermination campaign by Westminster City Council ten years ago involved laying 3214 poisoned baits in Westminster's sewers, the exterminators working in gangs of three – one lifting the manhole, one preparing the bait and one placing it in a tube – laying a hundred baits a day. The campaign failed, and a new 'super-rat', resilient to all the poisons Westminster City Council could feed it with, emerged under our seat of government.

No one really knows the GLC's rat population, but there are estimated to be ten million rats living under London. Rat-killing provides an exciting diversion for flusher gangs in the sewers, who have been known to kill 200 in a day's shift. The renovation and relining of London's sewers is expected gradually to decrease the rat population; but if money cannot be found to finance the renovation, then the population will have increased to epidemic proportions by the end of the century. This fear of rats has stimulated new innovations in rat control. One problem is the tendency of rats to take only small samples of food, then returning to it some hours later, thus avoiding many poisons. Recent research at Sussex University and McMaster

University in Ontario has shown however that rat packs have 'leaders', who take small samples of food, return to the pack, who can then smell it, then lead the pack back to the food. Thus more efficient methods of rat control will soon be used whereby 'leaders' are fed slow-acting poisons, then used as an unconscious bait to lure the rest of the pack to it. A new method of control is the use of supersonic sound, which drives the rats mad, so that they rush around killing themselves against the walls of the sewer (additionally killing off the Pied Piper of Hamelin by giving his magic a rational explanation).

London's subterranean life, which includes hundreds of eels in our sewers, living, burrowing, and multiplying, is a constant reminder that London under London is not a museum. Although the greatest days of empire building underground may be over, inevitably new systems will be built. We can be certain that with any new systems will come new oddities. The prophets of recycling will dream of whole new sewer systems powered by wind and producing gas! H J Leaning is bound to stand up and suggest optic fibre cash dispensers in every home. After all, there is something of Charles Pearson, or the woman who wanted to open sewage shops, or H J Leaning, in all of us.

# 10 Subterranean Futures: The 80s, 90s and Beyond

The colonization of subterranean London did not stop in 1984 when this underview of the municipal netherworld was first published. Like a tree whose roots must extend downwards as its branches spread upwards, London's growth above ground has been matched by London's growth below ground.

## THE LONDON RING WATER MAIN

The biggest capital project under London in the last ten years has been the completion of the London Ring Water Main. Costing £250 million, the Ring Main has completely transformed the distribution of water in London.

Previously the bulk of London's water flowed eastwards from the Thames above Teddington, with a smaller southward flow into East London from the River Lea. It was inefficient, requiring a large number of small and uneconomic pumping stations, and the mains from the Thames were being used to their capacity. The Ring Main is based on a new principle: a fifty-mile tunnel (twice the length of the Channel Tunnel), the deepest under London, with a diameter of 7.5 ft, fed with water from tunnels linked via water treatment works to the reservoirs above Teddington, and making a continuous loop, with twelve shafts at different positions on the loop lifting water up into the pipe network just below the streets. One control centre at Hampton controls the entire system.

Most of the Ring Main has been built in clay, and to dig through the clay Thames Water bought three tunnel-boring machines, each costing over £1 million. Using circular cutters and periphery trimmers, the machines dispose of the debris down a conveyor belt to narrow gauge railway wagons. Behind the boring equipment hydraulic arms carried on the machine lift and position the pre-cast concrete segments as it moves along. Using this method the tunnelling teams have broken world records: completing a quarter of a mile of tunnel in five days. Only beneath Tooting Bec where the excavators hit water-bearing chalk and the tunnel flooded, did engineers encounter serious problems; here they had to artificially freeze the chalk and water, and bring in a new tunnelling machine, and Earth Pressure Balance Machine, which works on the Bentonite principle (see page 120), before continuing.

*The Ring Water Main bored beneath London at an average of 100 ft per day.*

Most of the twelve vertical shafts that bring water up from the Ring Main into the below-street distribution network are hidden, or lie unnoticed on Thames Water land. But two of them are driven past by thousands of motorists daily. Both Shepherd's Bush Roundabout and Park Lane Roundabout hide beneath them vast pump-out shafts.

Half the Ring Main's loop, the south-eastern semicircle running from Hampton, via Surbiton, Merton, Streatham, Brixton and Park Lane, to Hampstead, is in operation. The other half, the north-western semicircle, running from Hampton, via Brentford, Hammersmith and Kensington, to Hampstead, has already been excavated and will be in operation by 1995. Until then, while the final work is being completed, it remains dry.

It is a strange experience walking through a dry water main. You expect tidal waves at the end of the tunnel, while the perfectly regular pre-cast concrete segments, going on and on, suggest Freudian eternity. Transportation is difficult along the miles of tunnel now that the narrow gauge railway has been taken up, and engineers use bicycles to get from one section to another. Indeed, a Thames Water engineer can bicycle from Hampton to Hampstead without seeing daylight. (It takes about one-and-a-half hours.)

When the entire loop is filled and in operation, the Ring Main will supply half of London's water needs, moving nearly 300 million gallons per day – enough to fill the Albert Hall eight times.

*An Earth Pressure Balance Machine at work for Thames Water.*

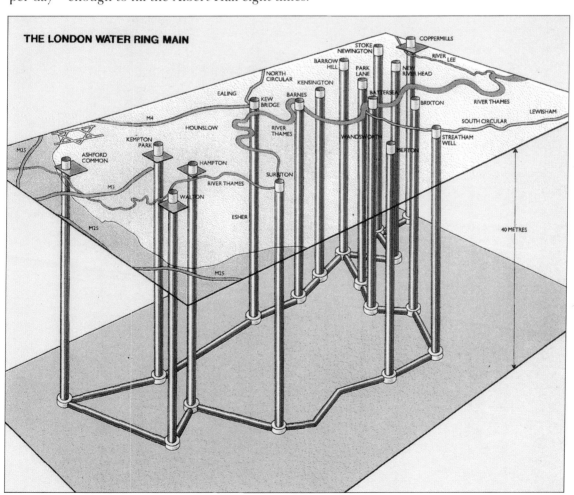

219

*The bicycle comes into its own in the Ring Water Main below London in the final stages of construction.*

## LEICESTER SQUARE ELECTRICITY SUBSTATION

While tunnellers were boring beneath the city to improve London's water supply, a gigantic, and virtually hidden, excavation was going on underneath Leicester Square to improve Central London's electricity supply.

The new subterranean electricity station, excavated in the early 1990s, took two years to build and goes down some forty feet beneath the Square.

Access is through a steel plate trap door at the Panton Street corner of Leicester Square. The station descends down three levels: at first level with an 'entrance hall' directly beneath the Square; a second level whose rooms are lined with transformers reducing the National Grid's 132,000 volts to the 405 and 240 volts required for the individual customer; and a third level containing the cables that are fed into it from a newly built tunnel running from London Electricity's substation at Duke Street near Grosvenor Square to Leicester Square.

Already it provides Leicester Square, Piccadilly, Covent Garden, Theatreland and the National Gallery with all its electricity; and already its operatives are obliged to lay down little saucers of rat poison in every corner of the station. Humans are not the only colonisers of underground London.

The Leicester Square substation is not the only new underground development involving electricity. Just as in the City and Docklands Mercury Communications have utilised 150 miles of cast iron pipes belonging to the old London Hydraulic Power Company to house their optical fibre cables (see page 190), so Citigen, the London-based energy company, is using old service ducts and the sides of underground car parks to spread a new cable network throughout the City, providing

*Completed in May 1991: silent, invisible and unmanned, this underground substation will supply the West End's electricity needs well into the future.*

office blocks with heat and power. From Citigen's generating station at 47–53 Charterhouse Street, powered by a combination of oil and natural gases, a new tunnel takes cables from Charterhouse Street, under Aldersgate Street, into the Barbican; and from Charterhouse Street and the Barbican they are distributed throughout the City.

If new water and electricity tunnels characterise the history of subterranean London in the 1980s and early 1990s, new railway tunnels will characterise the history of subterranean London in the middle and late 1990s. The last years of the century will see three new underground railway projects, five new twin tunnels under the Thames, and a major underground terminal for the Channel Tunnel railway. Already a new underground station has been built at the Angel costing £70 million and boasting the longest escalator in Europe.

In March 1988 the Government set up two transport studies: the Central London Rail Study and the East London Rail Study. The studies recommended:

1  an extension of the Jubilee Line from Green Park into Docklands, terminating at Stratford;
2  a high-speed 'Crossrail', similar to the Parisian RER, running west to

## NEW RAILWAY TUNNELS

*Map of the Jubilee Line extension from Green Park to Stratford promising to bring new life to Canary Wharf.*

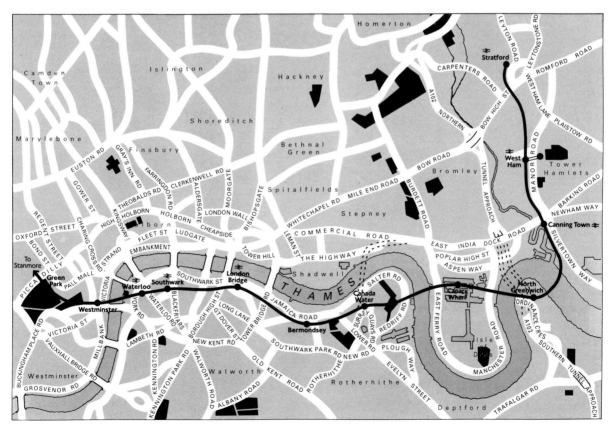

east from Aylesbury and Reading to Shenfield in Essex, with the Central London section from Paddington to Liverpool Street running underground;

3  an extension of the Docklands Light Railway west to Bank Station and south from the Isle of Dogs beneath the Thames to Greenwich and Lewisham.

**The Jubilee Line Extension:** The development of Docklands in the 1980s, and the almost total lack of underground transport in Southwark, Greenwich and Lewisham, subterranean London's Empty Quarter, made some sort of railway development in East London's Thames Corridor inevitable.

Docklands' largest developer, Olympia and York, proposed a new line running from Canary Wharf to Waterloo. Other suggestions were for a River Line and a Fleet Line. Finally in 1989 the Government decided that instead of a new line, a ten-mile extension would be built to the Jubilee Line, through Southwark, Docklands and North Greenwich, to Stratford, with four river crossings and twelve additional stations.

By then much of the major Docklands office developments, including Canary Wharf, was complete, but economic boom was turning into

*London Transport's Earth Pressure Balance Machine for excavating the Jubilee Line extension which will bore four new tunnels under the Thames.*

*A tunnel-cleaning train.*

deep recession. Property prices were falling. Brand new office blocks sat astride the wharfs and overlooked the waters absolutely empty. One property company even put full-size cardboard cut-outs of people against the windows, to alleviate the emptiness. Lack of transport discouraged firms from moving in, making the Isle of Dogs even emptier. Olympia and York's Chief Executive Michael Dennis told *Building Design* in October 1992 that potential tenants 'simply do not believe that the transport would be there on time. That more than anything else was the stumbling block for the success of Canary Wharf.'

In the March 1993 Budget the Jubilee Line Extension was given the final go-ahead, at a cost of £1.8 billion, some of the finance to be raised by private investment, the lion's share to be provided by the Government.

The line will run east from Green Park, through a vast new station at Westminster, under the Thames to Waterloo, along the South Bank, via Southwark, London Bridge and Bermondsey, to a new station at Canada Water. From there it will cross the River a second time to Canary Wharf, recross it to North Greenwich, then turn north, to make its fourth crossing, and continue through Canning Town and West Ham to Stratford.

To ensure that each of the new stations on the extension have their own unique identity, Italian architect Roland Paoletti, who worked on the creation of the Hong Kong Mass Transit Railway, has chosen different architects for each station.

'Instead of thinking how you decorate a station, think how you undecorate it,' Paoletti told his architects. 'Wherever you can, leave the civil works exposed, go for something simple and minimise the need for finishes.'

225

The two most adventurous of the new stations will be at Westminster and Canary Wharf. At Westminster the station will be designed by Michael Hopkins, beneath the new parliamentary annexe he has designed on the site of the present District and Circle Line station. The new station will be one gigantic box, bigger than the parliamentary annexe above it, with escalators weaving through cross-braces, like high-tech flying buttresses, from street level, to District and Circle Line level, to Jubilee level. To build the station, house the signalling equipment and the miles of cables and optical fibres, bore twin tunnels beneath the Thames, while keeping the District and Circle Line station open, will require skills closer to brain surgery than to underground engineering.

Canary Wharf is being designed by Norman Foster and Partners. The rectangle of water in West India Docks between Canary Wharf and Heron Quay will be dammed and drained, and the station will be built in the cut which will then be landscaped over. The two entrances to the station will be marked by two gigantic bubbles of multi-laminated safety glass, through which the passengers will descend down banks of escalators into a single continuous space lit by daylight through the bubbles. It will cost £60 million, and is expected to turn Canary Wharf into the third most busy interchange station in London.

Significantly, almost as much money is being spent on the less glamorous stations such as Bermondsey, North Greenwich and Canning Town, serving poor inner-city neighbourhoods, which has done much to win over local communities and soften suspicions about a line partly built with private capital. These new stations serving residential districts have changed the projected line 'from being a commuter drain linking the main interchange stations to Canary Wharf and the Isle of Dogs, to being a line that will allow local residential and working communities to profit from it as well,' said Simon Hughes, the local MP.

*The banks of escalators in Canary Wharf Station looking up to the glass entrance dome.*

*Opposite:*
*Diagram of the new prestigious Westminster Station showing the Jubilee Line below the existing District and Circle Line, with the projected Parliamentary building above.*

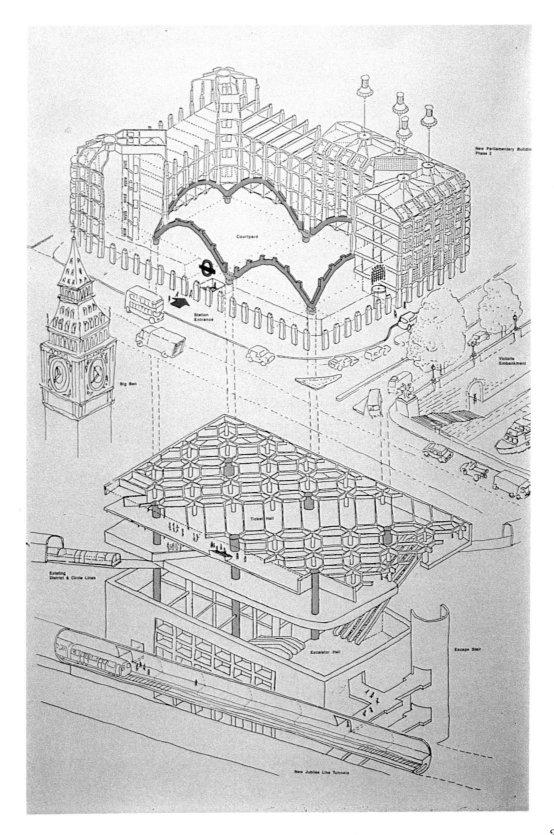

New Parliamentary Building
Phase 2

Courtyard

Station
Entrance

Big Ben

Victoria
Embankment

Ticket Hall

Existing
District & Circle Lines

Escalator Hall

Escape Stair

New Jubilee Line Tunnels

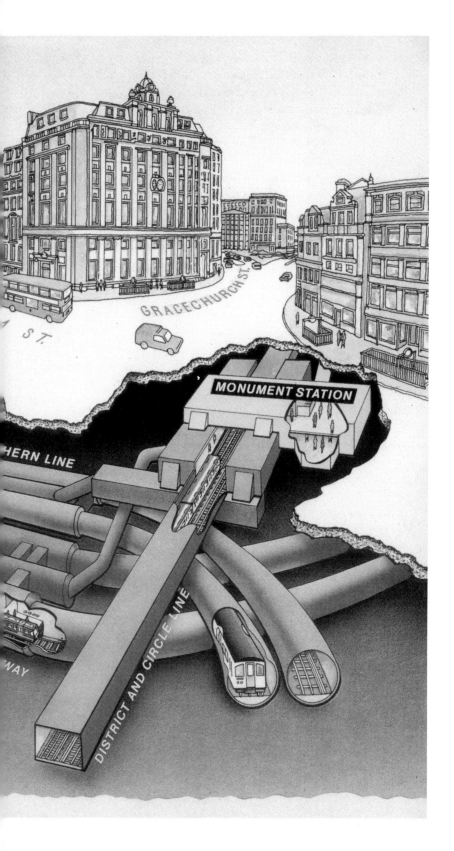

*A cross section of 'the Worm', the new combined Bank and Monument station.*

**CrossRail:** Another recommendation by the Central London Railway Study was that there should be a high-speed east–west line, linking suburban stations with central London. The result will be a new underground railway, running in twin tunnels from Paddington to Bethnal Green, bringing trains from Reading and Aylesbury in the west to Shenfield in the east.

From Paddington, where the line will descend underground into twin tunnels, trains will stop at Bond Street, Tottenham Court Road, Farringdon and Liverpool Street, before ascending to ground level and continuing through East London to Shenfield. The tunnels will be big: twenty feet in diameter, compared with the Victoria Line's thirteen feet; the stations will have high ceilings to offset feelings of claustrophobia among passengers; and they will be double-ended, with entries and exits at either ends of the platforms.

Excavating the tunnels and stations will yield some 1.5 million cubic metres of spoil, or approximately 16,000 London double-decker buses full of debris. The project is expected to cost £2 billion pounds and should be completed before the end of the century.

*Map of the proposed CrossRail, the underground section running from Paddington to Liverpool Street.*

*Opposite top:*
*CrossRail at Tottenham Court Road station.*

*Opposite bottom:*
*CrossRail at Bond Street station.*

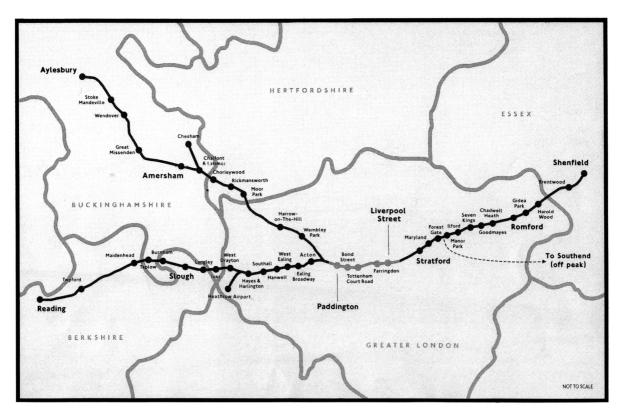

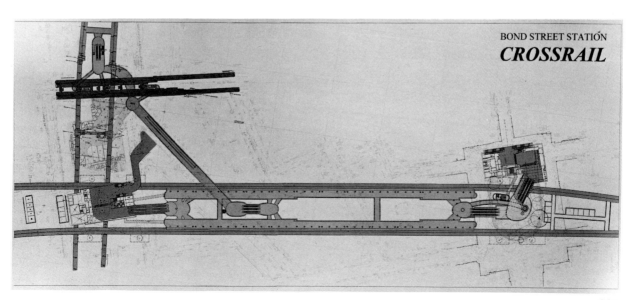

BOND STREET STATION
*CROSSRAIL*

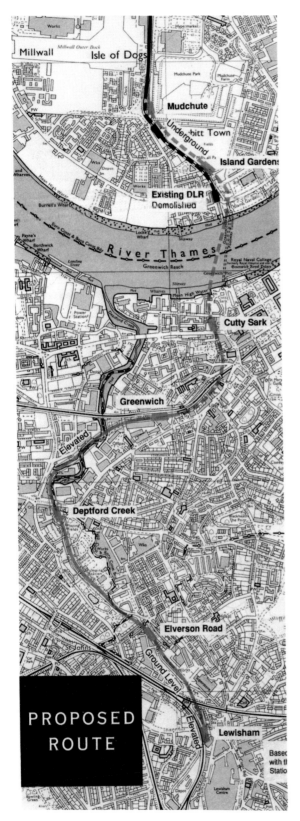

**The Docklands Light Railway Extension:** Since Docklands was developed in the 1980s the Docklands Light Railway has been the only rail link between Docklands and Central London. Already the railway has been extended to the west, dropping below ground into one-mile twin tunnels at Royal Mint Street and running to Bank Station, now so chock-a-block with underground infrastructure that it has been christened The Worm. Now it will be extended to the south, continuing from Island Gardens, where the present Docklands Light Railway terminates, beneath the Thames, and on through Greenwich to Lewisham.

The present Mudchute and Island Gardens stations will be demolished, replaced by a ground-level station at Mudchute and an underground station at Island Gardens. The line will drop down into twin tunnels at Mudchute, run beneath the Thames to a new underground station named Cutty Sark, then come up to surface level at Greenwich, continuing along the valley of the River Ravensbourne (see page 48) to Lewisham. Altogether the extension will cost £140 million.

In addition to these three railway projects, the King's Cross/St Pancras area – already one of the most overcrowded patches in subterranean London (even before the excavation of the new British Library's 70 ft deep basements) – will reverberate to new diggings excavating the proposed terminal for the Channel Tunnel railway, from which two new tunnels will be bored beneath London to take trains eastwards down the Thames Corridor into Kent.

*Map of the proposed south extension of the Docklands Light Railway running underground from Mudchute to Greenwich.*

# Bibliography

**Preface**

Fitter, R. S. R., *London's Natural History*, 1945
Hollingshead, John, *Underground London*, 1862

**1    The Underworld War**

Fitzgibbon, Constantine, *The Blitz*, 1957
Graves, Charles, *London Transport Carries On*, 1947
Hewison, Robert, *Under Siege: Literary Life in London 1939–45*, 1977
Moore, Henry, *Shelter Sketchbook*, 1940

**2    Smothered Streams and Strangled Rivers**

Aston, J., *The Fleet*, 1890
Barton, Nicholas, *The Lost Rivers of London*, 1992
Foord, A. S., *Springs, Streams and Spas of London*, 1910
Stow, John, *Survey of London* (originally 1600), 1980

**3    The Bowels of the Earth**

Balston, Thomas, *John Martin, His Life and Works*, 1947
Evelyn, Sir John, *Fumifugium*, 1661, reprinted 1933
Harrington, Sir John, *The Metamorphosis of Ajax: A New Discussion on a Stale Subject*, 1596
Jephson, Henry, *The Sanitary History of London*, 1907
Lambton, Lucinda, *Temples of Convenience*, 1987
Martin, John, *Metropolitan Improvement Plans*, 1842

**4    Patterns of Pipes**

*Hydraulic Power: A Review of the Services of the London Hydraulic Power Company*, 1964
Metropolitan Water Board, *London's Water Supply, 1903–1953*, 1953
Wylie, J. C., *The Wastes of Civilization*

**5    Tunnels Under the Thames**

Rolt, L. T. C., *Isambard Kingdom Brunel*, 1957
Pugsley, Sir Alfred, *The Works of Isambard Kingdom Brunel*, 1980
Lampe, David, *The Tunnel*, 1963

**6    Trains Underground**

Douglas, Hugh, *The Underground Story*, 1963
Jackson, Alan, and Croome, Desmond, *Rails through Clay*, 1962
Nock, O. S., *Underground Railways of the World*, 1973

**7    The Nerves of the City**

Hannah, Leslie, *Electricity Before Nationalisation*
—— *A Pioneer in Public Enterprise: the Central Electricity Board and the National Grid,
    1927–40*, Essays in Business History, Oxford, 1977

**8    The Defence of the City**

Ford, Ford Maddox, *Memories and Impressions*
Home Office, *The Protection of Your House Against Air Raid*, 1938
Haldane, J. B. S., *A R P*, 1938
Laurie, Peter, *Beneath the City Streets*, 1970, revised 1972
Webber, Philip (ed), *London After the Bomb*, 1982
Campbell, Duncan, *War Plan UK*, 1982

**9    Orphanage for Oddities**

Barker, Felix and Hyde, Ralph, *London as it Might Have Been*, 1982
Cromwell, Thomas, *Walks in Islington*, 1935
Harrison, Michael, *London Beneath the Pavement*, 1961

**10    Subterranean Futures**

Esther, Caplin, *London: The Underground City* (broadsheet), The Building Centre, 1992
Ostler, Tim, *Building Design*, 2 October 1992
Baillieu, Amanda, *Building Design*, 23 October 1992

# Gazetteer

**1 The Underworld War:** See **8.**

**2 Smothered Streams and Strangled Rivers:** Most of London's rivers can easily be walked in an afternoon. The simplest way to trace their routes has been suggested in the text. The most interesting of these buried rivers is the Fleet. It is also the longest. Nor should you neglect the various overground rivers: the Ravensbourne, the Lee, the Wandle and Beverley Brook. Their courses are clearly marked in the *A-Z*, and long stretches are flanked by tow-paths. Thames Water discourages visits to sewers constructed around underground rivers, such as the Fleet, the Tyburn, the Westbourne and the Effra, although historical societies can sometimes persuade the Board to allow a visit to their local underground river. Visits normally have to be confined to the summer.

**3 The Bowels of the Earth:** Individuals are not allowed to visit London's main sewers. Unlike the Parisian *égouts*, with their wrought-iron walkways, Bazalgette's sewers, with their rounded sides, are considered too dangerous for guided tours. Those with good reasons (authors of books on underground London, local societies) can often arrange a visit, but only in the summer. Officials of local societies should contact the Public Relations Office, Thames Water, Nugent House, Vastern Road, Reading, RG1 8DB (0734 593 364). Individuals who do not belong, or do not want to belong, to any society, should contact their local council, who can arrange visits to local sewers. Tours of Bazalgette's Abbey Mills Pumping Station are much easier to arrange. Thames Water has even produced a booklet for parties of schoolchildren. The embankment of the Northern Outfall Sewer, which runs from Hackney across the Lee, past Abbey Mills to Barking Creek, is now a public footpath. But be warned: it takes you through some of the ugliest industrial deserts in London.

**4 Patterns of Pipes:** Because of the threat of terrorism, the Greater London Council stopped the public from touring Bazalgette's pipe subways. But the old Grand Junction Waterworks at Kew Bridge, landmarked by its enormous water tower, has been turned into a museum, well worth visiting. Its relics of water history range from wooden water pipes to Cornish Beam Engines. (Kew Bridge Engine Trust, Kew Bridge or Gunnersbury Stations, open all week and Bank Holidays. For further details ring 081-568 4757.)

**5 Tunnels under the Thames:** You can still cross under the Thames in Brunel's tunnel. Metropolitan trains run through it over 100 times a day, and the lift at Rotherhithe Station rises and falls within the original shaft. Both Rotherhithe and Wapping stations have a series of illustrations posted on the platform telling the story of the tunnel. The Tower Subway, owned by the London Hydraulic Power Company – the only privately owned subway under the Thames –

is closed to visitors, but numerous other tunnels are open. Both the Greenwich and the Woolwich Foot Tunnels are worth walking through. Blackwall and Rotherhithe Road Tunnels are used by tens of thousands of vehicles each day. Of the two, Blackwall is the more interesting: travel from south London to north London and you will go through the original 1897 tunnel; travel from north London to south London and you will go through the modern 1967 tunnel.

**6   Trains Underground:** London's underground railways are easy to explore, as easy as buying a ticket. The oldest line – the Metropolitan – has the most interesting features. Stations from Edgware Road to Farringdon have at last been revamped and stripped down to their original Victorian bones. Visits to some of London's lost Underground stations can be arranged by local societies through the London Subterranean Survey Association. If you are doubtful where to end your explorations, try Covent Garden, where London Transport has its own museum, open daily 10am-6pm (for details ring 071-379 6344).

**7   The Nerves of the City:** Both London Electricity and British Telecom are nowadays reluctant to play host underground – tours of London Electricity's Thames tunnels, with their eighty-foot shafts, are considered too dangerous for the public, while tours of British Telecom's cable tunnels are considered too dangerous for British Telecom. Schools and societies can, however, arrange visits to the Post Office Underground Railway, although several weeks' advance notice is required. For details write to the Post Office Controller, Mail Rail, 148/164 Old Street, London EC1V 9HQ (071-250 2753).

**8   The Defence of the City:** Churchill's Subterranean War Cabinet Rooms underneath Whitehall are now open to the public (071-930 6961).

**9   Orphanage for Oddities:** Pleasure barges make regular journeys along the Regents Canal under Islington, although the canalside towpath, which runs from the zoo past Camden Lock, stops before the canal goes underground at Caledonian Road. Harrods Tunnel can be visited by shoplifters, crypts and the Chancery Lane Safe Deposit (now the London Silver Vaults) by all and sundry. Cardinal Wolsey's Wine Cellar in the Ministry of Defence is now open to the public (by appointment only 071-218 6015). Lastly, do not forget the Museum of London at the Barbican, which has a fascinating collection of relics from subterranean London.

# Index

Abbey, Mills Pumping Station, 73-5; Street, 47, 49
Abercrombie, Sir Patrick, 157
Abney Park Cemetery, 52
Acton, Assembly Rooms, 46; Station, 46; Wells, 46
Adam, Robert, 50
Adelaide Road, 39
Adison, Robert, 51
Admiralty, 195; Arch, 161
Aeolian Hall, 168
Albert Gate, 44
Albion Docks, 47, 92
Aldgate, 73, 142, 209; East, 162; High Street, 53
Aldwych extension, 11, 193, Station, 53, 73
Alexandra, Princess, 160
Alyndon, John de, 59
Amwell Springs, 86
Anderson, Sir John, 19
Angel, The, 129; Court, 29
Anne, Queen, 46
Antimephitic Company, 71
Archer, Thomas, 213
*Architects' Journal*, 214
Ardizzone, Edward, 14
Armstrong, Sir Thomas, 33
Arsenal Football Stadium, 52
Arundel Castle, 61
Ashford Common, 83
Askew Road, 46
Associated Electrical Industries, 185
Athens-Piraeus Railway, 145
Austin Friars, 211
Automatic Telephone & Electric Co, 185
Avenue Road, 39
Aybrook Street, 40, 43

Bagnigge Wells, 31; Road, 31
Bagster, Joseph, 96
Baker Street, 40, 129, 150, 161-2
Bakerloo Line, 13, 122, 150, 153-4, 159, 161
Baldwin, Stanley, 171
Balham, Hill, 75; Station, 12
Bank, of England, 29, 81, 141, 210; Station, 12, 149, 154, 228
Barbican, 191
Barking, Cable Tunnel, 9, 173-4; Creek, 75, 79, 174; Power Station, 127, 173; Road Bridge, 127
Barlow, Peter, 115, 117
Barnes, 91, 119, 121
Basevi, George, 44
'Bastion' Exchange, 119
Battersea, 52, 75, 181; Creek, 52; Dogs' Home, 52; Manor, 52; Power Station, 52, 121, 170, 173; Road, 102
Baynard Castle, 39
Baynard's Watering Place, 43
Bayswater, 26, 44, 73, 208; Brook – see Westbourne
Bazalgette, Sir Joseph, 71-3, 75-7, 79-81, 141-3, 165-6, 185, 191, 193, 196, 201
Beamish, Richard, 110-1
Beaton, Cecil, 21
Beaverbrook, Lord, 18
Becket, Thomas à, 23, 47, 49
Beckton, 58-9, 74-5, 79, 97-8, 173
Belair Park/House, 50

Belgrave Square, 44
Bell, Alexander Graham, 178
Belsize, Avenue, 39; Park Station, 19-20, 198
Bennett, Arnold, 137
Berkeley Square, 40-1
Bermondsey, 47, 49-50, 76-7, 173; Abbey, 47
Besant, Sir Walter, 50
Bessborough Gardens, 92
Bethlem Hospital, 27
Bethnal Green, 73, 186
Beulah Hill, 50-1
Beverley Brook, 23, 47, 52
Big Ben, 68
Bill of Sewers (1531), 60
Billy Brown of London Town, 12, 196-7
Binnie, Alexander, 125
Bishop's Bridge Road, 44
Bishopsgate, 186
Blackfriars, 30, 39, 75, 81, 192, 120, 122-3, 146, 166, 186, 197, 206-8
Black Hill, 31
Blackwall Tunnel, 125, 127
Blake, William, 44
Bloody Bridge, 44
Bloomsbury Square, 195, 213-4
Boadicea's Statue, 81
Bollo Brook, 46; Lane, 46
Bolton, Sir Francis, 90
Bond Street, 41, 64, 147, 161, 231
Boulton & Watt, 92, 94
Bouncing Bowler, Cousin Lane, 29
Bouverie Street, 210
Bow, 75, 100; Common, 68, 100
Bowater House, 214
Bramah, Joseph, 64-5, 93, 102, 127
Bramwell, Sir Frederick, 141
Branch Hill, 43
Brandt, Bill, 14, 20
Brewer, H W, 122
Brick Lane Gasworks, 97, 99
Bridewell, 35, 37, 39; Bridge, 35
Brigade of Guards, 198
Brinkley, J R, 185, 186
British, Archaeological Society, 210; Broadcasting Corporation, 189; Library, 198, 205; Museum, 7, 61, 166; Museum Station, 147, 162, 198; Rail, 122, 127, 149-50, 157, 205-6; Relay Wireless and Television, 189, 191; Telecom – see Post Office
Brixton, 50, 75, 157, 160-1; Road, 51
Broad Sanctuary, 18, 42; Street, 27; Broadway, 142
Brockwell Park, 50-1
Bromley, 47-8
Brompton, and Piccadilly Line – see Piccadilly Line; Cemetery, 45; Road, 73, 210; Road Station, 20, 150
Brook, Drive, 47; Green, 47; Mews, 44; Street, 41, 43
Brunel, Sir Marc, 105-8, 110, 113, 115, 121, 127, 174, 208; Isambard Kingdom, 110-111, 176
Buckingham, Duke of, 181; Palace, 41-2, 44, 158, 201-2
Bucklersbury, 29
*Builder, The*, 75
Bull, and Bush, Hampstead, 154, 198; Sir William, 46
Bulmar, Bevis, 85

Cable Street, 15, 124
Cade, Jack, 83

Cadogan Lane, 44, 215
Caledonian Road, 206, 208
Camberwell, 75
Camden, Catacombs, 205; Council, 214; Lock, 205; Town, 30-1, 91, 176, 205; Town Station, 19, 30, 198
Canada Docks, 47
Canary Wharf, 226
Cannon Street, 29, 75, 197; Station, 29
Carlton Club/House, 95
Caroline, Queen, 44
Carraras, Admiral, 203
Carthouse Street, 32
Castle, Barbara, 160
Cavendish Square, 159, 215
Central, Electricity Board, 171-3, 198; Electricity Generating Board, 19; Hill, 50; Line, 40, 73, 118, 147, 150, 153, 156, 172, 174, 197-8; London Electric Supply Company, 216; School of Speech and Drama, 39
Centre Point, 182
Chadwell Springs, 86
Chadwick, Edwin, 66, 68, 177
Champlain-Hudson Canal (USA), 106
Chancery Lane, Safe Deposit, 213; Station, 19, 162, 186, 198
Channel Tunnel, 145
Charles, Prince of Wales, 161
Charlton, 58
Charing Cross, Electric Supply Company, 216; -Euston- Hampstead Line – see Piccadilly Line; Loop, 122; Road, 81; Station, 120, 147, 161, 195-6; Clegg, 94, 96-7
Chartists, 100
Chaucer, Geoffrey, 49
Cheapside, 41, 59, 83, 140
Chelsea, 43, 153; Barracks, 45; Bridge, 45, 74; Bridge Road, 45; Creek, 46; Embankment, 74; Hospital, 88; Waterworks, 45, 88, 97, 216
Cheshire Cheese, Fleet Street, 210
Cheyne Walk, 74
Chiswick Park, 46-7
Christian Science, Third Church of, 41
Churchill, Gardens Estate, 122; Winston, 18-20, 198-9
Circle Line, 45, 142, 145-8, 174, 206
'Citadel' Exchange, 123, 186, 199
City, and South London Line – see Northern Line; Ditch, 28, 53; of London Corporation, 132-3; Ordinance, 28; Road, 27, 29, 92, 163, 197, 206
Clapham, Common Station, 19-20, 52, 196; High Street, 75; Junction, 52; North Station, 19, 57; Road, 51; South Station, 19, 198
Clapton, 52
Clayton, Rev John, 94
Clegg, Samuel, 94, 96-7
Clerkenwell, 26, 30, 32, 35, 39, 86, 140; Prison, 102; Road, 73; Tunnel, 129
Clissold Park, 52
Cliveden Place, 44
Coldharbour Lane, 50
Colombo House, 123, 186, 187
Commercial, Gas Company, 97, 100; Road, 15, 69
Commissioners of Sewers, 60, 62-3, 96, 100
Common Council, Acts of, 62
Consolidated Commission of Sewers, 66
Cooke, William Fothergill, 175-6
Coppermills, 83, 91

Cornhill, 84
Cornish Beam Engine, 75, 90
Counter's Creek, 23, 45-6, 74
Cousin Lane, 29
Covent Garden, 161; Exchange, 186, 187
Cowdray, Lord, 125
Cox, Graham, 79
Cox's Bridge ('Cokkesbougge'), 52
Cranbourne, River, 23, 53; Viscount, 53
Crapper, Thomas, 65
Cremorne Gardens, 96
Cricklewood, 195
Cripplegate, 84
Croll, Alexander Angus, 99-100
Crosby, Anthony, 37-9
Crossness, 77
CrossRail, 230
Crouch Hill, 52
Croydon, 157
Croxted Road, 50
Crystal, Palace, 141; Way, 140
Cubitt, Street, 184; Thomas, 44-5
Cummings, Alexander, 64
Cunliffe-Lister, Philip, 170-1
Curtain Road, 27, 97, 102
'Cutty Sark', 125

Daily, Courant, 32; Express, 152-3, 199;
   Telegraph, 139
Dalrymple-Hay, 120, 149, 181
Dalton, John, 94
Davies, Mickey, 15
Davisville Road, 46
Davy, Edward, 176; Sir Humphrey, 96
Dawes Road, 74
Decca Records, Kilburn, 43
Denmark Hill, 49
Denton, Rev William, 131, 139, 154
Deptford, 48; Power Station, 124, 169, 173;
   Pumping Station, 75-6; Tunnel, 173
Dickens, Charles, 49, 66
Dingwall's Discotheque, 205
Disraeli, Benjamin, 44, 66
District Line, 45, 141-5, 147-8, 152-3,
   157, 193
Docklands Light Railway, 232
Dodd, Ralph, 105
Dollis Hill, 18, 195
'Dolphin', 88; Square, 122, 210
'Donseg', 121
Dorchester Hotel, 21; Road, 43
Doré, Gustave, 100, 105, 130, 139
Dover Street, 47; Station, 20
Dowgate, 29
Down Street Station, 20
Drayton Park, 73
Dublo-Hornby, 181
Duke of York Steps, 161
Dulwich, 23, 50
Dundonald, Lord, 127
Dunstan, Archbishop, 39
Dutch and Rhenish Railway, 144

Earl's, Court, 45, 92, 129, 142, 154,
   156; Sluice, 47, 49-50, 69
East, Ham, 74-5; London Railway,
   115; London Waterworks, 88
Ebury Bridge Road, 45
Edgar, King, 39
Edgware Road, 73, 146-7, 182
Edison, Thomas, 169
Edward I, 29, 83; II, 29; IV, 53; VII
   (Prince of Wales), 76, 125, 127, 149
Edward and Edna, 172
Eel Brook Common, 45

Effra, River, 19, 23, 47, 50-2, 69, 75;
   Sewer, 75
Electra House, 184
Electric, Supply Bill, 171;
   Telegraph Company, 177
Elephant & Castle, 47, 176, 184, 208
Elgin, Avenue, 43; Marbles, 182, 193
Elizabeth, I, 50, 60-1; II, 159
Elliott, Sir John, 157-8
Ely Place, 213
Embankment, 71, 74, 81, 96, 122, 142-3,
   166-7, 193, 201, 207; Gardens, 45
English Illustrated Magazine, 146
Epstein, Jacob, 156
Equitable Gas Company, 42, 97-8
Erith Marshes, 76
Euston, Road, 73, 92, 135, 137, 150;
   Square, 133, 146; Station, 131, 157,
   159, 176, 179, 181, 184, 205
Evans, Admiral Sir Edward, 18
Evelyn, John, 62-4, 66, 169, 191, 208
Eversholt Street Post Office, 179, 181

Faggeswell Brook, 32
Falcon, Brook, 23, 47, 52; Grove, 52;
   Park, 52
Falstaff, Sir John, 32
Faraday, House Exchange, 18, 123,
   184, 186, 187; Michael, 100, 166
Farringdon, Road, 31-2, 182; Station,
   12, 131, 133, 138; Street, 33-4, 137
Fawkes, Guy, 201-2
Fenchurch Street, 53
Fenians, 101, 193, 195
Ferranti, Sebastian de, 168-70, 173
Ferry Approach, 127
Festival of Britain, 198
Finborough Road, 45
Finchley Road, 43
Finsbury, 195; Park, 88, 150, 157-8;
   Pavement, 27; Square, 214
Fire of London, 63-4, 84, 210
Fish Lane, 67
Fitter, R S R, 8
Fitzjohn's Avenue, 39
Fitzstephens, William, 23, 28
Five Fields, 44, 142
Fleet, Bridge, 32; Canal – see New
   Canal; Lane, 33; Line, 120; Prison,
   34; River, 23, 26, 30-9, 43, 49, 50,
   53, 64, 72-3, 81-3, 85-6, 129, 131,
   135, 137, 159, 182, 184, 193, 206;
   Street, 37, 39, 63, 161, 210
Folly Ditch, 49
Forbes, James Staats, 144-6
Ford, Ford Madox, 195
Forest Hill, 47
Forster, E M, 21
'Fortress', 186, 199
Foster, Arthur, 119
Fowler, Sir John, 132
Frankenstein, 96
Freston Road, 45
Frith, Richard, 53
Frognal Lane, 43
Fulham, 47, 74; Gas Works, 46, 96-7;
   Road, 45

Gaiety Theatre, 166
Galbraith, William Lyle, 98
Galleon's Reach, 97
Gants Hill, 197
Gardiner, Clive, 156
Garrick Street, 81
Gas, Light and Coke Company, 82, 94,

95, 96-8, 100, 102-3, 166-7, 216
General, Electric, 185; Strike, 182
General Electricity Review, 172
Geological Museum, 8, 18, 20
George II, 44; IV (Prince of Wales), 96,
   102; V, 193
Gerrard Street Post Office, 186
Gilbey family, 205
Gillespie Road, 52
Gladstone, William, 177
Gloucester, Place, 40; Terrace, 44
Godwyn, 43
Golden Lane Brewery Group, 97
Golders Green, 7, 154
Goldhawk Road, 46
Goodge Street Station, 19-20, 147, 198
Gower Street Station, 146, 195
Gracechurch Street, 53
Graham & Green, 96
Grand, Junction Water Company, 88,
   90; Union Canal, 42-5, 69, 84, 92,
   141, 166, 197, 205-6
Graveney, River, 47, 52
Gravesend, 105, 117
Gravett, William, 110
Gray's Inn, Road, 31, 186, 208; Wine
   Establishment, 212
Great, Central Gas Consumers'
   Company, 100; Conduit, 41, 83;
   Exhibition, 97; Northern Railway,
   132, 150, 153; Northern
   Underground Railway – see
   Piccadilly Line; Ormond Street, 84;
   Railway of Canada, 144; Smith
   Street, 18, 42; Stink, 66-7, 77;
   Victorian Way, 140-1; Western
   Hotel, 142; Western Railway, 132,
   176
Greater London, Council, 68, 93, 191,
   200, 209, 213-4; Council Economic
   Policy Planning Group, 191; Plan, 157
Greathead, James, 115-21, 123-4, 148,
   165; Shield, 7, 115-6, 119
Green, Finger, 88; Lanes, 88; Park, 41,
   159, 161; Walk, 47
Greenwich, 47-8, 97, 117, 124, 205;
   Foot Tunnel, 124-5, 127; High Road, 75
Grey, Lord, 33
Grosvenor Canal, 45; Gallery, 168-9;
   Hill, 41; Road, 74
Gunn Gwennet, W, 156
Gurney, Samuel, 68

Haca, 52
Hackney, 52, 73, 172; Brook, 52-3, 73;
   Downs, 52; Road, 27
Hainault, 153
Halcrow, Sir William, 83, 121, 158,
   160, 184, 186, 199
Hall, Sir Benjamin, 68
Hammersmith, 46-7, 69, 73, 121, 175;
   Bridge, 47, 121; Road, 47; Station, 47
Hampstead, 7, 23, 26, 31, 39, 44, 73,
   154, 202; Fair, 156; Heath, 43, 153-4,
   198; High Street, 153; Ponds, 30,
   85-6; Road, 150; Theatre, 39; Wells, 23
Hampton, 83, 91; Court, 67
Hanger Lane, 46
Hannah, Leslie, 170
Harewood, Earl of, 96
Harington, Sir John, 60-1
Harland Road, 45
Harper, Lord Mayor, 84
Harrington, Lord, 44
Harris, 'Bumper', 156

Harrisson, Tom, 15, 21
Harrods, 181, 210
Harrow, Air Ministry Citadel, 195;
    Road, 45
Hassall, John, 156
Hatfield House, 61
Hatton Garden, 186
Haverstock Hill, 30, 39
Hawkins, S T, 57
Hawksmoor, Nicholas, 149
Hawley Road, 30
Hawthorne, Nathaniel, 115
Hay Hill, 41
Hazard Bridge, 51
Heath Street, 43
Heathrow Airport, 161
Henry I, 43; III, 59-60, 116; VIII, 60
Hermit Place, 43
Herne Hill, 50-1, 75
Heyden, Sir Christopher, 33
Highbury, 52, 73, 84, 158; Place, 84
Highgate, 23; Cemetery, 52; Ponds,
    30-1, 85; Road, 30, 73; Wood
    Telephone Exchange, 187
High, Holborn, 33, 186; Holborn Post
    Office, 182; Holborn Telephone
    Exchange – see Kingsway; Street
    Kensington Station, 145
'Hildaburna', 52
Hoffman & Will, 71
Hogarth, William, 35
Holborn, 81, 83, 175, 186, 199; River
    – see Fleet; Station, 18, 198;
    Viaduct, 33, 53, 166-7, 179, 207
'Hole in the Ground', 18, 194
Hollingshead, John, 9, 40-3, 86, 133
Holloway Road, 73, 208
Holywell, 23, 26
Honor Oak, 91
Hopper Closet, 64-5
Horder, Lord, 18
Horseferry Road, 18, 97, 100, 102-3
Horseguards Parade, 195
Houndsditch Telephone Exchange, 186
Hounslow West, 162
Hoxton, 27
Hudson Tunnel (New York), 125
Hughes, Thomas, MP, 140
Hungerford Bridge, 71, 81, 122-3, 197
Hurlingham, 96
Hyde Park, 42-4, 141, 214
Hythe (Hampshire), 189

Iceland Road, 53
Illustrated London News, 97, 102, 181
Imperial War Museum, 47
Independent Gas Company, 97-8
Ingersoll, Ralph, 21
Institute, of Civil Engineers, 71-2;
    of Mechanical Engineers, 141
Ironmonger Lane, 59
Island Gardens, 124
Isle of Dogs, 124
Isledon Road, 52
Islington, 26-7, 73, 88, 206

Jablochkoff, Paul, 166-7
Jack Straw's Castle, 43, 154
Jacob's Island, 49
Jamaica Road, 49, 124
Jeanette Cochrane Theatre, 200
Jefferson, Dr Horace, 90
Jennings, Humphrey, 15
Johnson, John, 106
Johnston, Edward, 156-7

Joint Electricity Authorities, 170
Joinville (France), 94
Jonson, Ben, 29-30, 33
Jubilee Line, 120-1, 157, 161, 163, 224

Kansas City (USA), 185
Keith, John, 208
Kelfield Gardens, 45
Kelston, 60
Kempton Park, 83
Kennington, 50-1
Kensal Green, 45, 73; Cemetery, 94
Kensington, 73, 91, 150, 197; Lord, 45
Kent Waterworks, 88
Kentish Town, 73, 99
Kew Bridge Engine Museum, 90
Kilbourn, River, 43
Kilburn, 43-4, 73; High Road, 43; Park
    Road, 43; Priory, 43
Kinnear Moodie, 119
King Edward Building (GPO), 182-4
King William Street, 149;
    Station/Tunnel, 9, 11, 123, 148-9, 162
King's Cross, 30, 39, 73, 135, 176-7,
    184, 206, 208; Road, 31; Station, 12,
    52, 129, 131, 137-8, 146, 150, 157,
    158, 197, 206
King's Road, 44 – 5, 74; Scholar's Pond
    – see Tyburn
Kingsway, Telephone Exchange, 186,
    197-8, 210; Tram Tunnel, 200, 207-8
Knight, Dame Laura, 156
Knightsbridge, 44, 170, 208
Knight's Bridge, 44; Hill, 47, 50
Knockshinnoch (Ireland), 120

Lacey, Henry, Earl of Lincoln, 32
Lacon House, 199
Ladbroke Grove, 45
Lamb, Sir William, 84
Lambeth, 47, 50, 52, 90, 92, 140;
    Road, 47; Waterworks, 88, 90, 216
Lamb's Conduit Street, 84
Lamson pneumatic tubes, 18
Lancaster Gate, 44
Langbourne, River, 23, 26, 53
Lay, Samuel, 96
Lea, Bridge Waterworks, 88; River,
    52-3, 73, 75, 83, 91
Leaning, H J, 214-5, 217
Lear, Edward, 105, 113
Leathersellers' Hall, 85
Leicester Square, 53, 222
Leinster Gardens, 132
Lewisham, 161
Leytonstone, 197
Lime Street (Manchester), 175-6
Limehouse, 68, 93, 124, 176
Lincoln's Inn Field, 195
Lindsay, Sir Coutts, 168 – 70
Little, Carpenter, 108; Conduit, 83, 85
Liverpool Street, 27, 208; Station, 12,
    181, 186
Lloyd George, David, 213
Lockwood, 91
Lombard Street, 53, 84
London, and North-Western Railway,
    144; Bridge, 50, 59, 64, 85, 88, 106,
    123, 149, 166, 184; Bridge
    Waterworks, 85; Chatham and Dover
    Railway, 144-5; College of Fashion,
    27; County Council, 68, 91, 124-5,
    127, 147, 170, 179, 195, 213;
    -Croydon-Epsom Atmospheric
    Railway, 141; District Telegraph

Company, 177; Docks, 92; Electricity
    Board, 127, 165-6, 173, 215;
    Electricity Supply Corporation,
    168-70; Fever Hospital, 90; Gas
    Company, 97; Hydraulic Power
    Company, 92-94, 117-8, 216;
    Liverpool and Manchester Railway,
    175; Magazine 125; Manchester
    Railway, 176; Military District
    Command, 198; Passenger Transport
    Board, 120 – 1, 154, 156; Redivivum,
    63; Spy, 34 – 35; Transport, 129, 154,
    157, 165, 172-4, 181, 184, 191,
    196-8; Wall, 17-8, 59, 182, 186
Lords Station, 162
Lots Road, 45-6, 153
Lowndes Square, 44
Ludgate Circus, 39; Hill, 130
Lyndhurst Road, 39

Madge, Charles, 15
Maida Vale, 43
Manchester, Athenaeum, 144;
    Sheffield & Lincolnshire Railway, 144
Manners, Lord John, 178
Mansion House, 81, 150, 166, 208
Mapleson, Col J H, 193
Marble Arch Station, 12, 118, 156
Mare Street, 52
Marlborough Road Station, 162
Marshall, Charles, 175
Martin, John, 68-9, 71, 214
Marylebone, Lane, 40; Street, 208
Mass Observation, 15-17, 21
Mayfair, 40
Mayhew, Henry, 66, 68, 131, 140
McKnight Kauffer, 156
Mercury cables, 191
Mere, William & Adam, 60
Merton, Abbey, 51, 91; Bridge, 51
Metropolis Water Act (1852), 90
Metropolitan, Board of Works, 68,
    71-2, 91, 166-7, 170; Commission of
    Sewers, 71; Electric Supply
    Company, 216; Line, 31, 40, 47, 115,
    130-147, 150, 152-4, 156, 158, 162,
    206; Public Health Division, 77;
    Water Board, 91, 197, 215
MI5 Building, 18, 41
Mickey's Shelter, 15
Middle Lane, 47
Middleton, Hugh, 86-7
Millais, Sir John, 132
Millbank, 42, 69, 74; Prison, 97, 210
Mill Pond, 49
Millstream Road, 49
Millwall Docks, 173
Ministry of Defence, 196, 198-9, 210-1
Mithras, 29
Monmouth Rebellion, 33
Montagu House, 196, 210
Monthly Magazine, 95
Monument Station, 149, 228
Moore, Henry, 11-14, 16, 20
Moorfields, 28-9
Moorgate, 27, 150, 199, 206; Exchange,
    186
Moris, Peter, 85
Morning, Chronicle, 49; Lane, 52-3
Mornington Crescent Post Office, 184
Morrison, Herbert, 19, 170, 172
Morse, Samuel, 176
Mosley, William, 140
Mount Pleasant, 31, 135, 182-4
Munich Crisis, 184, 196

Murdock, William, 92, 94

Nagpore (India), 127
Napoleon, 96
Nash, John, 206
National, Bus Company, 208; Gallery,
    210; Grid, 165-6, 169, 171-3; Opera
    House, 193, 195; Safe Deposit
    Company, 27; Telephone Company,
    178-9
Neasden, 7
Neave, Airey, 202
Neckinger, River, 23, 47, 49-50;
    Wharf, 47
'Nellie 1', 19
Neva, River, 106
New, Bond Street, 168;
    Bridge Street, 39; Canal, 33-4, 37,
    45; Cavendish Street, 202; Covent
    Garden, 52; Cross, 75, 120, 164;
    Kent Road, 47; River, 85-8, 215;
    Patriotic Imperial & National Light
    & Heat Co, 95; Scotland Yard (new),
    93. 201; Scotland Yard (old), 42,
    193; Statesman, 187
Newcastle Lane, 33
Newgate Street, 172
Newman Street Post Office, 186
News of the World, 210
Nichols, Frank, 210
Nicolson, Harold, 15
Night, 156
Nine Elms, 52, 100, 102
Nock, O S, 144-5, 153
Nollet, Abbé, 166, 175
Norfolk Road, 39
North, Audley Street, 41; End, 154; Sea
    gas, 103; Thames Gas, 103, 215;
    Western Railway, 176
Northern Line, 119, 122-3, 148-50,
    153-4, 157-8, 206
Northumberland Avenue, 199
Norwood, 50; Cemetery, 50, 100
Notting Hill, 140

Oak Hill, 43
Offa's Charter, 42
Old, Oak Common, 46; Ford, 73, 77;
    Kent Road, 49, 76, 173; Street, 73
Oldbourne – see Fleet
Oliver Twist, 49
Olympia, 45
Ordnance Hill, 39
Orwell, George, 191
Osborne, Mr, 176
Osterley, 162
Oval Station, 19, 51
Oxford, 67, 78; Circus Station, 81, 140,
    158-9; Countess of, 45; Street, 40 – 1,
    71, 73, 81, 83, 182, 208

Paddenswick Road, 46
Paddington, 43, 132, 174. 187; Post
    Office, 182-4, 187; Station, 44, 131-3,
    135, 138, 140, 142, 176, 183
'Paddock', 18, 194-5
Page, Thomas, 113
Painter, 108
Palace Street, 42
Pall Mall, 95
Palmerston, Lord, 41, 137
Palumbo, Peter, 208
Pancras Way (Wash), 30
Paris, 94; Metro, 129, 148, 162-3
Park, Lane, 214; Royal, 162; Tower
    Sheraton, 44

Parliament, Houses of, 61, 67-8, 71, 74,
    81, 100-1, 140, 150, 193, 199, 201-2,
    210; Square, 42
Parr's Ditch, 47
Paxton, Sir Joseph, 140-1
Pearson, Charles, 99-100, 130-2, 137,
    139, 147, 214, 217
Peck, River, 69
Peckham, 49, 75
Pen, Sir William, 60
Pentonville Road, 73, 92
Pepys, Samuel, 60, 64
Père Lachaise Cemetery (Paris), 84
Peter, Robinson, 159; Street Gasworks,
    96-7; the Great, 169
Petty France, 42
Philips Ltd, 189
Phillips, John Orwell. 98, 100
Piccadilly, 41, 73, 81-2, 129, 150;
    Circus Station, 154, 159; Line, 150,
    153-4, 156, 158, 161, 193, 198, 206
Pick, Frank, 156-7
Pickwick, Samuel, 30
Pimlico, 45, 69, 121, 160
Pincher, Chapman, 199
Pinks, William, 33, 37
Piratin, Phil, 21
Plague, The, 43
Plaistow, 74-5
Plessey, 185, 197
Plumstead, 58-9, 76
Pneumatic Despatch Company, 181
Poe, Edgar Allan, 44
Political and Economic Planning, 157
Pope, Alexander, 30, 35, 37
Portsea Hall, 44
Post Office, 81, 121, 123, 165, 174-91,
    197-8, 199, 202, 206, 214-5;
    Pneumatic Railway, 179, 181;
    Railway, 121, 158, 175, 177, 181-4,
    189, 193; Station, 172, 198; Tower,
    186
Poultry, 29
Praed Street Station, 195
Price, John, 118-9
Priestley, Robert L Ltd, 120
Primrose Hill, 39, 96, 205
Prince Albert Road, 39
Prioress Street, 47
Prolock, Mr Justice, 178
Prologue (Chaucer), 49-50
Pudding Lane, 63
Punch, 88, 131-2, 141; Tavern, Fleet
    Street, 37; Tavern, Kilburn, 43
Putney, 75
Pye Ltd, 185

Quarterly Review, 177
Queensway, 199
Queen Victoria Street, 81

Radio Rentals, 189
Railton Road, 50
Railway Times, 176
Raleigh, Sir Walter, 50; House, 50
'Rampart', 123, 199
Ram, Thomas atte, 29
Ranelagh Gardens, 45
Ranleigh Sewer, 43
Ravensbourne, River, 23, 47-8
Ravenscourt, Gardens, 47; Park, 46, 73
Rediffusion Ltd, 189, 191
Redington Gardens, 43
Red Lion Square, 186
Red Lion, Turnmill Street, 32

Reed, Eric, 77, 79, 91
Regent Street, 81
Regent's Canal – see Grand Union
    Canal; Park, 40, 99, 170, 176, 197. 202
Ricardo, John Lewis, 177
Richardson, 111
Richmond, 91; Park, 156; Park, 47
Riley, Francis, 110
Ring Water Main, 218
Riverside Studios, 47, 121
Riversdale Road, 52
Robinson, William, 52
Ronalds, Francis, 175
Rosamund's Pond, 41-2
Rosebery Avenue, 86
Rose Tavern, Turnmill Street, 31
Rothschild, 93, 191
Rotherhithe, 47, 49, 69, 92, 123; New
    Road, 50; Road Tunnel, 92, 123-4,
    207; Station, 50, 105-6, 112, 115,
    123-4
Rotterdam Sub-Aqua Railway,
Rotunda, (Horseferry Road), 18, 97,
    199; Woolwich, 205
Route 'C' – see Victoria Line
Royal, Commission on London Traffic,
    208; Crescent, 45; Dockyard, 169
Ruegg, Henry, 96
Rush Common, 50
Russell, James, 82; Square, 182, 195
Ruston-Bucyrus, 19

Sabine, Ernest, 61-2
Sadlers' Wells, 96
Saffron Hill, 31
Saint, Agnes' Well, 23; Ambans, 67;
    Anne's Road, 45; Bartholomew the
    Great, Smithfield, 213; Bride's Well,
    23; Chad's Well, 23; Clement's
    Well, 26; Etheldreda, Ely Place, 213;
    George's Steps, 50; James's Park,
    41-2, 146, 156; John family, 52;
    John's, Smith Square, 213; John's
    Wood Chapel, 40; Katharine's
    Docks, 45, 93, 106, 197; Margaret's,
    Lothbury, 29; Mark's, Hennington,
    51; Martin's-le-Grand, 176, 179, 181,
    184; Mary's, Stamford Brook, 46;
    Mary's Station, 50; Mary
    Woolnoth, 12, 53, 149; Mildred's,
    Bread Street, 211; Pancras, 99, 131,
    203; Pancras Wells, 23; Paul's, 19,
    84-5, 90, 176, 181-2, 199, 212;
    Stephen's, Coleman Street, 211;
    Stephen's Walbrook, 29, 211;
    Thomas' Hospital, 47
Salford, 144
Salter's Hill, 50
Samaritans, 211
Sandford, Gilbert de, 83
Savoy Hotel, 21
Science Museum, 181
Scott, Sir Giles Gilbert, 170, 173;
    Harold, 16; Samuel, 34
Scudmore, Charles, 178, 188
Seacoal Lane, 33
Security Archives Ltd, 198
'Seerseal', 78
Seething Lane, 60
Serpentine, The, 42-4, 197
Seven Sisters Road, 52, 88
Shaftesbury Avenue, 81, 197
Shakespeare, William, 83
Shallow, Justice, 32
Sharebourne Lane, 53

Shaw, Norman, 193
Shelton, Sir Ralph, 33
Shepherd's Bush, 45, 118, 129, 176,
    187; Well, 39
Shepherd, T H, 99, 206
Shirland Road, 43
Shooter's Lane, 205
Shoreditch, 23, 53
Shore, Elizabeth, 53
Siemens, Sir William, 168
Sikes, Bill, 49-50
Sloane Square Station, 12, 45
Slochteren (Holland), 103
Smith Square, 213
Smithers, Mr, 96
Smithfield, 32, 213
Smollett, Tobias, 88
Snow Hill, 32, 35, 206
Soane, Sir John, 29
South, Dock, 50; -Eastern Railway,
    145; Kensington Station, 20, 142-3;
    Kentish Town Station, 162; Lambeth
    Road, 52; Lambeth Gasworks, 101;
    *London Press*, 50; Metropolitan Gas
    Company, 97
Southampton Row, 200
Southwark, 47, 49, 92, 95;
    Bridge, 92; Waterworks, 88
*Speculation on the Source of
    Hampstead Ponds . . .*, 30
Spender, Stephen, 172
Spring Grove, 163
Sprot, William, 60
Spurgeon Street, 47
Stamford, Bridge, 45; Brook, 23, 46-7,
    73-4
Standard, Conduit, The, 84; Telephone
    & Cables, 185
Stanley, Albert, 153-4
Stanmore, 161
Statute of the Streets (1633), 62
Stephenson, Robert, 66
Stepney, 75, 123-4
Stockwell, 50-1, 75; Station, 19, 148
Stoke Newington, 11, 52, 73, 86-7, 91
Stow, John, 26-9, 33, 44, 83-5, 94, 98,
    191, 199
Strand, 73, 161, 163, 166, 196
Stratford, 73
Streatham, 23; Hill, 47
Strowger Automatic Telephone
    Exchange, 185
Suez Canal, 203
Surbiton, 83
Surrey, and Kent Commissioners of
    Sewers, 51; Canal, 69, 141, 173;
    Docks, 124
Surte (Sweden), 120
Sussex University, 216
Swift, Jonathan, 35
Swiss, Cottage, 13, 162; *Cottager, The,*
    13, 17
Sydenham, 23
System X, 187, 188
Szechwan (China), 94

Tabard Street, 47
Tachbrook Street, 42
Talgarth Road, 47
Tate Gallery, 97
Taylor, Fred, 156
Teddington, 83, 90-1
Telegraph Hill, 43
'Telemole'/'Telemouse', 78, 120
Temple Station, 129

Tenniel, Sir John, 88
'Teo Burns', 39
*Teredo navalis*, 106
Thames, Barrier, 127, 199-201;
    Navigation Committee, 106; River,
    8-9, 23-5, 27, 29-30, 34, 39, 42-8, 50,
    52-3, 66-7, 72, 74-5, 79, 81, 83, 88,
    90-2, 96, 105, 108, 110-1, 117-27,
    141, 149-50, 160-1, 169-70, 173-4,
    184, 186, 196-7, 199-201, 210;
    Television, 189; Tunnel, 105-15, 123;
    Water Authority, 74, 77, 79, 86, 91,
    117, 121, 199
Thamesmead, 120, 127, 174, 205
Theobald's Road, 199, 207
Thomas-à-Watering, 49-50
Thorn EMI, 189
Thornbury, Walter, 117
Thornea Island, 42
Threlfall, George, 181
Thurlow Park Road, 50
Tilbury, 105; Shelter, 11, 15-6
*Times, The*, 51, 105, 110-1, 116, 142,
    153, 178, 185, 186,
Tite, Sir William, 33
Tooley Street, 115
Tooting Common, 52
Tothill, Street, 41; Fields, 42
Tottenham, Court Road, 102, 150;
    Station, 227
Tower, Bridge, 117, 200, 208; Bridge
    Road, 47; Hill, 75, 115, 117; Hill
    Station, 142; of London, 7, 53, 61,
    69, 93, 199; Subway, 92, 115-8, 120,
    122-3
Trafalgar Square, 81, 123, 161, 162,
    197, 210; Square Post Office, 186,
    187
Treasury, The, 18, 42
Trenck, Baron, 40
Trent Valley Railway, 144
Trevithick, Richard, 105
Trident Television, 93, 118
Trustees of the Middlesex and Essex
    Roads, 100
Tunne, The, 84
Turnmill, Brook – see Fleet; Street,
    31-2
Turpin, Dick, 32
Tyburn, Brook, 39, 43-4; River, 23,
    39-43, 83, 135, 158, 199, 201-2

Universal Private Telegraph Company,
    177
University College, 169
Upper, Mall, 175; Street, 84, 206;
    Thames Street, 29, 55
Uxbridge Road, 162

Vale of Health, 43, 85
Vanburgh, Sir John, 205
Varah, Rev Chad, 211
Vauxhall, 50, 52, 69, 75, 119, 121, 160;
    Bridge, 52, 92, 122, 160-1; Bridge
    Road, 42; Waterworks, 88
Vazie, Robert, 105
Victoria, Embankment, 75; Line, 119,
    121-2, 157-61, 202, 206; Park, 53,
    73; Queen, 106, 113; Station, 45, 97,
    157, 159, 195; Street, 42, 68
Vine Lane, 115, 117
Visionhire, 191
Volta, Alexandre, 166

Walbrook, River, 8-9, 23, 26-9, 59-60,
    64, 83

Waller, Joseph, 62
Walthamstow, 91
Walton-on-Thames, 83
Wandle, River, 23, 47, 52
Wandsworth, 47, 52
Wapping, Station, 105-6, 108, 111, 115,
    123; Wall, 92
Ward, Ned, 34-5
Warple, River, 46
Warren, Lane, 205; Street Station, 159;
    The – see Woolwich Arsenal
Warwick Road, 45
*Wastes of Civilization, The*, 88
Waterloo, 117, 122-3, 149-50, 184,
    187, 196, 199, 207; Bridge, 81, 92,
    166, 207; -City Line, ('The Drain'),
    120, 122-3, 149-50
Waterson Street, 27
Watkin, Sir Edward, 144-5
Watt, Gregory/James, 94
Wellington Barracks, 42
Wells, River of – see Fleet
West, Drayton, 176; Dulwich Station,
    50; End Lane, 43; India Docks, 106,
    166; London Railway, 45; *London
    Sketcher*, 46; Middlesex Waterworks,
    82, 88, 121
Westbourne, River, 12, 23, 43-5, 47,
    50, 74, 135, 142
Western, Gas Company, 97-8; Pumping
    Station, 74
Westferry Road, 173
Westland Heliport, 52
Westminster, 67, 69, 88, 95, 176, 199,
    202, 216; Abbey, 52; Bridge, 81;
    Bridge Road, 81; Palace of, 59, 202;
    Station, 142, 227
Westway, 44-5
Wheatstone, Charles 175-6
White, City, 162; Conduit Street, 84
Whitechapel, 75, 176; Road Post Office,
    181
Whitefriars, 39
Whitehall, 18, 42, 63, 117, 121, 123,
    161, 184, 186, 195-7, 199, 210
Whitestone Ponds, 43
Wick, Street, 53; Lane, 77
Wigmore Street, 40
Wilkie, Wendell, 15
Wilkinson, 'Red Ellen', 18
Willesden Junction, 43
William Street, 44
Willow Place, 42
Wimpole Street Post Office, 182
*Windsor Castle*, 156
Winsor (Winzer), Frederick, 94-5, 97
*Winter Sales*, 156
Woburn Square, 195
Wolsey, Cardinal, 211
Wood, Lane, 162; Street, 184, 186
Woolaston, W H, 96
Woolwich, 76, 96, 117, 127, 168;
    Arsenal, 173, 205; Foot Tunnel, 127;
    Reach, 127
Wormwood Scrubs, 45-6
Woronzow Road, 39
Wren, Sir Christopher, 33-4, 37, 63-4
Wylie, J C, 88
Wyllie, W L, 97

Yerkes, Charles Tyson, 151 – 3, 198
York, Building Waterworks, 82;
    Gardens, 52; Road Station, 162;
    Way, 150, 206

Zachs, Richard, 189